D0501953

WITHDRAWN
UTSA LIBRARIES

Both Sides of the Border

Both Sides
of the
Border

A SCATTERING OF TEXAS FOLKLORE

Edited by
Francis Edward Abernethy
Kenneth L. Untiedt

Publications of the Texas Folklore Society LXI

University of North Texas Press
Denton, Texas

©2004 Texas Folklore Society

All rights reserved.
Printed in the United States of America.

10 9 8 7 6 5 4 3 2 1

Permissions:
University of North Texas Press
P.O. Box 311336
Denton, TX 76203-1336

The paper used in this book meets the minimum requirements of the
American National Standard for Permanence of Paper for Printed Library
Materials, z39.48.1984. Binding materials have been chosen for durability.

Library of Congress Cataloging-in-Publication Data

Both sides of the border : a scattering of Texas folklore / edited by Francis Edward
Abernethy, Kenneth L. Untiedt.
    p. cm. — (Publications of the Texas Folklore Society ; 61)
Includes index.
  ISBN 1-57441-184-5 (cloth : alk. paper)
  1. Tales—Texas. 2. Talex—Mexican-American Border Region. I. Abernethy, Francis
Edward. II. Untiedt, Kenneth L., 1966- III. Publications of the Texas Folklore Society ;
no. 61.
GR1.T4 no.61 GR110.T4
398.2'09764—dc22

                    2004011885

Both Sides of the Border: A Scattering of Texas Folklore is Number LXI in the Publications
of the Texas Folklore Society

Text design by Carol Sawyer/Rose Design

Library
University of Texas
at San Antonio

CONTENTS

PREFACE

Tell me honestly, have you ever cleaned out your files? I don't mean picking through one pittance of a drawer of files while watching *As the World Turns*. I mean thoughtfully and meticulously going through cabinets and closets and garages filled with files that go back to your school days and even before. I thought not. The task out-daunted you, didn't it? You feared the cataclysmic emotional upheaval that would result from delving through the detritus of your past. I urge you to summon your true grit and intestinal fortitude and to do so now. Address yourself to the task so that those who follow you will not have that as one of their onerous duties at your eventual exit.

This "holier than thou" attitude is the result of my having cleaned out my Texas Folklore Society files as I prepare to pass the TFS editorial mantle on to Ken Untiedt. I had to do a massive cleanout and organization some years back when I organized and boxed all of the Society's records from 1971 to 2000 to be deposited with the rest of the TFS records in the archives at the Barker Center at The University. Now I have made the second round of cleaning out files to see if there was anything I missed, and I found some real jewels. These were papers and clippings from years past that had been lying around just looking for a place to make their literary debuts.

The result of all this cleaning out is that this year's PTFS is one of your ultimate bargains—four books in one!—a history monograph, a Tex-Mex book, a miscellany, and a *Family Saga* reprise. Now is that a huge hype or what!

We purposely highlighted the Tex-Mex section and christened this 2004 Publication of the Texas Folklore Society #61 *Both Sides of the Border: A Scattering of Texas Folklore,* because of its emphasis upon recently researched Tex-Mex folklore—and because the opening article is a beautiful autobiographical piece by Lucy West about growing up on both sides of the Rio Grande border. Additionally, we recognize that Texas has other borders besides the Rio Grande. In fact, we considered the ambiguity of the word "Border" as it applied to Texas with its several borders and will use that title with the folklorists' knowledge that all of this state's songs, tales, and traditions have lived and prospered on the other sides of Texas borders at one time or another before they crossed the rivers and became "ours."

The Texas Folklore Society has been publishing Mexican folklore from both sides of the border since its beginning. PTFS #1, now called *'Round the Levee,* included a Mexican border ballad— untranslated! Frank Dobie began his folkloric mission collecting and publishing Mexican folklore that had lived on both sides of the Rio Grande. His *Spur of the Cock* (PTFS #11–1933) and *Puro Mexicano* (PTFS #12–1935) were extensive collections of Texas- Mexican folklore as were Mody Boatright's *Mexican Border Ballads* (PTFS #21–1946) and Wilson Hudson's *Healer of Los Olmos* (PTFS #24–1951). More recently, Joe Graham edited *Hecho en Tejas* (PTFS #50–1991) and the Society published Al Rendon's classic picture study, *Charreada: Mexican Rodeo in Texas* (PTFS # 59–2002).

The above list does not include the fact that just about every volume of the Society's sixty-one publications has included Mexican folklore that has lived on both sides of the Texas Rio Grande border. Nor does it include Texas Folklore Society extra books such as Frank Dobie's *Coronado's Children,* Americo Paredes' *With His Pistol in His Hand,* Riley Aiken's *Mexican Folktales from the Borderland,* and John O. West's *Mexican-American Folklore.*

And we must conclude with the observation that Texas has a large population of individuals who have lived on both sides of the border and are now creating a folkloric mix that we will hear much of in the future. Thus, *Both Sides of the Border* is timely.

Both Sides was to have been a traditional miscellany, containing the best of papers presented at TFS meetings over the past few years, as well as casual submissions. We have used that meritorious miscellany of materials as the center of the book. We concluded *Both Sides of the Border* with "*The Family Saga* (Cont'd.)" because we had several rich family legends and studies of family legends left over from last year's publication. *The Family Saga* has stimulated a flow of family legends that will eventually require the publishing of a companion volume.

■■

I started editing my first PTFS, number thirty-seven, in the fall of 1971, which was before some of you were even born. I was determined to start the volume with something by my hero J. Frank Dobie, so I talked Bertha Dobie into sending me a hunting story from his unpublished files. You will notice that I start this, my last volume, with J. Frank Dobie also. I thought such a beginning tribute was fitting.

I bummed and borrowed enough articles to make a passable TFS miscellany in 1971, and I gave the material to Bill Wittliff at the newly founded Encino Press. Bill put it artistically all together in what we clumsily called *Observations & Reflections On Texas Folklore* (PTFS #37–1972). The title was accurately descriptive but it lacked euphony, or something. But Lordy! Was I ever proud of that book! Bill followed the footsteps of Carl Hertzog. He knew instinctively and aesthetically how to blend paper, print, pictures, text, etc.—all the elements that make a book—into a unified artistic whole. It is a rare talent, one much neglected in our fury to get books on the stands.

I started editing *Both Sides of the Border,* number sixty-one, with a full hopper of folkloric articles, much richer in material than I was that first year of this editorship. I realized again—for the twentieth time—how blessed the Society is with its wealth of writers and researchers. Folklore courses have lost their places in academe since the beginning of my editorship, but Society members have continued to collect and preserve and study folklore on their own. And the Society has been able to continue its publishing program, always with the support of its members. I take this opportunity to thank all members who have ever put their literary pens to paper for the Society's sake. You are the lives of the Society's publishing program, and future generations will bless your names as the carriers of Texas' folkloric torch.

I have not made a survey lately to see what other states have done in the way of preserving and presenting their folklore. But I would venture to say that Texas has done as well as any in maintaining a published record of its folklore studies.

So I am ending much as I began thirty-three years ago with a miscellany of observations and reflections on Texas folklore that I found readable and informative. I used a few old papers that had rattled around in my files for years because I could not find the exact place to use them. I paid tribute to some long departed

Texas Folklore Society Secretary-Editor Ken Untiedt, office secretary Heather Gotti, and Editor Emeritus Ab Abernethy

buddies who still remain dear to my heart. And I hope that ultimately I have organized a PTFS that has some worthwhile academic value.

The editors thank Heather Gotti, our office secretary, for her work in collecting and organizing the articles for this publication, and we thank Karen DeVinney, managing editor at the University of North Texas Press, for her editing.

I shall not sing a swan song until I find one that goes well with a country band composed of fiddle and guitar, banjo and bass—something like the East Texas String Ensemble. And as much as I like the perks more than the works, I will try to keep my hands off the TFS publications so that Ken Untiedt can start putting his stamp on the books of the next thirty-three years.

It's been a blast! It's been my life.

Francis Edward Abernethy
Stephen F. Austin State University
Nacogdoches, Texas
January 31, 2004

I

REMEMBERING
OUR ANCESTORS

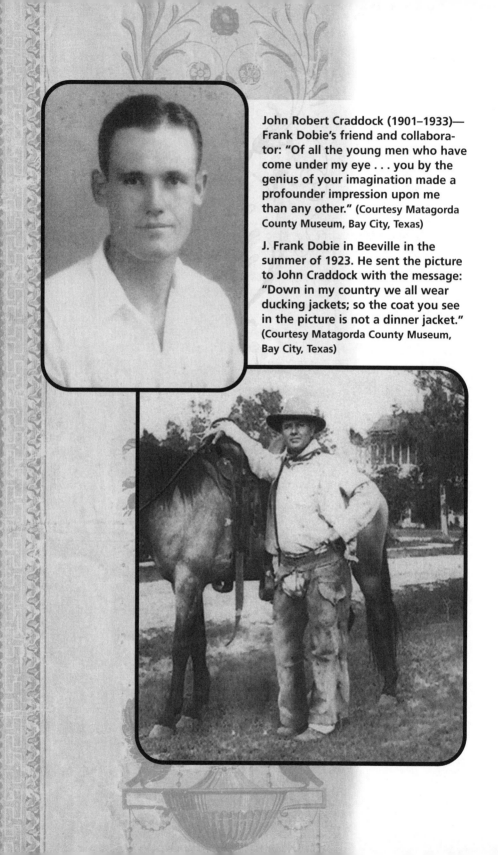

John Robert Craddock (1901–1933)—Frank Dobie's friend and collaborator: "Of all the young men who have come under my eye . . . you by the genius of your imagination made a profounder impression upon me than any other." (Courtesy Matagorda County Museum, Bay City, Texas)

J. Frank Dobie in Beeville in the summer of 1923. He sent the picture to John Craddock with the message: "Down in my country we all wear ducking jackets; so the coat you see in the picture is not a dinner jacket." (Courtesy Matagorda County Museum, Bay City, Texas)

LETTERS FROM J. FRANK DOBIE TO JOHN ROBERT CRADDOCK

Edited by Mary Belle Ingram, Historical Marker
Chairman, Matagorda County Museum Bay City, Texas,
with F. E. Abernethy

The Texas Folklore Society is forever indebted for its very existence to J. Frank Dobie, the Society's Executive Secretary and the
editor of its publications from 1922 to 1943. The Society, which
had been founded in 1909 and was stabled at The University of
Texas, was a casualty of World War I. Fortunately, J. Frank Dobie,
a young English instructor at UT, resurrected the dormant society
in 1921 and made it the bearer of his wealth of Texas legends as
well as a treasury of Texas folklore in general. Dobie led the Society for the next twenty-one years, established it academically, and
made it almost as well known as he was. For which reasons the
Society was pleased recently to receive the following collection of
J. Frank Dobie letters from Mary Belle Ingram, Historical Marker
Chairman and Archivist with the Matagorda County Museum, Bay
City, Texas.

Mrs. Ingram, who is in charge of the archives at the Matagorda
County Museum, discovered the Dobie letters among the collec-
tion of papers given to the museum by the Richard and Florence
Craddock Gusman family, prominent citizens in Bay City and
Matagorda County. Richard Gusman was longtime mayor of Bay
City, and his wife was the sister of John Robert Craddock, to
whom Dobie wrote the letters.

The letters from Dobie to John Craddock were written
between November 6, 1923, and April 16, 1932. The final letter

of August 30, 1933, is from Bertha Dobie to John's father, W. A. Craddock, expressing her sorrow and Frank's at the death of John at age thirty-two.

Most of the correspondence occurred between November 23, 1923, and November 9, 1924, during Dobie's two years of "exile" as head of the English department at Oklahoma Agricultural and Mechanical College at Stillwater. Aggravated with the condescending attitudes of some of his peers and superiors at UT, Dobie precipitously accepted an offer to head the English department at Oklahoma A&M. He was sorry he made that leap almost as soon as he landed, and a year later was working earnestly with his friend and TFS founder Leonidas Payne to get back to UT. Dobie returned to The University of Texas at Austin as an adjunct professor in the fall of 1925.

Unfortunately, we do not have much biographical information about John Robert Craddock during the time of the correspondence. We know that John was born in Rogers, Bell County, Texas, on November 20, 1901, to William Attress Craddock and Florence Punchard Craddock. Both parents were from old-time Texas families. So, John was twenty-two years old and a student at UT when the correspondence began. He was not a student of Dobie's, but Dobie considered John a collaborator. Dobie had already published John's "The Cowboy Dance" in PTFS II (1923), now called *Coffee in the Gourd*. John had also given Dobie three stories—"The Waiting Woman," "The Headless Squatter," and "The Legend of Stampede Mesa"—for PTFS III (1924), *Legends of Texas*. Dobie loved the Stampede Mesa story and used it many times in his storytelling speeches and in his writing.

Dobie, in the list of contributors in *Legends*, describes John as "a true product of the rangy West, and he is gathering all manner of folk material from the old-time Plains people. Only one to the manner born can seize a legend as he has seized 'The Legend of Stampede Mesa.' At present Mr. Craddock is ranching in Dickens County. He has written good ballads and has been a student at the University of Texas." The phrase, "has been a student" was written during the summer of 1924, when John was spending the summer at his father's ranch near Spur.

John was obviously a favorite young man for Dobie, who was thirty-six in 1924, and the planned camping trip for the summer of 1924 was the height of excitement for both of these young men. The adventure fell through for some undiscussed reason. John returned to UT in the fall of 1924 with a plan to study law but quit school at the end of the semester, in January of 1925, probably because of health problems. He returned to his father's ranch near Spur, where he finished his life as a victim of Parkinson's Disease. Dobie published John's "Songs the Cowboys Sing" in PTFS VI, *Texas and Southwestern Lore* in 1927, and "The Corn Thief— A Folk Anecdote" in PTFS VII, *Follow the Drinkin' Gou'd* in 1928. Dobie wrote his last letter (as far as we know) to John in 1932, at which time it appears that John's illness had reached such a state that his father had to write for him.

John's disease caused him to have trouble walking, and he drowned when he accidentally fell into the family well on August 23, 1933. Dobie was in Mexico at the time, so Bertha Dobie wrote the letter of condolence to John's father in which she said, "Frank has loved very few men as he loved your son." Frank Dobie did love John, as can be seen from the correspondence, and admired his family and the family's history and ranching culture, and his sorrow must have been great with John's passing. One of Dobie's last tributes to John was in his letter of 1932: "Of all the young men who have come under my eye since I have been in Austin you by the genius of your imagination made a profounder impression upon me than any other. This aside from the fact that I came to know you better as a friend."

John Robert Craddock was buried in Red Mud Cemetery, Dickens County, Texas. On his death certificate his profession was listed as "student."

The following letters, now residing in the archives of the Matagorda County Museum, reveal a lot about the young, cowboy-romantic J. Frank Dobie. He wrote these letters to John at a time when he was exploding with excitement and enthusiasm for collecting and writing about the legends of Texas. Dobie's career began with the popularity of the Society's *Legends of Texas* in 1924, it accelerated with his publication of *The Vaquero of the Brush Country* in 1929, and it reached national prominence with the publication of *Coronado's Children* in 1930. Frank Dobie went on to national fame and popularity as a writer and folklorist and character, but the years he spent in correspondence with John Robert Craddock of Spur, Texas, were the years of his making. It is interesting to discover in this most personal correspondence the mind and personality of Frank Dobie during the years of his maturation.

■■

OKLAHOMA
AGRICULTURAL AND MECHANICAL COLLEGE
BRADFORD KNAPP, President
STILLWATER

Nov. 6, 1923

Department of English
[*handwritten*]

Dear John:

Your explanation, with sketches, of the Haunted Spring and Stampede Mesa legends is fine. However, you did not say what is the place of the new legend, "The Waiting Woman." You say that "the wood cutter who hauls wood for the store" gave it __. What woodcutter, what store, where? What bills? This is a good little legend. Something over three weeks ago I was at T. C. H. and then before the Texas Poetry Society at Dallas telling and reading Texas legends. Among others I read yours—"Stampede Mesa"—and, believe me, it took.

It froze last night; there is no wind this morning and what heaven it would be to ride across the frosty grass now! How a horse would feel his oats! I am all lonesome for the outdoors. It is a farming country all around here, though the 101 Ranch and the Osage pastures are not so far away. What's the Texas news? Are you taking all Law this year?

Your good friend,
J. Frank Dobie

■■■

[OKLAHOMA A&M LETTERHEAD]

December 1, 1923

[*typed, with handwritten postscript*]

Dear John:

"I have started me a sour-dough keg, and settled down for the winter." When I read *that* the hot blood of sympathy flamed up in the back of my head as it does into your eyes sometimes when you hear something that appeals to you. Oh the mocking curse of civilization and of the necessity to "be getting on" that keeps us puling over poets and pupils when we might be listening to the more than poetic rhythm of spurs on frosty gravel these fine mornings. There is one humane thing that I learned in the army that I wish to pass on to you. Always these cold mornings rub your horse's bit to warm it up before you put it in his mouth. I never saw a cowpuncher think to do that. I never thought to do it before I learned it in the army.

The map is a good deal better. In your legend you say that Doakum Flats are to the south of the Mesa. In your map you show the Doakum trail running east and west and the squatter's house is north of the trail. Now where exactly are those flats? I imagine that the squatter must have had his squat near the Flats where his little bunch of cows was grazing, don't you? You see, I am as particular about particulars as old [Morgan] Callaway would be. If you happen to learn of the New Mexico Fort that the trail leads to, be sure to let me know. That would make an item of color.

I'll joy to get your ballad when it comes. Do not generally employ internal rhyme in your ballads as you did in The Wagon. You will never regret the winter you are spending out in the open. If I stay in a year, I grow more in three weeks out than I do all the year in. Nowhere but out of it can a man masticate and digest civilization.

Mrs. Dobie sends her regards. We had turkey Thursday, and I would have given a good deal to have had you with us. I hope that your father is out and mending. I should very much like to know him.

Always your good friend,
J. Frank Dobie

P.S. I am sending you a magazine in which you will find some things to your liking—especially the jump off of a 70 or 75 foot cliff! Please return magazine when you are done with it.

■■

[OKLAHOMA A&M LETTERHEAD]

March 9, 1924
[*typed, with handwritten postscript in right margin*]

Dear John:
Have I treated you like a stranger? Well, up to a few days ago I have been going for weeks on five hours of sleep—working on the legends. They are with the printer now and soon I shall be receiving proof to read. There will be over two hundred and fifty pages of them, and they will be read long after old Morgan Callaway is rotted and the worms have eaten his Anglo-Saxon infinitives.

[Dr. Morgan Callaway was the head of the English Department at The University of Texas at the time. He was condescending about Dobie's work in folklore, and Dobie returned the sentiment about Callaway's work in Anglo-Saxon grammar.] You can have as many copies as you want, but I am sorry to say that you will have to pay for them at about the rate of five dollars for half a dozen, or, if you want them bound, at the rate of two dollars a piece. I am running the Society three or four hundred dollars in debt getting out such a big publication. The volumes will be ready for delivery by the first of May I hope. Anyway, I am going to Austin May 2–3 for the meeting of the Texas Folk-Lore Society.

I have been too busy to consider my environments, but if I pause to consider it, I realize that I had as soon be in hell with my back broke as chained permanently to this layout. The majority of young people here seem to be descendants of Kansas sooners who squatted on 160 acres of land and lived on turnips and cornbread while they brought up a family. The country is so thickly popu-lated that rabbits can't exist. I see by the papers that your part of the state is settling up a lot. Well, we came on a generation too late.

Now, I always soak beans over night before trying to cook them. Then I put them in an iron pot the first thing when I get up, let them cook until I leave camp, leaving plenty of water on them and plenty of bacon in them, and plenty of fire around them. They will be done when you get back, but keep on cooking them for two or three days, and about the time you eat the last one it will be as black as ebony, as soft as a girl's kiss, and as palatable and digestible as ambrosia. It snowed here last night, and I have enjoyed myself today wearing my moderately high-heeled boots (which I bought last summer); but no amount of boots could fool my imagination into the idea that I was dragging a pair of spurs around, squatting gingerly so as to keep those spurs from hooking my stern, or catching an extra breath of the free, free air at the sound of twig's whirr of the rowel on my heel as I rode through the brush.

I have just read a great book: *Fifty Years on the old Frontier,* by James H. Cook. I think sometimes of our project. I think that we want to make it cover present cow people as well as those of the dying generation. Are any cowmen coming back, financially? Not many, I presume. For atmosphere, you ought to go to Houston to "the Convention." I am sending you a sheath of cowboy songs. Keep it, but send back to me that copy of the Pioneer Magazine I sent you, please. I want it for my file.

What is called civilization is a damned lie and delusion. Are you going back to it! I hope that you are not thinking of marrying soon. Write to me when you can—soon.

Your friend,
J. Frank Dobie

Are you getting any more songs? Keep your collection going. What about the ballad? I want to see it. Have you sent anything off? Any luck?

■■

[OKLAHOMA A&M LETTERHEAD]

April 28, 1924.

[*typewritten*]

My dear, dear Friend Craddock:

At last I can write you a line. For the last six weeks now I have not slept six hours a night, and I have made every waking hour count. I have been finishing the legends as they came from the printer, correcting proof, verifying notes—there are scores of them—and working on various material connected with the volume. I honestly think that this will be one of the three or four most significant books ever printed in the state of Texas. It will be nearly three hundred pages long. Your legend of the Stampede Mesa is the best legend in it. By the way, I have picked up two or three additional versions to that legend up here from some old "rusties."

It is costing us a cool thousand to print the book. We have about half that much money. I have so much confidence in the volume that I ordered 1250 copies run off and five hundred bound. I'll send you a bound copy. If you want others bound you will have to pay for then [*sic*] at the rate of $2.00 each. The binding costs money.

I am about to finish the index now. Wednesday night I leave for Austin, and never did a thirsty saddle horse trot towards the water hole with more eagerness than I am heading for Texas. May God curse and damn such a layout as I am in here. I hear that I am charged with 1, using profane language in class, 2, smoking in my office and on the campus (against which crime the president has issued special orders) 3, never attending chapel, 4, flunking too many students. I do not give a damn whether they like my ways or not; I do not intend to reform. Nor am I afraid of my job.

I am more or less counting on seeing you this summer, but as yet my plans are not certain, and yours are not either, perhaps. I can picture no greater happiness than owning your own land and living on it.

You ask for a kodak picture. I am sending one that my sister snapped of me at Beeville last summer. It would be better if the horse's head were showing. Down in my country we all wear ducking jackets; so the coat you see in the picture is not a dinner jacket.

I have laughed a dozen times at your horse's "interpreting his belly full of oats." How the cattle are lifting up their heads on the grass these days! I am glad to see that the price is up a little. Write me now when you can and let me see those ballads. I have several new songs also. I am thinking of making up an article of several versions of the stampede legend and trying to market it. Have I your permission to go ahead? We could write the article jointly, for you have already contributed the best version. Keep on the watch for other legends. Good night,

Your friend,
J. Frank Dobie

[OKLAHOMA A&M LETTERHEAD]
May 20/24

[*handwritten*]

Dear John:

I spent a glorious week in Austin, where I was treated like a king. [The Texas Folklore Society met on the UT campus on May 3. Even though Dobie was in Stillwater, he was still the secretary of the TFS.] Since returning I have been covered with mountains of dead timber—except Sunday when we went to the 101 Ranch rodeo, Indian dance and parade, and pioneer historical pageant. The 101 Ranch is only about 45 miles from here. We got out of these peanut settlements on the way over and saw some good pasture land and hundreds of Texas coast steers that had just been shipped in. Well the rodeo was fine, especially the bull-dogging, the bronco riding being rather a cut and dried affair, the mounting all being done in a chute and some of the horses doing little more than see-saw, though a couple of them were right hellish. As I admitted to you before, I myself am not *ginete* [sic. *jinete*] (bronco buster). Hundreds of real-Indians—they live all about the 101 Ranch—in old time garb and gait made a rare sight to me.

Now, did you get the package of legends that I had sent to you? What do you think of the book? The Society is in debt $500.00 on it but we have plenty of copies for sale at $2.50 and $1.50 respectively. You can convey this information to any one you see who wants a copy. You might give the paper at Spur a little write-up on the volume. We need to get some publicity! [The last sentence had a left side bar with the handwritten words "Do this."]

"Sweetened hot" was new to me. Thanks for the word! Yes, I have sniffed cigarettes along with burning grass. For my part, I like the smell of horses too. But of all sensations the sound of a lone Mexican whistling or singing as he comes in the darkness to a camp fire around which talk low other Mexicans is the most soul stirring.

I am too busy now to do anything with Stampede legends. I have learned a lot of things. I wish that I could go over your material with you and see what you have. Can't you get music to those songs? We must have the music.

How is your father now? Adios. Write ere long.

Your friend
J. Frank Dobie

■ ■

[OKLAHOMA A&M LETTERHEAD]

May 31, 1924

[*typewritten*]

Dear John:

I do not often answer a letter on the day that I get it, but I am in a great hurry to tell you that I think I shall arrive in Spur about the 22 of July if that date suits you. My school does not close here until about that time. I'll go with you and work for the S M S outfit if they will pay me forty dollars a month and board and not make me ride any pitching horses. Or, I'll ride with you towards New Mexico. I will not pitch hay or ride in an automobile. I have a Stetson hat, a pair of boots, a pair of spurs. Can you rustle me a saddle and a blanket in addition to the saddle blanket? I can not be around there more than three or four weeks, as I have to go home for a few days. I am due out in Santa Fe to talk on the Folk-Lore of the Southwest about the last of August, but may not go [He went.]. We have a warm invitation from a Boston friend of mine who is excavating Indian remains to camp with him and his outfit at Pecos, New Mexico. He is a bully good fellow—not of Boston origin, I think. Well, I want to see something of the plains life and something of you. I had as soon be one place as another when I get out there, and the business of riding and trying to rope will be my entertainment. Don't plan anything except to have me with you doing whatever you have to do.

No, you owe the Texas Folk-Lore Society only $5.00. I threw the bound volume in for a pelon, as the Mexicans say. By Gosh, but it pleases me to hear how much you like the book. I doubt if I shall ever do another piece of work in which I shall put so much of my heart. I do not know though. Be figuring out some way how you can get the music of cowboy songs transferred to paper. We can make a little book of them that will sell. My wife is pleased, too, with your liking her legends. She helped me on a thousand details.

God, but I will be glad to get away from here into an open country. Your friend always,

J. Frank Dobie

■ ■

[OKLAHOMA A&M LETTERHEAD]

June 28, 1924

[*typewritten*]

Dear John:

I am not out of the sage country, but a whiff of any kind of water will make a steer dying of thirst throw up his head. I am scheming now to get away from here if possible four or five days earlier than I expected. If anything develops you will hear from me soon. I suppose that there is no necessity for an exact date just yet.

I like the looks of my horse. If we make Mexico [Dobie meant "New" Mexico, not Old Mexico.] in three days we shall have to string out sure enough. I wish that we would strike a good sized herd of cattle trailing that way and that we might loaf along with them a day or two. [Dobie would have given his front seat in hell to have made a real trail drive.] I feel a sort of hunger for association with cattle. I have a few memories that will stand out in my life as long as I have memory; I know that this experience will make another such. I wish that we were going to be gone a month. I have to be down in Beeville about the middle of August to a homecoming. Then the last of August I have to be in Santa Fe, New Mexico, to read a paper on "Folk-Lore of the Southwest." Then back here about the fifth or tenth of Spetember [*sic*]. I won't think of this place when I get away from it.

Meet me in your car as I shall have a suit case or two. I'll bring my substitute for a slicker, a raincoat. I am glad that we won't have a pack-horse, and you won't have any trouble making me leave behind all vestiges of college garb. Shall I bring a wool shirt? If we get up into the hills we may strike some right cool weather. I have a good *morral* that I shall bring also, and when I step off the train I shall have on a Stetson hat.

Say, John, do you know a fellow in Spur named J. A. Putnam? He is reputed to know all about the famous "Lost Adams Mine" of Colorado, and may have a flood of legends on the subject to pour out. By the way, LEGENDS OF TEXAS has for a month been the best seller of non-fiction in Dallas. Eight weeks ago we were six hundred dollars in debt; the financial officer writes me that we shall soon be out. I think that we will have to go into a second edition. Last night I wrote to the Dallas News, or rather to one of the men I know on it, suggesting that you and I could furnish some interesting feature stories to the News. We'll take along a good notebook apiece, more or less write up our trip, and then after we come back see what we can sell. I'll be going through two or three of the cities this summer and can see the editors personally.

We have had rooming with us for two months now a couple, the man of which was a cowboy in Wyoming twenty years ago. He is the most interesting talker that I have met in Oklahoma and has given me some real pictures. Well, I pant like a lizard to see you.

Your friend,
J. Frank Dobie

STILLWATER, JULY 3/24

[*handwritten*]

Dear Craddock:

You can expect me to arrive on the noon train in Spur July 18. I intend to steal time and get away early. Am going through a new country (Lawton, Okla. and Wichita Falls) and it will take me only 2 1/2 days to make the trip! I am going to bring my six-shooter. I have some army blankets light and no better than cotton. Shall I bring one? I intend to let my beard grow on this trip.

I had thought of bringing a few books and a fish line or two, in case we should come to the Pecos or some other river. Shall I bring such or not?

There is a bare chance that my long absent brother from California may get home this month instead of in August as was planned. If so, I'll have to go to Beeville first. At any rate, I should get to Spur by the last of the month. I mention this contingency. I do not expect Elrich to come yet.

My blood dances hourly at our prospects.

Yours,
Dobie

[*postscript in upper right-hand corner*]
P. S. Do I need a coat of any kind; I do not know what kind of climate to expect, especially at night.

WESTERN UNION
TELEGRAM

RECEIVED AT
3 D S 16.NL

Stillwater Okla Jul 11 1924

John R Craddock
Craddock Ranch Mail Spur Tex

Cant reach you until Monday July Twenty One Look for me then
Will explain delay later.

J Frank Dobue [sic]

■■■

STILLWATER, OKLAHOMA,

July 12, 1924

[*typed, with handwritten postscript*]

Dear John:

Absolutely I feel cheated out of three or four days of my life. I
wired you kast [*sic*] night that I could not reach Spur until Monday, July 21. I figured that you might be in town today and would
get the telegram if the agent mailed it to you. I had been all primed
to come as per arrangement when an order came from the president requiring that nobody put up his examinations and leave
unless given awritten permission. I could not get the written permission. I am head a [*sic*] department and responsible for the conduct of six or eight other more or less human beings. Damn such
responsibility. Just now I am looking for an instructor to resign
and if he does I should fill his place before I leave. But I am going
to leave here next Saturday night or noon. And when I leave *I am
gone.* No mail for a month is my hope. However, I have to be in
Austin the night of August 11. I could weep at the time I am losing from your society and range.

I am bringing a good camera. Have not heard anything from the Dallas News people. Yours always,

Dobie

Three minutes after I received this came your letter. I am tickled at the prospect of seeing Stampede Mesa. We will get pictures of it. Andy Adams from Colorado wrote me of his admiration for that legend. Your letter vibrates with freshness.

■ ■

WESTERN UNION
TELEGRAM

RECEIVED AT
4 D S 49 NL

Stillwater OKLA Jul 14

1924
John R Craddock
Mail Craddock Ranch Spur Tex

Foiled again The villain had just received telegram My brother absent five years California is home He will remain only few days My mother expects me to come now I will go Am very much ashamed to putting you out so can reach Spur about August third Will write

J Frank Dobie

■ ■

STILLWATER, OKLAHOMA

July 15/ 1924

[*handwritten*]

Dear John:

The unexpected happened. A month ago I wrote you that I had a brother who might come home. As I wired you last night, he has come. I want to see him very much, but I do wish that he had accommodated his visit to the plans that the family had set. Well, Elrich "has seen the owl and the elephant." You would like him. He is about as regular in his methods as a [second part of the simile is scratched out and unreadable.]

Here for days I have been imagining: this time next week or two weeks hence, John Craddock and I will be riding up the bank of the Double Mountain Fork; we will be smelling the broiled bacon; I will feel the delicious feel of leaning back against my saddle as we smoke by the fire. I had not built so on an experience in years. What I am concerned with now is how all this affects you. I must say, that it seems to me I am treating you very shabbily for a host—though I have not played the hand myself.

I can get out there about August 3 if you are still able to go then on the trip. I would have most of the month left then to be with you. If you can't get off then, be frank & say so and if you have work, I'll come and help you do it. Write me at Beeville, Texas. I'll be there by the middle of next week. I guess.

I hope that you have not had the horses shod. I hope that you have got both my telegrams in time to prevent extra trips and preparations. I hope as I live that we go yet. Our appetites will be whetted—not dulled—by the delay. I am going to ship you a blanket and a few things so that I will not have to lug them around. Have read up a lot on New Mexico; have a good map of it also. What is the quickest railroad time between Austin & Spur? What best route? Write me quick at Beeville.

Got a letter a day or two ago from old Andy Adams—great frontier writer—who spoke fine things of your Stampede Legend. He knows the Dockums in Colorado, sons of old man Dockum, and says that he is going to check up the story with them. By heaven, we'll have to make some kind of camp at Stampede Mesa. We'll have to yell and shoot my six-shooter and stampede the jack rabbits. We'll have to celebrate. You have immortalized Stampede Mesa. Meet it is that we pay tribute to both Mesa and immortality.

Yours,
J. Frank Dobie

Regards to your father, please. If we take this trip still, and if the plan still holds to camp at Squatter's, I hope he will come with us. I have bought a good Eastman Kodak—3A

■■

[One wonders what happened between July 15 and October 20. I cannot believe that Dobie and John made that trip because Dobie would have made some mention of it in the following correspondence. Dobie had a hectic professional and family schedule, as referred to above, and he could have kept canceling and rescheduling the trip until they ran out of time. But I do believe that he dearly wanted that trip as a great adventure and as grist for his writing mill. I have a feeling that the reason for cancellation lay with John, and perhaps with John's physical condition. I base this on the idea that Dobie would have been too sensitive to mention the aborted trip had it been John's fault through his illness that the trip did not make.]

■■

[OKLAHOMA A&M LETTERHEAD]

October 20, 1924

[*typewritten*]

Dear Friend John:

I have time just to write a bit. I am still lookong [*sic*] for those ballads. Revise them all you can before you send them. Then I will rake them over and perhaps one of them will hit the fancy of Hubbell. Have you seen the new SOUTHWEST REVIEW? It is a thousand per cent improvement over the old Texas Review. [Jay Hubbell was the new editor of the *Southwest Review,* and he was interested in western themes. He and Dobie became good friends, and Dobie was a regular contributor.]

Do you have any cowboy pictures? Very much to my surprise I received a commission, so to speak, from a big outfit the other day to write a couple of articles on cowboys. They want pictures. I have a lot of pictures, but they are all of Mexican vaqueros. If you can possibly rustle me up some cowboy pictures, I would be eternally obliged to you. I like the picture you sent me. Would you mind if I ran it? If not, send me one without any writing on it. This picture is a little too self conscious though for my purpose. I wish that I had a picture of cowboys in camp along about sunset. I wish that I had one of them on herd. I wish that I had two or three of cowboy "characters"—long, lank, slouchy looking. If you know where these can be secured and will write for them, I'll be more than glad to pay good money for them. The thing is that I do not want posed pictures.

Watch and see if I do not get somebody to take your "Legend of Stampede Mesa" and pay for it.

I am busy as a cat. Give [historian Walter Prescott] Webb my regards if you see him. How is his book [*The Great Plains*] coming along? Are you taking any English? How do you like studying law? Craddock, take my advice and study like the devil. I have reached the point that I can be as methodical as a machine, drudge like a dead head, and yet never lose my zest for adventure. A man has to come to the place that he can control his lust for the open and for adventure if he is to do anything with a professional life; at the same time he need not kill those refreshing qualities in himself. Stevenson said, you know, that romance was not so much seeking adventures, as being ready to seek them. Stevenson knew a good deal about romance.

Your friend,
Frank Dobie

[Dobie never signs his letters to John with "Frank." Here for the first time, however, he leaves off the "J." Also, Dobie's salutation is almost sentimental, "Dear Friend John," which might be an indication of a new plane for their relationship.]

■ ■

[GUNTER HOTEL, SAN ANTONIO, LETTERHEAD] ON TRAIN, NORTH OF RED RIVER,

November 9, 1924

[*handwritten on both sides of paper*]

Dear John:

I have been intending for days to write you. I am going to do over two of your ballads and submit them to Hubbell of Southwest Review. By "doing over" I mean merely ironing down a few wrinkled places. The "Sunday Cowboy" is good stuff. You surely know your oats, but you must pay more attention to technique of English. That does not mean that you are to gut all flavor out of it. Gut nothing out that is flavor or savor.

I have been down to San Antonio to write an article on "The Old Trail Drivers" for *Country Gentlemen*. Was certainly glad to see Webb there reporting the meeting for the *Dallas News*. I wrote an article for *Country Gentlemen* on "Cowboy Songs." All the time I was writing it, I had in mind that you could be writing a better one. I'll send you a copy of the article when it appears.

I'm feeling my oats these days. Thank you for pictures. I do not believe that I can use them, however; they are too *posed!* I want them, though.

Craddock, no other people on earth can equal the old cowmen and cowboys. But their time is past. Be sure to go to San Antonio sometime when they are meeting. I'll write again soon.

Your friend,
J. Frank Dobie

■ ■

[We have no correspondence between Dobie and John Craddock for the next eight years. This does not mean that they did not write nor communicate. On November 11, 1929, Dobie remembered John with a newly minted copy of his *A Vaquero of the Brush Country,* inscribed "To my friend John Craddock." *Vaquero* is also from the Gusman collection and is in the Matagorda County Museum archives. The following letter from Dobie to John, written in 1932, is sent with all the warmth and friendship of a long-held and loving relationship. But, the two were no longer collaborating, probably because of John's poor health. It appears that John could no longer write and that his father wrote his letters for him. This is the approach to a sad conclusion.]

■ ■

402 PARK PLACE, AUSTIN, TEXAS

April 16, 1932

[typed, with handwritten postscript]

Dear John:

I hope that you won't think I do not think of you as seldom as I write. It is literally true that hardly a day goes by without my thinking of you. Of all the young men who have come under my eye since I have been in Austin you by the genius of your imagination made a profounder impression upon me than any other. This aside from the fact that I came to know you better as a friend.

Tonight I seem to be in a mood to review the life I have lived during the last several months. I can't remember what I did in January but be miserable with hay fever. February 1 I began teaching again, and I have done little but attend to teaching and meet the increasing routine of demands on my time since. I have written less during the last four months than during any other period of the same length for many years. I have gone about some "lecturing" as it is called—and honestly I have become very tired of listening to myself.

Your father writes me that you hear me every other Monday night over the radio. That information pleases me very much, though those radio talks never satisfy me. In the first place I don't seem to have enough imagination to visualize the audience; in the second place I am never for a momonet [*sic*], while talking, unconscious of the passing of time. One has to hew to the split second. In order to save time I have been writing out what I had to say and reading it. Then to get through I read too fast. I aim to sound as if I were talking instead of reading, but when a man is thinking about the time and not about his subject he can't do his best. I shall not go to San Antonio this coming Monday but am going to Lufkin to spout—"lecture." Mrs. Dobie is going with me as she wants to see East Texas flowers, and we are going in the car.

Well, ON THE OPEN RANGE did not get adopted as a text book and it has had not much of a run as a trade book. It has never been advertised as it should have been. The Southwest Press has about gone to the wall; in fact it has so far gone that it has never paid me royalty on Coronado's Children or paid the printer a big bill. Attempts are now being made to reorganize and refinance it; I hope they pan out. I have planned all along that you should receive a check for your Stampede story in ON THE OPEN RANGE whenever the Southwest Press starts to paying anybody anything again. My prediction is that that story will live a long, long time. [*On the Open Range* was adopted by the State of Texas as a supplementary reader in 1932, but Southwest Press had to sell it so cheaply that Dobie received little if any royalties from it.]

The Country Gentleman seems to have forgotten my existence. I don't expect that magazine to ever buy anything else from me. All its non-fiction is utilitarian now—the kind of thing I am not interested in and could not write.

I am getting a great deal of pleasure out of my course in "Life and Literature of the Southwest." The course was supposed to be limited to 50 students, but about 70 got in. A hundred and seventy would be in it if they had not been cut off. We read Bigfoot Wallace, Andy Adams, etc. and have a bully time. As usual the majority of the students are girls, though there is a good sprinkling of boys. Those girls had rather read about Billy the Kid than Alice in Wonderland. The way girls take to bloody deeds and men always puzzles me.

If you can use some more books I wish Mr. Craddock would write me. I have received some very good ones dealing with the West since you were here and should be most happy to make up a bundle to send out and loan you. Tell your father to write me right away if you want some. I sent you a copy of the last folk-lore publication the other day. It has been out only a week or so. I hope it has arrived all right.

Some time ago I had a long letter from a friend of yours, John H. Davis, who is as full of romantic ideas as an egg is of meat. Soon afterwards he came to see me. I am sending you his letter, thinking it might interest you. Send it back some time, as I may sometime follow its lead for a story. Almost daily I receive letters from people who think they have a buried treasure located but cannot "make out the signs" and want my help. And never, never can I give them the least help.

Perhaps you saw in the newspapers that I had been granted a Guggenheim fellowship for writing a book of tales out of Northern Mexico [*Tongues of the Monte*, 1935]. The grant affords $2000 a year and I shall consequently be on leave of absence next year. I am going to put the story of the Lost Tayopa Mine in the book, the story of the Onza, and some other yarns that I have. I have enough already for probably a third or a fourth of the book. In September I am going with a man down into the state of Tamaulipas, on the east coast of Mexico. He wants to hunt jaguars; I am going along to hunt stories also. We are going in a car and will be gone about two weeks. Soon after returning I plan to go into Mexico about Del Rio, outfit with horse, pack, and a Mexican and travel across the country towards Chihuahua City. This trip will be 400 miles or more. That is the way I will learn the country and its traditions. Later on Mrs. Dobie and I are going to Mexico City, where we have long wanted to go, and also to Torreon, Saltillo, and Durango. We may take a mule-back trip into the mountains out from Durango. I think I'll learn something. I hope I can write it.

If I had a book now I would not let it be published. The market on books, like that on everything else, is all shot to pieces [The Depression was at its worst in 1932.]. You never met my brother Elrich. He is the most interesting member of our family. After having been in Java for five years working for the Dutch Shell oil people, he came home last December—work having closed down in Java. He had saved some money. The first thing he did was to buy in with a fellow on a bunch of good cattle. I am mighty glad that the family is sgain [*sic*] represented in the cow business. I wish I had some money to go into it myself.

It is dry in this country as it it [*sic*] everywhere, but I wish you could see our yard. It is very beautiful and restful and we take a great deal of pleasure in it. One drawback to our situation is that our street has become almost a main thoroughfare between Speed-way and Red River, which is now paved from town out almost to the Country Club. The new boulevard along Waller Creek is being paved. Perhaps when it is opened up we shall not have so much dust and noise from traffic.

The annual Roundup for exstudents of the University was today. Sight of the horses made me homesick.

Well, John, I have enjoyed writing to you. Good [*sic*] bless you. I am, with affection,

Your friend,
Frank Dobie

Mrs. Dobie asks me to remember her to you. I send my regards to your father and mother. They are the *salt-of-the-earth* kind of people. The older I get the more I think of their kind.

■■■

402 PARK PLACE
AUSTIN, TEXAS

August 30, 1933

[*typewritten*]
Mr. W. A. Craddock
Spur, Texas

My dear Mr. Craddock:
In my husband's absence I am writing in reply to your letter announcing John's death. He will, of course, write you himself as soon as he comes home. Frank could not keep away from Mexico, and about two weeks ago went back to be gone until about the time the University opens.

I knew John too, and admired his noble ambitions and later sorrowed over the cruel disease that made any fulfillment of them forever impossible. Frank has loved very few men as he loved your son. Never did he write John or send him books out of any feeling of being kind but simply out of an affection and regard that the passing of years could not lessen. He has always regarded John's high appreciation of him as one of the gracious, good things in his life.

With sympathy for you and Mrs. Craddock, I am

Sincerely yours,
Bertha Dobie [signed]
Mrs. J. Frank Dobie

J. Frank Dobie in the Texas Folklore Society office at The University of Texas, ca. 1936 (Courtesy Barker Texas History Center, University of Texas)

Charles Leland Sonnichsen (1901–1991)—TFS president (1937–1938), prolific writer about Texas history and folklore, after-dinner speaker, and "one more hard-workin' sumbitch" (Courtesy University of Texas at El Paso Library, Special Collections Department)

"Leland saw me across the room, began singing 'Let the Lower Lights Be Burning,' motioned to you, and we met singing—you bass, me soprano, and Leland the tenor. Nice Memory!" *Joyce Roach* (T. I. L. meeting, 1988)

2

DOC SONNICHSEN HOLDS HIS OWN

by Al Lowman of Stringtown

On Sunday, June 2, 1931, a freshly-minted Harvard Ph.D. stepped off the train in the sunbaked border town of El Paso, prepared to assume responsibilities as an assistant professor of English at the Texas College of Mines and Metallurgy. The adjective "dapper" might have been coined to describe twenty-nine-year-old Charles Leland Sonnichsen. He was tall and good-looking, with elegant bearing, and trim of both build and mustache. The El Paso assignment would, of course, be temporary; after all, Harvard Ph.D.s surely commanded such status in academia that he would soon be summoned to the ivy-draped colossi of better-watered soil, both literally and figuratively. But a funny thing happened on the road to his destiny. Several funny things, in fact. We'll get to those shortly.

For one thing, he swam against the current. He made his reputation as a teacher of English and a writer of history. He served at different times as president of the Western Literature Association and then as president of the Western History Association. As an English professor writing history, he learned that nothing so enrages history faculty as a colleague from another department successfully challenging them on their own turf. "Historians don't like outsiders crowing on their dung-hill," he once put it.

So, who was this rabble-rousing upstart? His roots were in Minnesota, but he was born in northern Iowa on September 20, 1901, into a family of farmers. Although the name sounds Danish, the immigrating ancestor considered himself German. Leland

Sonnichsen described his mother as a tough-minded, resilient frontierswoman; his father as kind-hearted, patient, and unafraid of hard physical labor. He also made time to tell his grandchildren stories. When Doc was two his family moved to Minnesota, where he grew to maturity. After graduating from high school in Wadena, he headed for the University of Minnesota, where he received a Bachelor of Arts in English in the spring of 1924.

At Minnesota he seemed concentrated on maximizing opportunities to become a well-rounded human being. He supported himself with odd jobs, played tennis, and developed enough proficiency at fencing to become team captain. He did not make the cut for the drama club, but found his métier on the staff of the campus humor magazine. ROTC was compulsory, but he was never tempted by an army career. He developed a love for classical music by attending concerts of the Minneapolis Symphony Orchestra and cultivated an appreciation of art with frequent visits to the Walker Art Gallery. The only reason he didn't graduate magna cum laude was because he gave an interviewer the wrong answer to a simple question. Asked what was the most vital ingredient of great literature, Sonnichsen foolishly replied that he thought it should be interesting.

He launched his teaching career with a two-year stint at an Episcopalian-sponsored military school in southern Minnesota. Next step: Harvard. En route to an MA, he gained admission to the Harvard Glee Club. He gave himself whole-heartedly to its activities and continued to enjoy that pursuit for the rest of his long life. I recall a TSHA meeting of some twenty years ago when Doc and the irrepressible Joyce Gibson Roach decided to enliven proceedings by staging an impromptu recital of church tunes while standing amidst the book displays. It was a capella, of course. The hymns were all familiar at the Baptist Church in Jacksburr, Texas. [Does anyone foolishly think it's pronounced Jacksborough?] Suddenly, Doc hoisted his voice into a falsetto register in order to simulate the effect of a second soprano. This continued until Doc came down with a sore throat.

Meanwhile, back at Harvard, Sonnichsen finished his masters, and then headed to Pittsburgh, where he joined the English faculty at Carnegie Tech. While there, he made the acquaintance of Haniel Long, who would shortly depart for Santa Fe and a glorious Indian summer producing such classics as *Interlinear to Cabeza De Vaca and Piñon Country*. Not satisfied that he had reached his potential, Sonnichsen returned to Harvard in the fall of 1929 to obtain a doctorate in what was then called English philology—according to Webster, "the study of literary texts and of written records." Samuel Butler was to be his specialty. Parenthetically, philology sits almost adjacent to philogyny, which means "love of or liking for women." In his three-volume history of the Texas Folklore Society, Ab Abernethy remembers Doc as "being a continual attraction to ladies of all ages."

While at Harvard the second time around, Sonnichsen was vitally influenced by the legendary George Lyman Kittredge, noted student of English folklore and Shakespearean scholar. Kittredge was also a pillar of the American Folklore Society who had encouraged his disciple, John A. Lomax, to initiate a society that would do the same for Texas folklore. Lomax had done so, with help from Leonidas W. Payne, in 1909. J. Frank Dobie became secretary-editor of the Texas Folklore Society in 1922; it wasn't long before Dobie parted ways with the academics of the American Folklore Society and became estranged from Kittredge. These undercurrents would be felt for years to come. And Sonnichsen was awash in them.

Sonnichsen seemed oblivious to these strains during his time with Kittredge, and upon graduation from Harvard's doctoral program in 1931, he departed for the Texas College of Mines and Metallurgy in El Paso. Hopes for an ivy-league assignment dwindled as the Depression deepened. But what the heck; in two short years he was chairman of the English Department, where he remained until 1960. Nineteen thirty-three was also the year that the college president, John M. Berry, informed his young Harvard man that beginning that fall, he would be teaching a course in the

Life and Literature of the Southwest, patterned presumably on the one that J. Frank Dobie had crafted at The University of Texas in Austin. One suspects that Sonnichsen might have been laying the groundwork for this assignment because he was spending an increasing amount of time investigating early-day Texas family feuds—a far cry from Samuel Butler. In the summer of 1933, for example, he spent a month researching the Jaybird-Woodpecker affair at Richmond, Texas, southeast of Houston. Relocation to a new environment had compelled him to revise traditional approaches to research—from the intoxicating must of ancient tomes to dusty courthouse documents, tombstone inscriptions, census reports, church and family records, oral interviews, and the like.

So here he was in 1933—a department chairman albeit in a remote location, a new course to organize and teach, and research initiated in a subject that would sustain him for the next three decades. What else? Marriage. To Augusta Jones, by whom he had three children before divorcing in 1950. Six years later he married Carol Wade Sonnichsen, who survives him in Fort Worth.

Meanwhile, Sonnichsen gained wide and favorable response to his course in Life and Literature of the Southwest. So much so that in 1938 and again in 1939, he was invited to pinch-hit for J. Frank himself on the Austin campus. Dobie had the habit of leaving the Austin campus in springtime ostensibly to seek relief from hay fever, leaving his classes to Mrs. Dobie who, by general acknowledgment, was better organized than he. Cynics suspected that he was at work on his next book. Sonnichsen was amenable to a continuation of the arrangement provided it might lead to a permanent position on the Austin campus, but this was not to be, as English department barons made clear their preference for someone with more traditional interests—roughly the same argument that Dobie had encountered years earlier when he had first proposed a course in Life and Literature of the Southwest.

Be that as it may, Dobie's approval of Sonnichsen opened yet another door. For many years Dobie had made the Texas Folklore Society in his image. Beginning in the mid-1930s, Dobie and others were seeking a joint meeting with its New Mexican counterpart known, interestingly, as the New Mexico Hispanic Institute, whose luminaries included the likes of Ruth Laughlin Barker, Arthur L. Campa, Gilberto Espinosa, Paul Horgan, Edgar L. Hewitt, Alice Corbin Henderson, Matt Pierce, and Nina Otero-Warren. The meeting was foreordained to happen in El Paso. A local arrangements coordinator was needed, someone who would assume the presidency. That someone proved to be none other than Doc Sonnichsen. As he himself put it many decades later, "as soon as a comparatively sane, able-bodied El Pasoan showed up, he was going to be president, whether he liked it or not."

That 1938 Texas Folklore Society meeting was held at Hotel Paso del Norte. Doc recalled that Dobie appeared in full glory. Carl Hertzog remembered Dobie attired in a white suit working the crowd. For this occasion Hertzog turned out the handsomest program the Society had had to that date; it was enhanced with a sketch by Tom Lea, whose acquaintance he had made only short months earlier. Sonnichsen thought the $1.10 cost of the banquet ticket was exorbitant, "but it was the best I could do."

Doc's first book was obscurely published in 1942 at Caldwell, Idaho, by a most respectable regional publisher, the Caxton Press. *Billy King's Tombstone* was built around the life and times of a Tombstone, Arizona, bartender cum lawman. Or was it the other way around? Although published sans annotations, bibliography, and index, the book had a good reception. His next was the ever popular biography of *Roy Bean: Law West of the Pecos,* but prior to publication by Macmillan in 1943, it had more rejection slips than any other. Sonnichsen's immersion in folklore, especially of the Texas variety, was rationalized as "a branch of history," and, "what people agree to believe about the facts is a fact in itself, often more influential than the reality." Bean was a case in point. In 1950 came a survey of the mid-twentieth-century cattle industry—*Cowboys and Cattle Kings.* The reception was mixed and J. Frank Dobie was a lump in the batter, but as Dale Walker has observed, "the cattlefolk and their publications loved it."

Perhaps this is the place at which to talk about the schism between Sonnichsen and Dobie. In brief, Sonnichsen was a George Lyman Kittredge disciple. Kittredge's shadow had hovered over the 1909 founding of the Texas Folklore Society largely through the influence of John A. Lomax, another former pupil. But after Dobie's assumption of the secretary-editorship in 1922, relations between the eastern establishment and him grew frosty. Matters were not helped by the condescending review that his first folklore compilation—*Legends of Texas*—received in the *Journal of the American Folklore Society*, a review that may have been written by the sainted Kittredge himself. Dobie soon scoffed openly at scientific folklorists and proclaimed himself a storyteller, nothing more, nothing less. "Any tale belongs to whoever can best tell it," he asserted. And if a story needed embellishing for improvement's sake, so be it. Sonnichsen, well-grounded in the nationally accepted canons of folklore scholarship, was affronted by Dobie's attitude. With advancing age and an unassailable reputation as Mr. Texas, Dobie's position became even more calcified. A quarter century ago Sonnichsen told me that, having read *Apache Gold and Yaqui Silver*, he confronted Dobie concerning his purported discovery of the Lost Tayopa Mine. Dobie brushed aside the query, asserting, "When you are writing history, you have to stick to the facts, but when you are telling a story you have to make it a good story." Replied Sonnichsen in disbelief, "In that case somebody will have to do your work over, won't they?" Sonnichsen's great gift was his ability to stick to the facts and still tell a good story.

About 1948, as Doc was getting under way with *Cowboys and Cattle Kings*, J. Evetts Haley, Panhandle rancher and author, while on a trip through El Paso, expressed a desire to meet Sonnichsen in the flesh. Carl Hertzog made the appointment and drove Haley to the Sonnichsens' residence at the corner of Cincinnati and Piedmont Streets, snug against Mount Franklin. Sonnichsen had been left in charge of the household and its three children. Hertzog and Haley were welcomed at the front door by an apron-clad professor who ushered them past an upright vacuum cleaner whose whining sound they had heard moments earlier. As Sonnichsen led them to the kitchen, Haley observed paper in the typewriter on the dining-room table and neatly stacked typescript next to it. Lunch was cooking on the stove. The sink was half filled with freshly washed dishes. Even as he paused to wipe a snotty nose, Sonnichsen never missed a beat making his guests feel welcome with animated conversation. After a ten-minute powwow, the visitors returned to their vehicle. Once inside Haley beamed his approval to Hertzog, "That is one more hard-workin' sumbitch."

This ability to make every minute count characterized Sonnichsen to the end of his days. His English department colleague, James Day, long ago remembered how Doc, then back to teaching, would peck away at this office typewriter until five minutes before the bell, grab his notes, rush to class, give a fifty-minute lecture, return to the office, then pick up where he had left off at the typewriter. The day before he died at ninety-one he was on the roof of his Tucson home patching tiles.

After *Cowboys and Cattle Kings*, the next book was a sure 'nuff classic, *I'll Die Before I'll Run*, first published in 1951, then revised, expanded, and additionally illustrated by José Cisneros in 1962. This book was my introduction to Doc Sonnichsen; it also answered the childish question that my maternal grandmother had been unable to: why had my great-grandfather left Goliad County in 1875? The Taylor-Sutton Feud had boiled over, creating significant stress for this devout Baptist who wanted only to live at peace with his neighbors. A second feud book was published in 1957, with a rather prosaic title: *Ten Texas Feuds*.

It would be no surprise that Sonnichsen would prepare and periodically update a reading list for his course on Life and Literature. From 1934 to his 1972 departure from El Paso, he wrote endless book reviews for sundry journals and for El Paso newspapers—notably the *Herald-Post*. He resisted importuning to use these writings as the basis of an annotated bibliography of Southwestern Americana. But in 1962 he published an anthology: *The Southwest in Life and Literature*.

Three years after that he expanded a chapter from *Ten Texas Feuds* into a small book of its own about the Truett-Mitchell flare-up in Hood County in 1874. It was Sonnichsen's personal favorite of his many books, and one of mine, too. Twenty-five years ago my wife and I drove from a bed-and-breakfast on the courthouse square in Granbury out the Old Mambrino Road toward Mitchell Bend in the Middle Brazos Valley. With Sonnichsen's book in hand, the setting seemed strangely untouched since the heyday of the feud a century earlier. As the country lane dipped into the bed of wet-weather Contrary Creek, it was easy to visualize exactly where the feudists were positioned as the climatic ambush took place. One could readily imagine the echoing gunfire on the soft breeze that blew that afternoon. In the bend itself we spotted the Mitchell family cemetery and the grave of patriarch Cooney Mitchell himself, whose lynching had set off the deadly aftermath.

Doc used to tell people he knew enough secrets to write a social history of El Paso guaranteed to get him shot within twenty-four hours of publication. When he got around to publishing that El Paso history in 1968, he pulled enough punches to escape retribution. The most excitement occurred when Doc lost his grip on a bundle of galley and page proofs while entering the Texas Western Press building at the west edge of the UT-El Paso campus, where the book was being printed. He retrieved his hat from a gusty March wind all right, but the proofs went flying down a deep arroyo beside the press building and, according to Carl Hertzog's recollection, some even flew across the Rio Grande below Hart's Mill, which prompted Hertzog to announce: "Leland, this book of yours is an instant success. Not even published yet, it already has international distribution."

So much for Sonnichsen and his books. Time is up. When I think of Doc I always recall events at two consecutive meetings of the Western History Association in the early eighties. I asked Jack Rittenhouse at one of these conferences which of his numerous Stagecoach Press publications had been the best seller. Without hesitation he replied, "*Act of Enchantment,* that talk Larry Powell gave to the Historical Society of New Mexico in 1960. I think everybody in the audience must have bought one." This was another of Powell's paeans to the joys of good reading.

The next year I was recounting my conversation with Rittenhouse to Doc. "*Act of Enchantment, Act of Enchantment*," he repeated, as if trying to summon up the memory of an elusive title. Suddenly his face brightened and he exclaimed, "Ah yes, a rather *thin* little book as I recall, but I never read it. I just supposed it was Larry's attempt at a sex manual."

Doc had a granddaughter who grew up in Lubbock, became a model, and had considerable success in the Miss USA competition. She later married a Swiss diplomat. You may recall the flap last year when the Swiss ambassador to Germany was briefly recalled because his wife had posed for a German fashion magazine in a skimpy swimsuit. Guess whose granddaughter that was?

II

TEXAS-MEXICAN

FOLKLORE

The International Bridge that connects both sides of the border, El Paso and Juárez (Courtesy Skip Clark)

The El Paso-Juárez International Streetcar (Courtesy Skip Clark)

3

GROWING UP ON BOTH SIDES
OF THE BORDER

by Lucy Fischer West of El Paso

~~

My mother was born in Camargo, Chihuahua, a scant ten years after the turn of the twentieth century. She was only a few months old when the Mexican Revolution erupted and pushed her family north to Ciudad Juárez in 1910. The Rio Grande flowed furiously in those days, following the course it had carved out for itself. When her father, Jesús Lara Rey, felt the Revolution's violence come too close for comfort, he would move the family north of the river temporarily into El Paso, at one time smuggling some of the younger children in trunks to get them across the border. Family history relates that my grandfather died of a botched appendicitis operation at the hands of a drunken doctor. Antonia Lara Rey Mendoza, who bore twelve children for him, was left with the five survivors who ranged in age from one in the womb to the eldest who was nineteen. Lucina, my mother, was twelve. By the time she was fourteen, she had her first teaching job and was one of the teachers who inaugurated the *Centro Escolar Revolución* in the *Colonia Chaveña* several miles southeast of where she lived in Juárez.

In 1946, a German blue-eyed sailor came to the border, remembering that a psychic in Shanghai had told him he would have to go to a Latin American country to find the woman who would become his wife. He took the streetcar across the Stanton Street bridge and wound up at the *Plaza Alberto Balderas*. There, he found a Lion's Club dance instead of the bullfight he went looking for. As foretold, he also found the love of his life: my raven-haired, spirited mother. They danced into the wee hours, and on their date the following night, ate supper at The Oasis next to the Plaza Theater. Within days he proposed, gave her a ring, and she accepted. He left shortly thereafter to finish his tour of duty with the Merchant Marines, and for two years she received love letters with postmarks from all over the world. In 1948, she stopped teaching, married Martin Frank Fischer and the year after went across the country with him to New York State where they moved into a makeshift tarpaper shack in the woods. I was born in the Catskill Mountains. In the fall of the same year, culture shock and the cold drove my mother back to the border, where she and I settled in with my grandmother in Juárez until my father retrieved us in February of the following year.

All of her adult life my mother had been terrified of living on the north side of the Rio Grande. During her lifetime on the border, her excursions north extended only as far as downtown El Paso, especially to the Popular Dry Goods Store where she shopped for shoes to fit her narrow feet and took knitting lessons in English, although she didn't speak the language. To get to the Popular, she'd walk up El Paso Street, eyeing the tenements in the *Segundo Barrio*. She was convinced that all Mexicans who ventured across the border wound up living in those tenements, a belief which then wasn't far from the truth. About the time of my third birthday, we moved to the *Barrio del Diablo,* reputedly one of the worst neighborhoods in town. My father had purchased a three-room adobe house for $3800 from a Mr. Brown. It sat in the middle of the 3300 block of San Antonio Street. Across the empty lot out the front door we saw the traffic on Paisano Avenue, the last street before the chain link fence that separated El Paso and Juárez. Beyond that was the Chihuahuan Desert with its bounty of *chamizos* and *nopales.* Behind us flowed the Franklin Canal which carried water down from the north.

Our block was one which in today's language we would call culturally diverse. Llewellyn Thompson, a jazz pianist, lived across the street with his wife. The Greens—she Mexican, he African-American—lived next door with their two girls. Melvin White, who worked for the Southern Pacific, and his wife Estelle, a nurse, lived two doors down. My family's German-Mexican mix was unique to the neighborhood; the rest of the families on our block were Mexican. Judging from the state of our houses, in my perception at least, we must've all been about equally poor; practically every yard was part junkyard, part farmyard. My father brought home every conceivable scrap of anything even remotely usable, and it mostly sat there and rotted or rusted, much to my mother's chagrin. We raised chickens and rabbits, and kept the customary Easter gift chicks and ducklings until they grew to become Sunday dinners. Living that close to the border was an everyday adventure, and while the neighborhood had a reputation for being one of the worst in terms of gangs, I don't recall anyone voicing any apprehension. Nor did anyone seem to mind the steady stream of people coming from across the border through holes in the chain link fence looking for work. In the hobo tradition of the Depression Era, many a man was fed by my mother. These men repaid her kindness by helping her in the garden or by doing odd fix-it jobs around the house. She built a room onto the house entirely with the help of sporadic, itinerant workers. It was her favorite room, with large, light-giving windows and a room-length brick planter which in time was overflowing with jasmines, bougainvilleas, and shrimp plants, most of which she smuggled across the border. The sounds of children playing in front yards went well past dark in the summers, under the watchful eyes of parents sitting on porches to escape the inside heat since none of our houses were air-conditioned. If the teens who gathered under the corner streetlight were doing anything other than playing their instruments and singing, I certainly didn't know it.

My father worked for the McKee Construction Company during my early childhood, sometimes no more than three days per week; he lied about his age and found steadier work at Falstaff Brewery in 1956, at the age of 65. Somehow managing a home with very little money, my mother divided her time between house and garden, always with a song on her lips. She'd tell me that the reason we had no furniture was because it gave us more room to play. What we did have were books and a piano, which she played every morning after she came in from the garden.

When it came time for me to go to school, my mother decided I should go to school in Juárez. Some of the children on my block went to Zavala Elementary, others to Beall. The Greens were bussed to Douglass, in the days before integration. It was my mother's wish that I do at least kindergarten through the sixth grade in Juárez. It was her intent to take me to school and just wait for me, but the principal talked her into teaching fourth grade. The school was the *Escuela Primaria Agustín Melgar*, behind the first *Escuela Secundaria* on *16 de septiembre*, and in front of *El Parque Borunda*, then carpeted with grass and shaded by weeping willows. Every morning my mother and I would get on the #10 Paisano bus going downtown, get off and board the green, white, and yellow streetcar to go across the border, get off on *16 de septiembre* and get on the eastbound *Parque Borunda* bus to reach the school. The whole process took over two hours each way, each and every day; she felt that strongly about the value of the Mexican education, which she'd been a part of for nearly a quarter of a century.

My time at *Escuela Agustín Melgar* was a wonder that I shall never cease being grateful for. The first year there, I spent the morning in kindergarten, and the afternoon sitting on the windowsill outside first grade while my mother got through with her teaching day. When winter came, Srita. Luz Armendariz, the principal, decided that I might as well go into first grade, since I already knew how to read. We went to school ten months out of the year, and sat two and three in desks intended for one. Learning to print was not in the curriculum; script taught with the Palmer Method was. The classrooms were covered with maps for a solid foundation in geography, both Mexican and worldwide. We learned multiplication tables aloud, and the sounds of classroom voices wafted far into the park. Our physical education took place under the weeping willows. Music was a vital part of every day's activities, as was poetry. At the beginning of the year, the focus was patriotic, in preparation for *Las Fiestas Patrias* on Independence Day. I can still sing the Mexican National Anthem when the occasion calls for it. But the best times by far were the preparations for *Día de las Madres* on the 10th of May. We were all part of the school choir, which paid tribute to motherhood in song, and we were coached in the fine art of reciting heartfelt poetry complete with appropriate gestures. The following comes to mind:

> *Pañuelito perfumado, que me dio mi mamacita,*
> *bien lavado y bien planchado, me lo pongo en mi bolsita.*
> *Cuando llora mi muñeca, cuando juego a la momita,*
> *yo saco mi pañuelo, que me dió mi mamacita.*

Little hanky, perfumed hanky, that my mommy gave
    to me.
Nicely washed and nicely pressed, I keep it in my pocket.
When my little dolly cries, when I play like I'm a mommy,
I take out my little hanky that my mommy gave to me.

No mother went home without flowers: red carnations for those whose mothers were still alive, white for those whose mothers had passed away. No mother went home without gluey, glittery gifts made by small hands. No mother went home without echoes of melodies and poetry ringing in her ears. There was an abundance of pictures taken, not by parents because cameras were scarce, but by street photographers who went from school to school capturing special moments.

My time at *Escuela Agustín Melgar* was short-lived. El Paso school authorities didn't think too kindly of my mother transporting me across the border to get an education. The summer after second grade, the powers that be insisted I go to Zavala School. Not surprisingly, since I was raised in a bilingual home and had two years of solid schooling by age seven, I could read and write in both languages equally well, and knew how to add, subtract, multiply, and divide. The principal thought I should be in third or fourth grade, but my mother was adamant that I should be in a classroom with children my own age, and so I did second grade again, learned—very poorly—to print, and became the teacher's errand runner because she didn't know quite what to do with me. The transition to this side of the border became easier with time and excellent teachers: Miss Ross, Mrs. Wiseman, Mrs. Harrison, Mr. Yturralde.

One teacher who stayed with me throughout the time I was at Zavala was Mrs. Josephine Nagel. She was tall and slender, wore glasses, and kept her long blonde hair pulled back in a bun. Almost year round, she wore a bright red hibiscus from her garden tucked behind an ear. Mrs. Nagel traveled through the school's two floors pushing a cart replete with sheet music, musical instruments, a portable record player, and an autoharp. At least two times a week, we had music in the classroom, and after school twice a week there was choir. My musical debut took place in the cavernous Magoffin Auditorium at Texas Western College during a Trans-Pecos Teacher's Conference. From the uppermost center spot on the choir stand, dressed in a pale blue chiffon dress made by my mother, with confidence I gave voice to the cat's "meow" from the Brementown Musicians' song. It was Mrs. Nagel who took me back to the campus for my first experience at the opera to see a performance of *Tosca*. It was she who introduced me to traditional American folk music, spirituals, and musical theater, as well as the European classics. Perhaps because music had played such a vital role in my Mexican schooling, her dedication gave me a sense of security in a new environment while it enriched my knowledge of the universal language of music.

Because my grandmother lived in Juárez, the connection to the city continued to be a strong one. At least once a week, my mother and I would take the bus downtown, then the streetcar to downtown Juárez, and finally get on a bus going east to the *Colonia Bella Vista* to see her. My mother had several rent houses in the

Lucy Fischer (West) with her family in a 1956 photo taken by a Juárez street photographer

Lucy Fischer (West) doing a math problem at the board in the second grade at Escuela Primaria Agustín Melgar, Ciudad Juárez

same neighborhood and every time anyone moved out of one of them, she and I refurbished the place and readied it for the next tenant. We did most of our grocery shopping in Juárez—bought beef, sugar, and canned goods from *La Florida,* a Chinese-owned downtown store, fruits and vegetables at the *Mercado Cuauhtémoc.* On *Día de Los Muertos,* All Soul's Day, we cut the zinnias and marigolds from our garden, bought more *zempasúchil* and *crisantemas* along the way and joined the throngs of people who made the yearly pilgrimage to clean and decorate family grave sites. Afterwards, we lined up to eat corn on the cob boiled in #10 washtubs, served with an ample amount of butter, sprinkled with salt and chili powder, and peppered with cemetery dust. We satisfied our sweet teeth with chunks of sugar cane that we chewed all the juice out of. Year after year, the ritual trip connected me to those relatives who had died long before I was born, and most especially to the grandfather who had brought his family to the Rio Grande border.

My mother's and grandmother's speech was amply sprinkled with proverbs in the tradition of Sancho Panza. When I tried to do two things at once, they admonished, *"No se puede chiflar y comer pinole"* (You can't can eat ground toasted corn and whistle at the same time.). If a dress my mother made fit perfectly on the first try, it was *"Te cayó como anillo al dedo"* (It fit like a ring.). And if a hand-me-down fit well: *"Tu tienes cuerpo de limosnera"* (You have the body of a street urchin.). Of one of the Juárez neighbors who talked far too much, they said, "Habla hasta con los codos" (She speaks even with her elbows.). When going out to play, they'd warn, *"No te vayas a meter en la boca del lobo"* (Don't go into the head of a wolf.). And to keep me from getting caught up in others' mischief, they sent me out with *"Acuérdate que tanto peca el que mata la vaca, como el que le ata la pata"* (Equally sinful is he who ties the cow's feet as he who kills her.). These proverbs and far more than I can cite here became part of my folk speech and have remained with me.

I also became well versed in folk medicine because my mother, whether for lack of money, or because she had more faith in traditional cures than modern ones, always tried home remedies first. A precocious and gregarious child, I attracted attention and when I came down with an unexplained fever, she was sure it was *mal ojo*—evil eye. She proceeded accordingly, sweeping me with an egg and then breaking it into a bowl and putting it under the bed where I slept. Sure enough, an eye formed in the yolk and my mother decided that a favorite cousin had looked admiringly but not touched me, as is the Mexican custom. So she sought him out to break the curse by passing three mouthfuls of water to me.

To cut down the chances of a sore throat, she'd put warm saliva on her hands and spread it on my bare feet. If I still got a sore throat, it was lime juice combined with honey she poured down me. If I'd gotten my feet wet, she made sure that I also moistened the top of my head to keep me from getting blisters on the roof of my mouth or catching cold. When I got sick and she didn't know what to do, she'd call for my grandmother's wisdom. On one occasion, after several days of a fever that wouldn't break, my grandmother took a handful of Snow Cap lard from the kitchen, stripped me and rubbed me from head to toe with it. The fever broke as the chicken pox sprung. Less dramatic cures in my house included *yerba buena* for stomach upsets, chamomile for calm sleep, cinnamon tea made with *canela entera* for a cough, oregano tea for a croupy cough. Aloe vera gel squeezed out from a leaf spread on a wound served for most of my childhood injuries. A sliced wedge of garlic brought a splinter to the surface and drew out any toxins left by thorns. Like my mother, and my grandmother before her, I use and trust *remedios caseros*, home remedies passed down to me.

Besides the close bond with my grandmother in Juárez, the most important linking thread in my upbringing in El Paso was the ongoing contact to my mother's teaching community. Walking to or from the *Mercado Cuauhtémoc* beside the *Catedral de Guadalupe* to the *Mercado Juárez*, in a city whose population was then almost a quarter of a million people, we regularly encountered several of my mother's ex-colleagues, and the conversation would span decades. Most had spent longer than my mother's twenty-four years teaching, some at the *Escuela Revolución* where they had started their careers together. Rarely speaking to each other by phone because the cost was prohibitive, they came together only on each other's birthdays.

They called these occasions *"convivios"*—from the Latin "to share life." Whoever had the birthday prepared whatever meals they could afford, got dressed to the nines, and waited. About sundown, teachers would start trickling in, bringing simple gifts and sometimes food and drink to add to the repast. Raul López would make fun of Otilia Rombach, his former principal, because all she ever had was *"Pan Bimbo"* sandwiches sparsely filled with meat; only ample amounts of beer would make them palatable, he said. Her specialty was *"rompope con piquete"*—spiked eggnog. It was amusing to see all five-foot-two of her taking those tiny steps on the worn, bare hardwood floor back and forth to the sparse kitchen to get something for someone. At Margarita Ibañez de Salgado's house there was always loud dance music and lots of food. She'd been quite a tango dancer in her youth, and in her late fifties, she still had a figure she could brag about, especially in the bright dresses she loved to wear.

Most of these teachers were women. Some had married, but most had not, dedicating their lives to hundreds of children over the decades. When they got together, these women spoke not of their *achaques*, their maladies, but of how in their youth the Mexican government had treated them to free hotels in Mexico City and passes on the railroad from Juárez to anywhere the railroad went. My mother's favorite tale was of the regularly derailing trains in Chihuahua. *"Las Muchachas"*—the girls—were so well known as a group that the engineer would send them to the nearest town on a hand car to bring back food for the passengers; if they were stuck somewhere for a night, no town, however small, lacked enough musicians to put together a dance in their honor. These women spoke of the thrill of teaching with a zeal that lasted their whole lives. They broke into song as easily as they broke into laughter.

By the time I was ten, it was understood that I would be baking the cakes for the occasions. How my mother and I transported sheet cakes across the border on the streetcar, I don't remember, but we did. On October 21st we'd take one to Srita. Otilia, whom everyone respected for her integrity as a principal. On November 4th, it was for Srita. Carolina, whose specialty was scolding children and boxing ears, but whose garden was bountiful with violets with which she'd make nosegays for her table. As they grew older and it was more difficult to get around, the crowd got smaller and smaller but no less lively. When I got old enough to drive, I'd do the rounds in Juárez picking them up. I think that one of the things my mother missed most about not living south of the river was the freedom to go anywhere she wanted on the bus, to see her friends, to minister to them as they got older. Many of them couldn't come to El Paso to sing my mother the traditional *"Las Mañanitas"* on the Feast of Candlemas Day, February 2nd, when her birthday came. Some had never acquired passports. There was one gathering that I do remember, after my mother had bought a Magnavox console at the Union Furniture Store on South Stanton Street. Margarita led a conga line, weaving it in and out throughout the rooms in our house and then outside, filling the *barrio's* winter night air with laughter and music.

On the summer night that my mother lay peacefully still at the age of eighty-one, those women who were still alive came to pay their last respects, gathered around her casket, and sang the songs of their youth to wish her a joyous farewell.

When I go to Juárez now, following much the same shopping route as I did with my mother so long ago, I sing her praises for the rich cultural border background that was her inestimable and enduring gift to me. Outside the *Mercado Juárez,* I buy meat from a butcher who was her student, and inside I get spices, chilies, nuts, and vanilla from another, who reminds me every time I see him that Srita. Lucina was his favorite teacher. Traveling north, I drive over the nearly buried streetcar rails on *Avenida Juárez,* and once over the border, I eye the tenements that are still there. The house on San Antonio Street, long since sold, is nearly unrecognizable and no longer has my mother's well-kept garden around it. Red-bricked Zavala School sits beneath the freeway connecting to the Bridge of the Americas. My memories of the *Barrio del Diablo* and of growing up with one foot on either bank of the Rio Grande flow as freely as the river did in its wildest days.

[*"*Growing up on Both Sides of the Rio Grande*"* will be included in Lucy Fischer West's book *Child of Many Rivers: Journeys to and from the Rio Grande,* forthcoming from Texas Tech University Press.]

Lucy with her mother (right) and her second grade teacher at
Escuela Primaria Augustín Melgar

THREE GENERATIONS OF STORY TELLERS

"Welito" Sixto Dominguez

Bertha Dominguez

Sixtito Dominguez

4

WELITO: A MEXICAN-AMERICAN FAMILY IN SOUTHWEST TEXAS

by Bertha Dominguez of Del Rio

[Bertha Dominguez (1941–1997) was a student of Elton Miles in his Southwestern Literature class at Sul Ross State College in 1972. She and Elton sent me her paper to consider for publication the following year. This was during my earliest spasm of activity with the idea of a family saga book. I did not use it, for some reason, but I did like it and filed it away for future use. "Future use" arrived with our decision to include a separate collection of Texas-Mexican papers in this 2004 miscellany. After all these years, I was able to locate Bertha's mother and sister, Luisa and Estela Dominguez of Del Rio. From them I learned that Bertha Dominguez received a degree in English and P. E. from Sul Ross and that she taught high school classes from 1970 until her death in 1997. Bertha taught Greek and Roman mythology, and in 1997 she and her sister Estela made the grand tour to the classical hearthstones of Greece and Rome. That pilgrimage, I feel, is a most fitting conclusion to an academic life.—*Abernethy*]

This is a brief biography of my grandfather, Sixto Dominguez, as told to me by my father, Sixtito Dominguez, with recollections of old tales and true life happenings which are told in my family. They are rather typical of the average Mexican-American family in the Del Rio area, which is wool and mohair ranching country. The Spanish word for grandfather is *abuelito,* but most Mexican-American children pronounce it *welito.* Therefore I will use that word in referring to my grandfather.

Welito Sixto Dominguez was born of Mexican parents on a ranch called Bigotes, close to Jimenez, Coahuila. His father, Don Manuel Dominguez, was a wealthy rancher and had several ranch hands. When Welito was twelve years old, his mother fell in love with one of the ranch hands, Manuel Salazar. She divorced Don Manuel and married the ranch hand. She kept her children, but they had to move off the Dominguez ranch. Manuel Salazar decided that the best place for him to get ahead and support a family would be in the Estados Unidos, so he packed up their meager belongings and crossed the Rio Grande into Del Rio.

Times were hard, and Manuel could find only a few odd jobs, trying to keep the family going. One day Welito's mother decided that it was time for Welito to go to school and learn the language of the gringo.

At the age of thirteen, dressed in faded overalls, and wearing a pair of old boots that had been mended by his stepfather, Welito was enrolled in the first grade. Welito was afraid and he suffered during the first day of school because the kids made fun of him. The second day was no different from the first, and the taunts grew worse, because the kids thought it was funny for a thirteen-year-old boy to be in the first grade. He took as much as he could from them, but all too soon the Dominguez temper exploded. He beat up a couple of kids and knocked some teeth out of one of them. That same day he was expelled from school. That was the extent of Welito's formal education; yet he learned to read and write on his own and later learned math from an old Mexican who had been a schoolteacher.

Being expelled from school didn't bother Welito. He was ready to explore around La Loma de la Cruz, and now he had the time to do it. He had heard about the legend of Round Mountain, as the Anglos called it, from the old folks who got together after dinner to spin yarns. It was said that when the Spaniards came through the area, they had been burdened by a large amount of gold and jewels, and they had decided to bury it on the Loma de la Cruz, which is a steep cone-shaped hill with a big cross standing on a peak.

Somewhere close to the cross, there was supposed to be an opening that a few people claim to have seen, with a voice that came from within and invited the outsider to take the riches hidden there, with only one condition: the treasure must be taken out in one trip, all or nothing. It is said that if the person took off down the hill in search of a bag to carry the gold in, the opening would never again be found. Welito never could find the opening.

A few years later, Manuel found a job as a ranch hand for the Charlie Clark ranch, by the banks of the Rio del Diablo. Welito had to work to help out, because the family had grown and now there were ten kids to feed. He helped out for a while, and at the age of twenty-two, he decided to go out on his own and become a sheep shearer. Four years later, Welito met and married our Welita Trine—Trinidad Olivarez de Leon. She bore him three sons—José, Sixto Jr. ("Sixtito"), and Belizario—and a daughter, Oralia.

Welito worked very hard to get ahead, and soon he had his own shearing machine. He was a very ambitious man and he branched out into fencing and road building. He had contracts all over the area around Pumpville and Comstock and as far north as Pandale.

Once, while his crew was building a fence at the Hal Hamilton Ranch, he took his son Sixtito with him when he went to check on their progress. Mr. Hamilton was a breeder of Indian ponies, and one of them caught Sixtito's eye. Sixtito had always loved horses, and he knew he just had to have that one. He tugged at his father's pants leg and begged him to ask "El Soldado," as Mr. Hamilton was called, to sell him the pony. His father asked El Soldado, and El Soldado said, "Sixto, your boy has been going to school for a year now. If you can get him to ask me in English, I won't sell him the horse, I'll give it to him." Sixtito never got the horse because he refused to ask for the horse in English.

Welito had a lot of irons in the fire. On one occasion, while he was spending a few days with one of his shearing crews at the Wesley White Ranch, a few miles above the Pecos River, a pure bred Quina sow and her young brood wandered into camp. The crew was through for the day, and decided it would be good sport to try to lasso the little Quinos. The hooting and hollering scared the old sow, and she ran into a post by the water trough. She hit so hard that she fell over and grunted heavily for a while.

Mr. White rode into camp a short while later and wanted to know what had happened to the sow. The cook came over and told him that she had come staggering into camp and just collapsed. "Must be that loco weed they have been eating," he said. "I've had a few of them die on me in the last few days. You might as well kill it and use the fat at least, if nothing else, for making soap." The cook was overjoyed, he killed the Quina, knowing she had died from the blow on the head and not from the loco weed. That night he made *chorizo*—Mexican sausage—*chicharrones,* and everything else he could think of. The next day they had a meal fit for a king: fresh meat *chicharrones,* cooked with green chiles, tomatoes, and onions, fresh *pan de acero* baked in a Dutch oven covered with hot coals, frijoles, and Spanish rice, washed down with a pot of hot steaming coffee.

Between shearing jobs, Welito and a couple of friends decided to go fishing out by Howard Canyon. They camped by the spring at the foot of the bluff, which was surrounded by oak trees. They slept close together because they knew that as soon as the moon came up, the legend of the jewels would come alive. The ghostly wagon, driven by an overexcited man, would come tearing down the bluff. The noises were heard, but the wagon was never seen. The men knew that it was connected with the hidden treasure, and that it never hurt anybody. Besides, the fishing was good so they didn't mind the noise.

Everybody knew there was a sackful of jewels hidden around there somewhere. People came from far and near and dug up the place until it looked like a plowed field. The only sign they had to go by was a cedar peg stuck into an old oak tree trunk about five feet above the ground. People measured and counted from that peg in all directions, and dug holes everywhere but never came up with anything.

Welito found out about twenty years later that the jewels had actually been there and that they had been found. One day, while talking to Mr. Mills, the owner of the property, the conversation somehow turned to the old jewel legend, and Mr. Mills told Welito that an old couple had come down to the ranch one day to ask permission to camp out by the spring for a few days. A couple of days later one of Mr. Mills' ranch hands, who had been working in that area, came by and Mr. Mills asked him if he had seen the old couple out there by the spring. The cowboy said, "They are gone, but I noticed something odd about the old oak tree with the peg. It's dying out." Mr. Mills became curious and on his way to town one day he stopped by the spring. The cedar peg had been removed from the tree, and the hole revealed a hollow space inside the tree. Mr. Mills figured that it must have been the hiding place for the jewels. "You know, Sixto," he told Welito, "the ghost wagon hasn't come tearing down the bluff since then."

Welito was a good fence contractor with an honest head on his shoulders. His men liked and worked well for him. He was offered a job by the Southern Pacific Railroad to build fences for the right-of-way. Once, when Welita Trine was very sick with tuberculosis, he received word that a special train was coming through. Welito had so many things on his mind that he forgot about the train. When he heard the whistle he remembered, but the train was only a couple of miles away. Welito had two handcars on the trains and the track had to be cleared. The crew quickly set about removing the handcars. When one had been removed there was barely enough time to move the other one, but Welito gave the order for the men to clear out. The engineer saw the handcar and managed to stop the train in time, but he told Welito to take down the engine number and the time of the incident, because he was going to report him to the company.

Welito's headquarters were in Langtry at the time, and it was there that he received word that he had been fired by the railroad. He was also asked to appear at a hearing in El Paso a few days later. In El Paso, Welito was told that he could have his old job back if he decided to put the blame on his crew foreman and a few laborers. Welito told them that he had not asked Southern Pacific Railroad for the job, that the job had been offered to him by the SP. Besides, he had two crews out building a rock tank and a ranch road, and two more shearing crews out, so he really didn't need the job that badly. "The men need the job more than I do, and I'm not about to accuse innocent people of something I did," he said.

The Southern Pacific Railroad offered him the job again sometime later, but he again refused because he said that the Southern Pacific had too strict rules. Soon after that, Welita Trine died.

A year later, while on a visit to Monterrey in Nuevo Leon, Welito met and married Petra Arredondo. Petra turned out to be a very mean stepmother who hated my dad, his brothers, and sister. They were living in Del Rio.

My Uncle José, who was eighteen years old at the time, and five-year-old Oralia were very close. One day, Petra became enraged because little Oralia worked too slowly, and she picked up a piece of firewood to hit her. Uncle José came in about that time and grabbed the club from her and quickly ordered her to pack. He was fed up with all the injustices of crabby old Petra, and the Dominguez temper had flared up again. He told Petra that he was taking her back to Mexico, and that she would not return unless he died.

Eighteen months later Petra returned and it was for Uncle José's funeral. While driving a load of feed out to one of the ranches out toward Juno, his truck overturned five miles from Comstock and he was killed instantly. Petra was back to stay, and she continued to make life miserable for the rest of the family.

When my dad was sixteen years old, Petra decided that it was time for him to quit school and start earning a living by helping Welito out, taking charge of the crews full time. My dad was a football player and pitcher for the San Felipe High School baseball team at the time. He was also above average scholastically, and would more than likely graduate with honors the next year. Petra was not to be denied, and Dad left school his junior year, to work with Welito full time in the shearing camps.

Once when Dad and Welito were delivering a load of feed for the cattle at the Ingram Ranch, they arrived late in the afternoon and were tired and hungry. They had been on the road for two days because of tire trouble, and they hadn't eaten much. The first thing they did was to look for the foreman so he could give them something to eat. The foreman was not at home, so they walked in to see what they could find. They found a few gallons of fresh milk, some stale bread, and a few green chiles. Over in the corner of the kitchen hung a little *sarzo,* which is like a little cage where meat and such is kept cool and away from any animals that might wander in. In it they found some fat and some meat *chicharrones.* They ate heartily, and washed it down with the sweet milk.

While unloading the feed awhile later, they were told by the foreman that they had just eaten skunk chicharrones. He told them that he had fixed them because a friend of his had needed the fat of a skunk for a home remedy. It was too late for them to do anything about the whole thing, since they had already eaten it. Besides, it had been a good meal.

Dad recalled the story of the sheep-herder named Pedro de Luna, who came down to the old Tanque Quemado every day to water his herd. One day Welito had gotten some mountain lion meat from a trapper who worked for Mr. Jones down at Bullis Gap. Welito put the meat out to dry and made some great *cecinas,* or jerky. The cook made a great meat *quiso* and everyone had a good meal. Pedro told them that it was the best meal he had ever had, and asked if the jerky had been venison. When he was told that it was mountain lion, he stuck his finger in his mouth, trying to throw up what he had eaten, but the rest of the crew told him that if he had enjoyed the meal he shouldn't ruin it like that. They finally convinced him there was nothing wrong with mountain lion, and he went back to his herd.

Once while constructing a bed for a turbine that would produce electricity along the Pecos River, Welito and his crew were told that they could use an old rock cottage, which was standing nearby. The cottage had been built by Marcos Ausejo, a Spaniard, and was still in good shape. The men decided to sleep inside and keep a little warmer, but two old men who were working with the crew advised them against it. Lino Santiago and Sixto Lazaro had both slept in there before, and they both claimed that there were *duendes* in the house. *Duendes* are spirits that take your covers at night, and if they feel like it, they carry you outside cots and all. The old men claimed that they had been carried out one night, and they accused the other men of playing jokes on them. They offered no explanation for the *duendes,* but told the men if anybody doubted them, they could go ahead and try sleeping in the cottage.

Welito spent the last few years of his life working as a caretaker in a cemetery, and died a few years back [this was written in 1972] while visiting his old birthplace, the Bigotes Ranch in Jimenez.

TEACHING MATH
Social Satire from the Computer

Teaching Math in 1950:
A logger sells a truckload of lumber for $100. His cost of production is 4/5 of the price. What is the profit?

Teaching Math in 1960:
A logger sells a truckload of lumber for $100. His cost of production is 4/5 of the price, or $80. What is his profit?

Teaching Math in 1970:
A logger exchanges a set "L" of lumber for a set "M" of money. The cardinality of a set "M" is 100. Each element is worth one dollar. Make 100 dots representing the elements of the set "M." The set "C," the cost of production contains 20 fewer points than set "M." Represent the set "C" as subset "M" and answer the following question: What is the cardinality of the set "P" of profits?

Teaching Math in 1980:
A logger sells a truckload of lumber for $100. His cost of production is $80 and his profit is $20.
    Your assignment: Underline the number 20.

Teaching Math in 1990:
By cutting down beautiful forest trees, the logger makes $20. What do you think of this way of making a living? Topic for class participation after answering the question: How did the forest birds and squirrels "feel" as the logger cut down the trees? There are no wrong anwers.

Teaching Math in 2002:
A logger sells a truckload of lumber for $100. His cost of production $120. How does Arthur Anderson determine that his profit margin is $60?

Teaching Math in 2010:
El hachero vende un camion carga pr $100. La cuesta de production es. . . .

Gregoria Arispe Galván (1901–1997) in 1940, a professional midwife certified by San Antonio's Board of Child Hygiene, who practiced in that city for sixty-two years

5

FOLKLORE OF A SAN ANTONIO MIDWIFE

by Alicia Zavala Galván of San Antonio

Gregoria Arispe Galván was born in 1901 in Laredo, Texas, and moved to San Antonio when she was eleven years old. She came from a poor working class Hispanic family. She married at the age of eighteen, and in the late 1920s decided to become a midwife to help provide additional income for the education of her three children. She attended midwife classes that were given by local physicians, as was dictated by state and city regulations at the time. After three years, she was certified by the city's Board of Child Hygiene to practice midwifery in San Antonio, where she did so actively for sixty-two years, from 1929 to 1991.

Gregoria always strove to attain and project a personal and professional image of expertise and sophistication. This was done by serious study—her main reference was a well used 1901 obstetrics text—competent practice, and attention to appropriate fashions of the day. She also conveyed her status through the firmness of her convictions, expressed whether or not one wanted to hear them.

Her professional life was well organized. She kept her certifications up to date, and was proud of the documents that testified to her training and authorized her occupation. While there was no standardized uniform, many midwives then wore a white dress that seemed suitable to the station. Hers were of "puckered nylon," and with a set of five uniforms, she always had a clean and fresh uniform for every visit.

She carried with her on her house calls a black leather valise of a size that any physician would be proud of. In it were the tools of her trade: one rubber glove (right hand only), paraffin-encased silver nitrate eye drops for the new infant, antibiotic eye ointment nicely kept in a small box from Joske's—then San Antonio's most fashionable department store—scissors and hemostat for cutting bandages and umbilical cords, clean towels, a spool of encased sterile umbilical tape for tying the cord, a pull-scale from which was hung the newly diapered infant, a single pink tissue, and a small record book in which was recorded the vitals of new mother, father, and baby. (Or babies—she once gained local newspaper attention by delivering quintuplets, a litter of five healthy children.) All of these items except the lone pink tissue and the Joske's box were required by city and state rules. The right-hand rubber glove was all she felt she needed, as it was the right hand that massaged the vaginal opening and received the infant at birth while the left hand pressed the mother's abdomen. "The right hand does all the work," she once said.

Along with the up-to-date scientific and medical knowledge that she applied in her consultations, home visits, and deliveries, she also carried with her a parallel stream of religious and traditional folk beliefs. The practices and outlooks of both worlds came to bear on her patients, many of whom were familiar with and had confidence in the procedures and remedies that came from a strong Hispanic Catholic tradition. She would often adapt standard medical practices of the day to forms—or philosophies—that were more comfortable and acceptable to her clients. These understandings generally fell into four areas: fertility, prebirth/prenatal care, the birth event itself, and post-partum care.

Fertility was something either to be encouraged or discouraged. To promote fertility, an all-natural herbal tea was developed by Gregoria. The tea was to be drunk for ten days, with the patient avoiding sexual intercourse during this time. After the ten days were up, one was allowed intercourse no more than twice a week until the next menstrual cycle. I truly regret never learning all the ingredients of this special tea which, according to written testimonials, was said to be ninety-nine percent effective.

A "cold uterus" (*frialdad*) was believed to be the cause of menstrual cramps and thought to impede fertility. Belladonna ointment was used for cramping of the uterus; the ointment is known to be an anticholingeric, a smooth muscle relaxant. Cardui's Tonic, a homeopathic preparation no longer available, made of herbs and iron, was also recommended for this, as well as for treating the symptoms of menopause. Patients were also asked to use Lydia Pinkham Tonic for the menstrual irregularities in menopause and infertility, another homeopathic medicinal liquid made from herbal blends and an iron supplement, a preparation still available and popular.

To treat a delayed menstrual period or prevent a possible pregnancy shortly after intercourse, a homeopathic preparation readily available in pharmacies then and still to be found today was Humphrey's 11 tablets. A strong laxative of castor oil was another treatment for delayed menses or possible pregnancy to be used in the first two weeks. Gregoria never performed an abortion, but she did provide recommendations in times when women had much more restricted choices and information.

Prenatal beliefs were many and widespread, and Gregoria adhered to some but not others. One she affirmed was that if one hears a baby cry before it is born, that is a sign that the infant will carry a distinctive talent. However, no mention should be made at all by either parent until after the birth to ensure the child will fulfill its special ability.

Other folk beliefs were that one must wear a key during an eclipse and avoid going out during any eclipse to prevent birth defects, such as cleft palate, Down's syndrome, or similar anomalies. Further, one must avoid eating bananas, for they are too heavy to digest and might provoke a miscarriage or cause a stroke. Some of the mother's food cravings could be allowed, but Gregoria discouraged excessive intake of fattening foods. She advised her patients to eat a balanced diet, but she didn't care for the phrase, "eating for two." The child could always get fattened up after birth, she observed. Still thought to be good sense today, we also know that a large and heavy baby made for a more difficult and prolonged labor and delivery. It was also advised that mothers should avoid over-stretching during pregnancy, such as reaching overhead, for this might cause fetal strangulation within the womb or at birth by leading the umbilical cord to become tightly wound around the baby's neck.

The birth event, of course, was the focus of Gregoria's training and care. Another set of traditional beliefs and practices came into play if a thin transparent membrane that completely covered the head of the fetus, known as *El Velo* (the veil), appeared at birth. An infant born with the tissue was predicted to have a special ability or talent; the membrane became a signifier (*El Don*) of this. The parents were to wash the membrane very carefully, wrap it and save it in a box, and give it to the child when it became an adult.

Gregoria used olive oil to lubricate the vaginal birth opening to facilitate the passage of the child's head, and also used it to cleanse the baby after birth. Olive oil is a natural plant product, not artificially produced in comparison to petrolatum, which is a chemical by-product. In the delivery, she felt forceps were not necessary for a normal home birth (as all of hers were), unless there were complications, in which case a doctor would be called or the patient would be taken to a hospital. Though she carried a set of home stirrups, a decidedly frighteningly looking apparatus, she felt they were also unnecessary and could even be counterproductive emotionally and physically for the patient. Staying in bed one whole day after birth, except for going to the bathroom, was insisted upon, for this allowed the mother complete rest after childbirth and prevented hemorrhaging. For many women, this was a decided luxury!

After delivery, a cotton abdominal binder fastened with large safety pins was prescribed to be worn for forty days to help preserve a woman's physical appearance and to restore muscle tone. Elastic was not recommended because the skin could not breath, and also the cloth binder could be adjusted according to the decreasing abdominal girth of the woman as the weeks went by. A similar cotton binder was also put on the baby to prevent an umbilical hernia. For lack of other material in many homes in that time, the binders were often made of old clean sheets, but they had to be without colors or dyes.

On the second day after birth, the breasts engorge with milk and the flow begins, and a fever may also occur. In Spanish, this is known as *El Golpe*. For many women, breastfeeding was not a realistic option as they had to work many days and long hours and could not take the baby with them. Some did not want to breastfeed at all. To discourage the flow of milk, a natural regime was prescribed in which fluid intake was decreased and a cotton binder was wrapped snugly around the breasts to gradually decrease the production of milk. During Gregoria's time, women who wanted to speed up this process went to a physician who prescribed the drug Diethystilbesterol, abbreviated DES. Years later this was discontinued due to tragic side effects suffered by these women.

After delivery, the woman was directed to avoid sexual intercourse for forty days to help cleanse and restore the uterus to its pre-pregnancy state. This is now an accepted theory by many physicians. The traditional idea of "Bitter Mother's Milk" does represent an actual condition where the milk is in fact bitter. It was said, however, that when a baby rejects the mother's milk for this reason, it could mean that the child will be very headstrong or have a difficult personality. The mother was told to switch to standard commercial baby formulas and not to force the baby to breastfeed.

Gregoria Arispe Galván, the woman who raised me and home-delivered two of my own three children, continued consultations from 1991 to 1993, and died in San Antonio in 1997. By her wishes, she was buried with her official midwife's pin.

6

RELIGION, SUPERSTITIONS, AND REMEDIOS IN THE MEXICAN-AMERICAN CULTURE

by Gloria Duarte of San Angelo

~

The saying *"Sana, sana, colita de rana, / Si no te alivias hoy te aliviarás mañana"* (Get well, get well, little frog's tail, / If you don't get well today, you'll get well tomorrow.) or some variation of it was frequently heard in our Mexican-American community, especially when small Mexican-American children fell and hurt themselves. Along with the rhyme, the bruised or hurt area would be delicately touched and saliva applied. Watching a recent television commercial for health insurance and remembering the rhyme reminded me of the reason for the adherence to remedios—no insurance coverage! Because of lack of insurance coverage and because of cultural isolation, many Mexican-Americans have relied on a curandero and basic home remedies to take care of injuries or illnesses among the residents of the community. In some instances, immigrants consult *curanderos* or unlicensed practitioners for several reasons, including lack of money for insurance, preference for the type of care they had in their native country, and in some cases the fear of having their immigration status checked.[1]

Religion, superstitions, and remedios contribute to the conglomeration involved in folk healing beliefs and practices of such maladies as *mal de ojo, susto,* and *empacho* to name a few.

Religion has always been an important part of Mexican-American culture. In most Mexican-American communities, it is common to hear numerous mentions of God in reference to a variety of daily occurrences in life. For example, when people want or expect certain things to happen they leave it in God's hand: *lo que diós quiera* (what God wants), *que sea la voluntad de diós* (May it be God's decision.). Even in times of tragedy, we heard *así lo quiso diós* (That's how God wanted it.). Things happen because that is God's design. They feel that they have no control over life's occurrences, so if bad things happen, it is because God wants them to. In sum, God takes care of His people and His people are not to question God's design. If things do not work out as planned, it means that better things are in store because *Diós cuida a sus hijos* (God takes care of his children.), and He will provide.

All of these sayings became common refrains in Mexican-American culture. Even in saying good night, *Hasta mañana* (until tomorrow or good night), to our parents and siblings, the response was *Si diós quiere* (if God wills it). A similar phrase was used as a morning greeting, *Buenos días le de diós* (May God give you a good morning.). These traditional phrases indicate that the Mexican-American people see many occurrences in life as beyond man's control. Understanding this state of mind helps one to understand why the feelings of guilt and acceptance are somewhat different in this culture from American Anglo-Saxon culture.

Carryover of religious beliefs from the church to the homes in the form of saints is common. Every home in our community, and I dare say in most Mexican-American communities, has a crucifix, a picture of the Virgin of Guadalupe, patron saint of Mexico, and some holy water used in curing. Statues of other patron saints, as well as blessed palms, can usually be found in the homes. Even now in Catholic homes and even in restaurants, one finds crosses made from blessed palms and a statue of a favorite patron saint like San Martín de Porres or San Martín Caballero, who is believed to protect the place and bring it good luck. The blessed palms are usually burned during severe storms or other calamities to insure good luck. Many homes have their own small altars, also.

The same faith that is placed in God to explain simple occurrences applies to folk healing beliefs and practices, which include both superstitions and traditional remedies—and the use of good common sense. Because the nearest doctors are usually located miles away from the small communities and because many Mexican-American families do not have medical insurance coverage, they depend on themselves or someone in the community to heal minor illnesses, and they often depend on curanderos to look after more serious illnesses. This does not mean they never consult a physician, but these traditional approaches are familiar and comfortable to use.

Prevention of illness is extremely important in Mexican-American communities, and children are raised hearing much well-meaning advice. My mother and grandmother warned my siblings and me against going to bed with wet hair because that would cause us to have sore throats. Another piece of advice we heard was that we should never go out in the cold after taking a bath or shaving; otherwise, they warned us, our mouths would turn. They could usually show us someone who had gone outside too soon and whose face was paralyzed as a result.

We were also to avoid going out into the cold weather without covering our heads since earaches were a certainty if we did so. If we ignored this advice and got air in our ears and a resultant earache, the cure was rather unusual. My grandmother would fashion a funnel out of paper, place the pointed part inside our ear, and with a match light the wide part of the funnel. As the heat reached the inner ear, we could hear a pop, and the air would rush out and extinguish the flame. As unusual as using the paper-funnel earache cure may sound, the *Chicago Heights Star* featured an article on ear coning, which involves essentially the same process but for a different result. According to the article, ear coning derives from the Native American culture and Mexican culture. Santarra, a healer from Sedona, Arizona, has practiced ear coning for several years. She devises the cones herself out of muslin, dips them in beeswax, and adds sage. The process softens the ear wax and vacuums the wax onto the cone.[2]

A few superstitions we grew up hearing became part of our cultural upbringing. We were never to leave shoes at the head of the bed because to do so insured having nightmares. My mother always covered mirrors in the house and warned us to stay away from the mirrors during lightning storms. Nor did any of us ever cut our nails on Sunday because we were raised believing that if we did we would certainly be socially embarrassed sometime in the next few days. *Antojo* is another belief associated with sharing food. If a person craves or desires a certain food and does not taste it, *le sale un grano en la lengua* (a sore on the tongue results). Thus, in a Mexican-American home, a guest is always expected to at least taste whatever the others are eating.

Another superstition was the belief that if a person's ears turn warm and red, then someone is talking about him. We said, *Nos están sonando los oídos* (Our ears are ringing.). We immediately knew someone was talking about us. In addition, we knew whether what was being said was good or bad. If it was the right ear that was burning, whatever was being said was complimentary, whereas if it was the left ear, it was not. The proper vocal response if the left ear was burning was *que se muerdan la lengua* (May they bite their tongue.).

During the time when we had no telephones we knew when to expect company. If a piece of silverware or a dishrag fell to the floor, this meant company was coming.

With Mexican-American enculturation, these beliefs, superstitions, and *remedios* have lost their relevance. The success of folk healing depends almost entirely on faith, on believing that one will be cured by a particular remedio. Many of the *remedios caseros,* or home remedies that we grew up with, involved infants. For instance, a common cure for hiccoughs included placing a piece of red thread on the child's forehead. Placing a wooden match behind an adult's ear was the grownup's cure. Another remedy and belief applied to newborn babies was giving them cumin tea to instill common sense in them. Eliseo Torres recommends cumin seeds boiled to make a mild and soothing tea for teething babies.[3] Another remedy for newborns was to place a silver dollar wrapped in gauze around the baby's bellybutton with an abdominal binder to prevent umbilical hernias. The binder was kept in place until the hernia was reduced. As infants grew and started teething, the mothers hung a dime threaded with a string around the baby's neck to prevent fussiness. To eliminate coughs, mothers would rub Vicks Vaporub on the baby's chest and then cover it with a warm towel, which had been heated by ironing and folding it several times. Finally, to eliminate diaper rash on babies, dry starch was applied on the baby's bottom. These two cures move from remedios to modern over-the-counter medicine.

Another more serious illness associated with infants was *capada de mollera,* or fallen fontanel. Some believed that the sunken "soft spot" on the top of an infant's head could be caused by the child's having been dropped or having the mother's breast or the nipple of the bottle pulled too abruptly out of its mouth.[4] Accompanying symptoms may include diarrhea and irritability. A recommended treatment included wetting the baby's head with warm water and soaping the soft spot. The healer then gently placed his fingers inside the baby's mouth and pushed up on the palate, with the other hand gently pulling the hairs on the baby's soft spot.[5]

Probably one of the most common superstitions associated mainly with infants is *mal de ojo,* or evil eye (literally "bad eye"). Looking admiringly at a child without touching him can cause a listless condition in the infant. This condition is not inflicted through malice but rather through excessive admiration of those too weak to absorb it.[6] One of the most common charms worn as protection against *mal de ojo* is the *ojo de venado,* or deer's eye.[7] To counteract the potential of *mal de ojo,* the admirer of the child must touch it.[8] For this reason, strangers make a point of touching babies they come in contact with.

The symptoms of *mal de ojo* are similar to those of colic—irritability, drooping eyes, fever, headache, and vomiting.[9] One cure involves *barriendo* (sweeping) the child with a whole egg. Robert Trotter explains, "The sweeping is done by forming crosses (*crusitas*) with the egg on the child's body, starting at the head and going to the feet. While sweeping, the healer recites the Apostle's Creed three times, making sure that she/he sweeps both the front and the back."[10] "The egg is then broken into a saucer and placed under the child's bed overnight, usually under the place where the child rests his head. If the child has *mal de ojo,* then an eye will form on the egg yolk. Then the envious one, or the one who looked too admiringly at the child, must pass three mouthfuls of water to the sick one."[11] Trotter recommends burning or casting away the egg in the form of a cross the following morning at sunrise.[12]

Although these beliefs and remedies used by Mexican Americans to care for their young children seem far-fetched, they're not in some cases. The people used traditional methods and cures handed down through their families that involved using basic materials at their disposal.

Some pediatricians today use their own versions of home remedies with their own children. Antonia van der Meer in "How Pediatricians Treat Their Own Kids," reveals that for a cold, Dr. Andrade, a pediatrician in San Jose, California, gives his children saline nose drops made from one fourth of a teaspoon of table salt and four ounces of hot water. To soothe the throat and reduce coughs, Dr. Schweitzer, a pediatrician in Washington, D.C., gives her children decaffeinated tea with lemon and honey. Another pediatrician, Dr. Simon, sprays his children with Niagara spray starch rather than calamine lotion when they have chicken pox. Dr. Simon also rubs Maalox on his children's diaper rash to coat the skin with an antacid.[13]

Among Mexican Americans, *empacho* is another common ailment that can be treated at home with traditional doctoring. *Empacho* is caused by poorly cooked food or poorly digested food sticking to the abdominal lining, which then causes swelling. Eliseo Torres' explanation of empacho is that it

> reflects the need for balance that is expressed in
> the theory of humours—thought to be caused by
> improperly mixing hot with cold foods, or eating

> such foods in improper sequence. Eating too
> quickly and thus not chewing food completely is
> another act thought to cause *empacho*.[14]

Symptoms of *empacho* include diarrhea and a feeling of weight in the pit of one's stomach and sometimes loss of appetite.[15] Treatment involves rubbing the stomach with oil (or *volcanico*), and then *estirando la espalda*, or pulling the back. The patient lies flat, face down with arms outstretched, and then the healer pinches the loose skin from the back and pulls it in small folds straight up about every third vertebrae and then releases it. The process is repeated down the entire back area until three pops are heard, signifying the release or dislodgment of a bolus. The back is then massaged with a soft pounding after the pulling is repeated. The process concludes with a cup of *tea de estafate* (larkspur) or *manzanilla* (chamomile). This procedure was a favorite cure among the young children because of the comfort brought about by the massage.

Mal de susto (fright), an uncommon illness, requires a curandero for a cure. *Susto* can be caused by a traumatic experience, by receiving bad news, or by something supernatural. *Susto* is sometimes translated as "loss of spirit or even loss of soul,"[16] because supposedly at that point the spirit leaves the body. *Susto* must be treated immediately; otherwise, it can lead to a much more serious version, called s*usto pasado,* which is much more difficult to treat because more time has elapsed between the cause and the illness.[17] Symptoms may include shakiness, nausea, headache, palpitations, depression, irritability, insomnia, and an overall feeling of anxiety.[18] Healing the patient involves laying the patient on the floor with his arms outstretched in the semblance of a cross. At that point, the curandero, while reciting the Apostle's Creed, sweeps the patient's body with branches and herbs, urging the spirit to return and re-enter the body. This cure involves three sessions.[19]

Although many of these superstitions and remedios are no longer as prevalent in Mexican-American communities as they were a generation back, tragic incidents are still reported. A recent news-paper article reported the death of a Salvadoran immigrant who had turned to a faith healer to cure his rash. After suffering for two years with a rash that caused his legs to swell and his skin to peel, Roberto Caceres desperately turned to a curandero to cure him. The faith healer ordered an assistant to inject Caceres with a mix of vitamins and steroids, causing the Salvadoran to react violently and die. Previously, the Salvadoran had consulted a healer for back pain and had been cured. On this fatal occasion, fearing he would lose his job because of the severity of the rash, he resorted to a faith healer only to die.[20]

Although Mexican-American communities still have their own curanderos, none have attained the recognition or veneration that was accorded Niño Fidencio Constantino and especially Don Pedrito Jaramillo. Don Pedrito lived at Los Olmos near Falfurrias, Texas, and was widely known for his common cures, and became a folk saint.[21] Tales of Don Pedrito's cures were published in *The Healer of Los Olmos* (PTFS #24–1951). Typically, the curandero realizes his divine power late in life through a dream, a vision, or the development of a deep understanding of the sick. This healing ability is seen as a gift from God, so the curandero typically does not charge for his healing; however, patients can leave an offering or a gift. Mexican Americans, comfortable with their culture's tra-ditions, tend to seek medical help from curanderos first and seek out the modern medical physician only as a last resort.

ENDNOTES

1. "Man's Death Highlights Danger of Immigrants' Faith in 'Healers,'" *San Angelo Standard-Times,* 2 December 2002: A4.
2. Anita Pfeifer, "Ear Coning," *Chicago Heights Star,* 17 September 1992: H1.
3. Eliseo Torres, *Green Medicine: Traditional Mexican-American Herbal Remedies* (Kingsville, TX: Nieves Press, 1983), 33.

4. John O. West, comp. and ed., *Mexican American Folklore: Legends, Songs, Festivals, Proverbs, Crafts, Tales of Saints, of Revolutionaries, and More* (Little Rock: August House, 1988), 139.

5. Robert T. Trotter and Juan Antonio Chavira, *Curanderismo: Mexican American Folk Healing* (Athens: U of Georgia P, 1981), 91.

6. Torres, 13.

7. Ibid.

8. Ibid, 14.

9. Ibid.

10. Trotter and Chavira, 92.

11. West, 139.

12. Trotter and Chavira, 92.

13. Antonia Van der Meer, "How Pediatricians Treat Their Own Kids," *Bottom Line,* 15 December 1993: 9–10.

14. Torres, 14.

15. Ibid, 15.

16. Ibid, 14.

17. Ibid.

18. Ibid.

19. Trotter and Chavira, 90.

20. "Man's Death," A4.

21. West, 140.

Louis Jimenez of Lubbock prepares a pan of *pan dulces* for his day's customers (Photo by Ken Davis)

7

PEPE'S PANADERIA: BREAD FOLKLORE

by Kenneth W. Davis of Lubbock

Years ago somewhere between Crystal City and McAllen in a small community, I saw a sign on a weathered adobe building: Pepe's Panaderia: Bread of All Kinds. On a simple wooden table placed near the building's only window were curiously shaped loaves of bread, all of which looked to be made with yeast. There were anatomically correct small bears, horses, cows, an angel or two, and even a genderless owl. Called *pan de muertos,* these loaves are generally available from about November 2, the Day of the Dead, until after old Christmas, January 6, in many bakeries all over Texas and the Southwest. *Pan de muertos* loaves are baked sometimes in cast iron molds. Or they can be carefully shaped by hand. Frequently such loaves are placed on graves and at shrines. They are but one of many types of bread in Texas associated with the lore of the folk. *Pan de muertos* is associated with religious as well as with pagan traditions. As an aside, I note that in a concordance to the NIV edition of the Old and New Testaments there are 267 listings for the word "bread."

About ten years ago, I began baking bread. I've collected at least a hundred cookbooks since then. Some are devoted exclusively to bread; others have all sorts of recipes. There are a few recipes in the books for baking bread in the shapes of animals, but not many. The cookbooks and lore from Texas oral traditions are the sources for this study of some facets of the lore of bread.

The cookbooks range from the high-toned volume of the legendary Helen Corbitt's best recipes, a handsome book done by the

University of North Texas Press, to coffee-table types replete with enticing color photographs, to the more nearly authentic folk tradition cookbooks, the ones done by various church and/or social groups for the purposes of raising money. I have in this collection, for example, cookbooks assembled by the Houston and Dallas Junior Leagues, the Episcopalian ladies of Fredericksburg, the Women's Society of Christian Service at Salado's First Methodist church, and one titled *Amazing Graces,* a product of the true folk communal efforts of the Methodist ladies in Slaton. And I have relied on a number of commercial ventures.

Common to all of the Texas cookbooks I have are recipes for breads of various sorts. Consider the following list of kinds of bread found in *Our Texas Heritage: Ethnic Traditions and Recipes,* assembled by Dorothy McConachie (published in 2000 in Plano by Republic of Texas Press): Apple Dumplings, Buttermilk Biscuits, Challah, African American Cornbread, Mexican Cornbread, Dark Irish Soda Bread, Easy Basic Dough Bread, Finger Bread, Hushpuppies, Indian Ceremonial Bread, Matzo Balls, Potato Dumplings, Soda Bread, St. Joseph's Bread, and of course, Tortillas. To this list I add Sour Dough Bread, Kolaches, Hot Water Cornbread, and Southern Cornbread—the real kind, made not with white flour as a recent article in the *Dallas Morning News* for Valentine's Day says is the only way to make authentic Southern-style cornbread, but SOUTHERN CORNBREAD, made with honest-to-God yellow cornmeal and with NO flour. Mark Twain said that the North thinks it can cook cornbread, but that the notion is mere fiction. Only the uninformed or Yankees put FLOUR in cornbread. If my personal prejudices stemming from my misspent youth in old Bell County offend, I am sorry, but not much. I will, of course, be glad to share with you a recipe or two for REAL Southern cornbreads.

We have all been told that bread is the staff of life and as the reporter in the recent *Dallas Morning News* article noted, man does not live by bread alone. The reporter added that most Texans given the choice would attempt to live, however, by bread alone.

Bread is all-important in the world of working folk such a ranchers and cowboys, truck drivers, farmers, plumbers, and hog drovers. In *Texas Cowboy Cooking,* Abilene master chef and restaurateur Tom Perini wrote: "There is a story from a nearby ranch about a cow boss who, whenever he hired a new cowboy, would always ask, 'Can you cook?' If the cowboy said yes, he asked him if he could make bread. Because if a cowboy can't bake bread, he can't cook."[1]

Most chuck wagon cooks have their special if not secret recipes for making biscuits—sour dough, buttermilk, or sweet milk, usually cooked in a Dutch oven over a bed of hot mesquite coals. Some attempt to cook cornbread, but because of the sustained high heat required for baking edible cornbread, most prefer soda, baking powder, or sour dough biscuits.

Various types of bread are, of course, associated with the numerous ethnic groups that make up modern Texas. Several years ago, *Southern Living Magazine* included a recipe from a woman in Dallas for challah somewhat modernized and made easy for cooks not as adept at baking as are Jewish women who yet bake challah, a rich egg bread, on Friday before the Sabbath begins so that they can have fresh bread for the time when work is supposed to cease. The only place in the world where I have found breads that rival the best of Texas cooks is Israel. In Israel I ate at least sixteen different kinds of bread. All were good.

In my youth, hot water cornbread was a favorite among the black families with whose children I played. Among our German and Czech neighbors yeast breads were preferred. Kolaches, yeast biscuits, yeast rolls, and loaf breads made many kitchens veritable aromatic heavens—especially for hungry children and men who did hard manual labor in the fields and pastures. In Belton, Texas, in the Twenties and Thirties there was a Greek candy shop and bread bakery. Somewhere in my collection of bread recipes I have one for Greek Easter Bread, a feast or festival bread that has candied fruit in it. It is similar, I am told, to bread baked in the Greek bakery. This bread resembles bread with another strong ethnic connection:

pantone—Italian bread served at Christmas as well as at Easter. Pantone can be purchased in bakeries in larger Texas cities.

Cornbread, of course, is very much a part of the favored cuisine of Mexican Texans. Numerous recipes for Mexican cornbread are in almost all of the Texas cookbooks in my collection. Most Mexican cornbread is made with basic recipes to which are added chopped green chilies or even the fiery jalapenos and perhaps canned or fresh corn. I've eaten Mexican cornbread that had finely chopped fresh green onions in it. And at the home of the black friends from my youth, I ate cornbread made with crisp cracklings. Believe me, if you have never had a thick pie-shaped wedge of crackling bread fresh from the oven of a red-hot wood stove, you don't really know what good bread can be.

The imaginative genius of Texas cooks—males as well as females—becomes apparent in the names of some popular cake-like breads made for the most part with soda or baking powder as leavening. Consider the following: banana, apricot, pecan, walnut, pumpkin, carrot, zucchini, cranberry (surely a New England import), apple, orange, lemon, and Welsh bread made with freshly brewed tea. Table or working-folks breads include seven grain, and a host of whole wheat breads. Long before the makers of bread machines provided recipes that allowed cooks to put all sorts of exotic ingredients including tomatoes and other vegetables in breads, Texas cooks knew that including various herbs and spices in bread was good cooking practice. My late neighbor, a few years before her death, baked what she called "dilly bread" that had dill in it. Almost all cookbooks have recipes for bread made with many other herbs and/or spices.

Dessert breads such as sweet rolls, kolaches, and coffee cakes may include cinnamon, all spice, ground cloves, and grated fresh lemon or orange peel. Dessert breads made with dried fruits—peaches, apricots, apples, and prunes—have been popular with Texans since before the founding of the Republic. In a collection of handwritten recipes I have from the late nineteenth century are

pan blanco

pan muertos

pan dulces

(Photos by Ken Davis)

ones for loaves of bread that have in them sun-dried peaches and dried plums.

My late grandmother, Laura Weatherford Perkins of Bartlett, was renowned for her fried pies made with rolled out biscuit dough. These delicious concoctions had generous amounts of home dried and then cooked and seasoned peaches, sealed with fancy crimping in the pie-crust-thick pieces of dough. They were fried in hog lard until the dough shell was just the right shade of mottled brown. These pies were often included in the lunch pails (syrup buckets, usually) or paper sacks my cousins and I took to the two-room country school we attended.

The mention of hog lard brings to mind various other traditions about Texas breads and bread baking. Experienced cooks know that hog lard is the best shortening for making a memorable pie crust. Hog lard is also absolutely the only shortening for the making of biscuits really fit to eat. Never mind the cholesterol concerns of learned cardiologists and dieticians: when it comes to good biscuits and for the greasing of skillets, there isn't anything that can equal lard from hogs fattened on white corn. Yellow meal is indeed the best for true cornbread, but white corn puts whiter fat on Poland China hogs or even Berkshires than does the better tasting yellow. The lard from a hog fed with white corn is a perfect white and heats better than that from hogs fed yellow corn or maize. My grandmother forbade the feeding of maize to her "lard" hogs. In her advice to young married women, she passed on this essential wisdom.

The care and use of yeast as a leavening agent is one of the most interesting of the many facets of lore associated with bread baking through the centuries. Jesuit Brother Rick Curry, in his collection of bread recipes titled *The Secrets of Jesuit Bread Making*, says that the Egyptians were among the earliest to discover that unleavened bread left unbaked would in time sour and there would be considerable swelling. When the swollen mixture was baked, the taste improved and the texture was much like that of our yeast breads today.[2]

Many cooks in the several ethnic groups in modern Texas have preferences about the kinds of yeasts to use and how to store them. Few cooks in my childhood in the 1930s used powdered yeast, for example. The Germans and Czechs in old Bell County used cake yeast if indeed they did not make their own from scratch. I have never seen anyone make yeast, but I have eaten bread baked with homemade yeast and potato water that feeds the yeast to make it grow. Nowadays, if cooks wish to use cake yeast, they often must buy it from a bakery. Seldom are those small cakes of yeast wrapped in silver paper found in supermarkets. But if you are in the camp of true believers in cake yeast, you can get it in pound blocks from most small bakeries like Pepe's Panaderia. In the Lubbock area, I have two sources for cake or block yeast: the Slaton Bakery and a downtown Mexican food place called the Jimenez Bakery and Restaurant, owned and operated by Señor Louis Jimenez. Señor Jimenez and his helper bake what are surely the best rolls and loaf breads to be found other than those from one's own home oven. This yeast is inexpensive. In Slaton I pay $1.25 for a pound; in Lubbock, the cost is $1.50 for the same amount.

Bread lovers with deeply ingrained preferences swear that they can tell the difference between bread baked with cake yeast and that done with active dry yeast. These seasoned veterans of bread consumption also believe they can tell the difference between breads baked with active dry yeast and those containing instant yeast, the sort that doesn't require proofing. I am a lover of good breads, but I have not the sensitivity of taste to make such fine distinctions. But real cooks have their preferences. Cooks older than I am have solemnly assured me that unless active or cake yeast is proofed with some sugar added to the warm water or milk, the dough won't rise adequately. I've been told also that the sure way to get the best rise in dough made with powdered yeast is to use honey in the warmed proofing liquid rather than sugar. I have good results using honey as the sweetener for proofing.

Another belief about yeast baking transmitted mainly in the oral tradition is that potato water causes a loaf of table bread to rise and to have a really good texture as well as flavor. Potato water is the water left over after the thorough boiling of a medium-sized white potato. The oral lore associated with the use of potato water sometimes includes such distinctions as the superiority of boiling a whole potato over slicing the potato prior to putting it in the boiling water. I was told by my next door neighbor Helen Braun, whose ancestry was German, that I should never put a potato in cold water. She insisted that a potato to be used for making potato water had to be dropped in water that was in a "hard" boil. I've used that method and I've put potatoes in cold water before bringing them to a boil. I can't tell the difference, but I haven't baked bread for more than eighty years as did my neighbor.

Other bits of lore from the oral tradition include directions for the proper way to cook cornbread. I have said that the only real Southern cornbread is made with yellow meal. And real cornbread does not have sugar in it, nor does real cornbread have any flour in it. Add flour to a cornbread recipe and with luck, you will have a baked substance that might be edible, but it won't have the flavor and texture of real cornbread. A proper cast-iron skillet is also essential. The one I use has been reserved exclusively for the baking of Southern cornbread for almost ninety years.

A final custom about bread is one I have observed only in contemporary West Texas. The patriarch of a large, ethnically mixed family in Lubbock believes that he and his wife must barbecue a goat whenever there is a wedding involving any member of the clan over which he presides at all ceremonial events—weddings, funerals, church festivals, and the like. At weddings for members of this particular clan, it is a matter of pride to have not the delicious home-baked bread the matriarch bakes, but instead to have loaf after loaf of store boughten bread. You know the kind: it comes wrapped in waxed paper or in a plastic film sack and is warmed in or near the barbeque pit. Such bread is, of course, about as tasty as facial tissue. The rationale for the use of this inferior product is this: family pride demands that the guests be shown that the patriarch can afford to buy so-called fancy store bread for the wedding. But at funerals for members of this group of relatives, the bread brought to the house for the funeral meal must be home baked. To bring store bread is to show callous disrespect for the deceased and for the grieving family.

Bread is indeed the staff of life. We Texans venerate breads of all sorts. In my case, I bake my own bread not only because bread smells so good baking and tastes so good fresh from the oven with real butter on it, but also because I choose not to consume the chemical preservatives found in commercial bread. I discovered by trial and error that if I bake my own bread, I don't have allergy problems the way I once did. Hooray for bread. Hooray for wheat farmers, and growers of corn—especially yellow corn. And hooray for yet surviving small bakeries.

I hope Pepe is still in business and his panaderia is flourishing.

ENDNOTES

1. Tom Perini, *Texas Cowboy Cooking* (Alexandria, VA: Time Life Books, 2000), 115.
2. Rick Curry, *The Secrets of Jesuit Bread Making* (New York: Harper, 1995), 5.

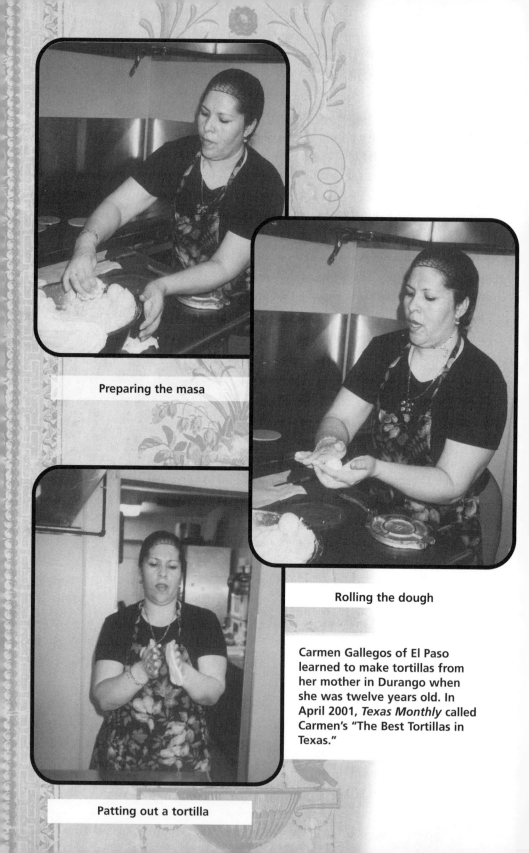

Preparing the masa

Rolling the dough

Patting out a tortilla

Carmen Gallegos of El Paso learned to make tortillas from her mother in Durango when she was twelve years old. In April 2001, *Texas Monthly* called Carmen's "The Best Tortillas in Texas."

8

A TORTILLA IS NEVER "JUST" A TORTILLA

by Lucy Fischer West of El Paso

～～

On my mother's stove, there sat a *comal*, a flat, round, cast-iron griddle with a handle, always ready to heat tortillas for at least two meals out of the daily three that she would prepare. On days when she was not too harried, those tortillas came not out of a plastic bag from the corner grocery store, but rather were hand-patted from lime-soaked and finely-ground *nixtamal*. Occasionally, she would use either a wooden or cast aluminum tortilla press lined with wax paper to speed up the corn tortilla-making process. For her flour tortillas, she'd use a red-handled rolling pin that she'd gotten at the old Cuahtémoc Market in Juárez. I remember vividly that whenever she worked in the kitchen, I was at her side; that she would hand me my own child-sized ball of *masa* to make my own *tortillas de maíz*; and that I had a child-sized rolling pin with which to turn my wad of flour dough into a *tortilla de harina*. I developed a healthy respect for the hot comal on which I placed my creations. It was my job not only to watch over my own creations, but also to mash down her flour tortillas with a round wooden press when they puffed up.

Growing up as I did on the border, in a home heavily infused by my mother's culture, the foods that were our mainstay were Mexican. I took great pride in participating in the preparation of food and contributing to the simple family meals eaten on our red and gray formica table with the chrome frame—you remember— the kind with the *faux* marble pattern. That unmistakable aroma of a fresh tortilla browning on a cast-iron surface is evocative of a treasured childhood in the kitchen. I've eaten tortillas since my four front teeth came together to take bites out of them, but I had never given much thought to their history, or their significance until lately.

Within the last three years, I have discovered complexities of the kitchen and food in ways that I never imagined existed. I would say in jest that perhaps I have been stuck in the kitchen far too long and that my education has suffered, but that would not be an accurate statement, nor would it be fair to what I believe about what I have chosen to do with my talents in what amounts to a "traditional" household setting. A fortuitous introduction to food studies is helping me articulate what I have done over the years and place a greater value on it.

Meredith E. Abarca received her Ph.D. in Comparative Literature from the University of California at Davis in December 2000 and has been teaching at the University of Texas at El Paso since January of 2001. Her dissertation is titled "Voices in the Kitchen: Hearing Subaltern Women Speak." It speaks to how countless women throughout the ages have created a space for themselves in the kitchen that is their domain. It speaks to how the kitchen is the "room of their own" in which women could exercise their acts of agency, manifesting that agency through cooking. It speaks to how those acts of agency *in* the kitchen have empowered women to find modes of self-expression, sometimes *only* within the confines of the kitchen, but in ways no less valuable than women writers and artists. I wholeheartedly believe, as Dr. Abarca does, that "the practice of cooking is a mode of expression just as valuable as the written word or the painted image."[1]

Dr. Abarca's dissertation combines the analysis of literary works with a series of *"charlas culinarias,"* culinary chats, with twenty-five working class Mexican and Chicana women from the ages of twenty to sixty-five living in Laredo, northern California, Michoacán, Veracruz, Jalisco, and Puebla. As I read the dissertation, it occurred to me that it is a fascinating way to tie together folk ways and oral tradition with literary works.

Dr. Abarca begins her dissertation as I began this paper, with a tribute to her mother. Liduvina Vélez, a woman with only two years of formal schooling, went from answering questions either monosyllabically or with *"yo no se hablar"* ("I don't know how to speak.") to becoming a field assistant conducting academic research alongside her daughter. "Duvi," as she is known to everyone who meets her, was married in Michoacán, Mexico, at age sixteen to a man she scarcely knew and, as was the custom of the time, went to live with her husband's family. In that rather intimidating setting, she had to find her place and create her space. She did that in the kitchen. Specifically, she did it by making tortillas.

Duvi remembers that her mother-in-law and sisters-in-law made "really ugly corn tortillas . . . ugly, too thick, full of holes." She, on the other hand, with an already practiced hand, made "beautiful ones, thin ones, puffy ones." She'd put her *tortillas bonitas,* her beautiful tortillas, in a basket as part of her contribution to family meals. Her tortillas became "the subject matter of her artistic expression," her source of pride. And thus, she began to find her place and create a space for herself. She affirmed "her *self,* and asserted herself as a teen-age woman to face her life's circumstances." While tortilla-making might seem like a simple task, those of us who have ever attempted it know it is an art. More importantly, however, it is significant to recognize that when Duvi describes both the process of making *masa* and creating tortillas out of it, she is making a connection with her cultural-ethnic, ancestral past.

Corn tortillas were an integral part of Mesoamerican diets thousands of years ago. Chicano essayist José Antonio Burciaga says that "over the centuries, the tortilla has served as the spoon and the fork, the plate and the napkin."[2] Their origin predates Mayan civilizations:

> According to Mayan mythology, the great god Quetzalcóatl, realizing that the red ants knew the secret of using maize as food, transformed himself

into a black ant, infiltrated the colony of red ants, and absconded with a grain of corn. Quezalcóatl then put maize on the lips of the first man and woman, Oxomoco and Cipactonal, so that they would become strong.[3]

Victor and Mary Lau Valle, food journalists and professors of history, call tortillas the "pillars of American civilization." I quote from their book *Recipe of Memory: Five Generations of Mexican Cuisine:* "From about 1000 B.C. until the 1930s, the technology of tortilla making had gone quite well with simple Stone Age technology."[4] In other words, with the *metate,* what Dr. Abarca calls the "Aztec blender."[5] Duvi's way of making tortillas in her youth is identical to the way women have made tortillas since pre-Columbian times. Fray Bernardino de Sahagún's *Historia general de las cosas de la Nueva España* supports the idea that the culinary arts were in the hands of women, since men are rarely mentioned as cooks.[6] It was women who "dedicated themselves to the artful presentation of food," according to Jeffrey Pilcher in his *¡Que Vivan Los Tamales!: Food and the Making of Mexican Cuisine.*[7]

Food for the Aztecs was not merely a source of nourishment for the body. The act of eating was associated both with pleasure and as a source of virtue and an act of goodwill. Quoting once more from Dr. Abarca's work:

In Nahuatl, the word *cua* means to eat [and] the adjective *cuali* means [both] beautiful and something good to eat. The etymology of these roots is found in the Nahuatl phrase that describes a woman who knows how to make beautiful and good tortillas: cual-tlaxcalchihuani-ni. The act of making tortillas in pre-Columbian times was seen as an act of virtue and good will.[8]

While Tonacaltecuhtli, a male Aztec god, is credited with creating corn, it is Xilonen, the goddess of maize, who nurtures its growth. Once again, for me, the connection is made between ancient civilizations and Duvi's tortillas bonitas, which nourished her children.

Long after the tortilla's origin and long before Duvi came into the world, the Mexican government trespassed into the kitchen. It was during the dictatorship of Porfirio Díaz at the turn of the century that "The Tortilla Discourse" took place, changing the course of history. It was Díaz's intent for the discourse to modernize Mexican cooking and elevate it to the standard of European cuisine by exchanging wheat for corn, and prohibiting the consumption of corn tortillas. In 1899, Senator Francisco Bulnes had published *El Porvenir de las Naciones Hispano-Américas* (*The Future of the Hispanic-American Nations*), in which he divided people "into three races: the people of corn, wheat, and rice." He determined that the "race of wheat is the only truly progressive one," and that maize "has been the eternal pacifier of America's indigenous race and the foundation of their refusal to become civilized."[9] Bulnes decreed that women's cooking habits needed changing in order that all indigenous and *mestizo* people could become civilized. While this century-old argument may sound far-fetched today, Dr. Abarca points out that a similar effort took place in the United States during the Thirties and Forties when a federally funded program was organized to assimilate Mexicans to mainstream cultural habits, substituting white bread for tortillas, arguably because Mexican children did poorly in school due to their inadequate diet of beans and tortillas.

Even though wheat did become a part of Mexican cuisine, it certainly did not replace corn. What did happen was that the focus of colonization changed: the new target for colonization became the method of converting corn into masa for tortillas. In 1899, Don Luis Romero Soto was one of the first inventors to obtain patents for a tortilla machine called "La Malinche," named after

Hernán Cortés's native mistress who assisted in the conquest of the Aztec capital Tenochtitlán. The selling point for the mechanical mills was the idea of liberating women from the arduous task of grinding corn on a *metate*. The purpose of modern technology in rural areas was to improve the well-being of peasants. Hand-made tortillas were indeed replaced by factory-made ones during the 1930s.

Women, however, did not own either the corn mills or the *tortillerías* and lost whatever control they might have had in the tortilla industry. The "tortilla discourse," and the replacement of the stone *metate*, tampered with a centuries-old cultural practice. While it freed women from the chore of grinding corn for tortillas, it made them slaves to a male-dominated capitalist society in Mexico; decades later, men still control the very profitable tortilla production industry. I cannot buy factory-made tortillas without considering the struggles inherent to producing them, nor witness a woman slapping *masa* into tortillas without admiration. While Duvi struggled to find her place in a household that was not hers to manage, women along the border and elsewhere continue to struggle to make decent wages in all areas of food production.

I enjoy both cooking and eating Mexican food as millions of people throughout the country do, whether it be a beautifully presented plate in a restaurant or a warm tortilla wrapped around a fresh *azadero* and wedges of avocado at home. Uses for tortillas are endless. I liken the basic tortilla to an artist's palette from which creations emanate. Sandwiching Mennonite or *azadero* cheese and slivers of long green chili between two of them and heating them until the cheese melts creates a *quesadilla*. *Tostadas* (The literal translation is "the toasted one.") is a tortilla that has been fried either in wedges or whole. Tostadas appear on restaurant tables with accompanying *salsa* or *chile con queso* to keep you happy while you wait for the main course. A *tapatía*, or *topopo*, is a whole crisp tortilla which serves as a showpiece for a slathering of beans to keep the subsequent layers of meat, the ubiquitous iceberg lettuce, tomato, and grated cheese from sliding off into your lap. *Tacos* are traditionally made by putting the chosen filling onto one half of a tortilla and folding it into shape as it fries, adding lettuce, tomato and cheese at serving time. Tortillas first softened in hot oil, then dipped in red or green chili sauce, then filled with meat, chicken, or cheese and onion, then rolled or stacked flat and topped with cheese and baked, become *enchiladas.* "Patricia Quintana wrote in her 1989 cookbook *Feasts of Life* that 'Tortillas are to Mexican cuisine what the sun is to the day and the moon to the night.'"[10] I agree.

For those of us who grew up in homes where the tortilla was an integral part of our meals, the aroma of a fresh, hot tortilla evokes memories that are infused with profound significance. Exploring their historical roots deepens the connection with the people of corn like my mother, Duvi, and myself. To know the struggles of the people who provide them for our tables gives me a deep sense of appreciation for their labor.

For me, a tortilla is never "just" a tortilla.

ENDNOTES

1. Meredith E. Abarca, "Voices in the Kitchen: Hearing Subaltern Women Speak" (Ph.D. diss. University of California, Davis, 2000), Chapter IV: 158–93. Quotations elsewhere are from this section.
2. José Antonio Burciaga, *Weedee Peepo* (Edinburg, TX: Pan American University Press, 1988), 96.
3. Ibid.
4. Victor Valle and Mary Lau Valle, *Recipe of Memory: Five Generations of Mexican Cuisine* (New York: The New Press, 1995), 1.
5. Abarca, 162.
6. Fray Bernardino de Sahagun, *Historia General de las Cosas de Nueva España* (Ciudad Mexico: Porrúa, 1979), 159.
7. Jeffrey M. Pilcher, *¡Que Vivan los Tamales!: Food and the Making of Mexican Cuisine* (New York: The New Press, 1995), 6.
8. Abarca, 8.
9. Francisco Bulnes, *El Porvenir de las Naciones Hispano-Americanas ante las Conquistas Recientes de Europa y los Estados Unidos* (Mexico City: Imprenta de Mariano Nava, 1899).
10. Judy Hevrdejs, "Tortillas Are on a Roll," *El Paso Times,* 6 March 2002: 3D.

III

MISCELLANEOUS
MEMORABILIA

The Headless Horseman as depicted in 1867 by artist R. Orr in Mayne Reid's *The Headless Horseman: A Strange Tale of Texas* (Courtesy Steven Butler of Richardson)

9

THE EVOLUTION OF A LEGEND:
THE HEADLESS HORSEMAN OF TEXAS,
OR IT MAY NOT BE TRUE, BUT IT MAKES
A GOOD STORY

by Lou Ann Herda of Cypress

It is late at night. The meeting you attended in Cuero did not let out until nine p.m., and your drive towards San Antonio along Highway 87 starts out as a peaceful ride. The dark sky is full of twinkling stars and traffic is light. As you drive along, lightning flashing out of the corner of your left eye draws your attention. Puzzled, you glance in that direction, only to see that the lightning is not coming out of the sky but is, instead, coming from the ground. Suddenly, the lightning intensifies, coming closer to your car. You slam on the brakes as a horse gallops across the lanes in front of you. The lightning that you saw is coming from the hooves as they hit the ground. You see that there is a rider mounted on the horse, but that something is eerily missing from this rider. *It is his head!* Then you see that the head is dangling from the pommel of the saddle, thrust inside a sombrero, the eyes flashing as coals of fire. The rider dashes across the road and flashes off over the horizon. You have just experienced one of Texas' more illustrious legends, El Muerto, the Headless Horseman.

In 1928, J. Frank Dobie called this lone rider "The Headless Horseman of the Mustangs," but that was after the August 1924 *Frontier Times* edition where editor J. Marvin Hunter called him simply "the Headless Horseman." However, since its first telling in the mid-1800s, the headless horseman of Texas has evolved into quite a legend that gets better each time the story is told.

Over a period of twenty years in the late 1800s, Texas historian and writer J. Warren Hunter learned about Texas history first-hand from his friend Creed Taylor at Creed's home in Kimble County. Creed, who is best known for his role in the Sutton-Taylor Feud, the longest and bloodiest feud in Texas history, told Hunter a great many stories about when he fought in so many of Texas' early battles with the Mexican army.[1]

One of these stories concerned what two of Creed's friends, William "Bigfoot" Wallace and John McPeters, had done. By the year 1848, when Creed said the action took place, Bigfoot Wallace was already a legend because of his role in the fateful Mier Expedition and as a survivor of the Black Bean incident. His days as a Texas Ranger under legendary leader Captain Jack Hays were just beginning, although his prowess as an Indian tracker as well as Indian killer kept the man busy for decades. John McPeters, an almost unknown now, fought at the Battle of San Jacinto and also became a Texas Ranger, serving under "Mustang" Gray as well as others. Creed, himself a former Texas Ranger who served with Gray the same time as McPeters, seemed to tell the story as an aside, something that he happened to remember when he was talking about his friend McPeters. Hunter listened to the quick tale of how Wallace and McPeters had caught a band of horse thieves and had used one as an example of why horses shouldn't be stolen. Creed may have told this story in an off-handed way since he was not there when it happened; thus, he did not have any vested interest in the story. It was simply a relating of events, out of context, because he himself had once met the thief many years before.[2]

As the story goes in Hunter's 1898 manuscript called *The Life of Creed Taylor, Eighty-Six Years on the Texas Frontier,* Wallace and McPeters had tracked and killed a number of Mexican horse thieves near the Nueces River, south of present-day Uvalde. Wallace had decided to use the ringleader's body as a warning for anyone else who wanted to follow his example. After being shot and killed, this man, called both Vuavis and Vidal in the story, was decapitated by Wallace. His body was put onto a wild stallion that the two men caught and tied between two trees, and his head was thrust inside his sombrero, secured with a strap, and tied onto the pommel of the saddle. Then the horse was let loose to ride across the hilly countryside. Over time, either Wallace or McPeters or perhaps both of them could have related this story to Taylor. However, a story as good as this bears repeating by the deed-doer, Bigfoot Wallace, who was described by writer Sam Haynes in *Soldiers of Misfortune* as "a colorful character whose anecdotes about life on the frontier in later years make him something of a Bunyanesque character in Texas lore." Strangely enough, though, neither John Duval nor A. J. Sowell, who each listened to Wallace's stories and wrote about his life in Texas, included this most curious crime in his biographies.[3]

In this earliest rendition of the tale, Creed did not put himself at the scene of the crime; however, he had had his share of killing Mexican men. In 1824, when he was a boy of four years, his family settled in DeWitt's Colony near Gonzales, where he later took part not only in the fracas over the Mexican cannon, but was also at the Siege of Bexar, fighting alongside famous Texan martyr Ben Milam. It was at this battle in December 1835 where he met the man who would later be known as El Muerto.

During the siege, Creed relates that Bate Berry, a longtime friend of Creed's, found a Mexican deserter on a hill near where the Texians were holed up inside a house in San Antonio. Berry, who years later was reprimanded by General Andrew Jackson for scalping Mexicans in the Mexican War, brought his frightened captive into the house where the Texians demanded his life. The officer, whose name was Lieutenant Vuavis under General Woll's command, pled for his life in exchange for information about Woll's future activities against the Texians. He especially appealed to fifteen-year-old, dark-skinned Creed, who he mistakenly took for a Mexican. Taylor, who spoke fluent Spanish, interpreted for the officer, but the Texians already knew the information he divulged. For whatever reason, the officer was allowed to live and, later, to be set free, but his appearance made a lasting impression on the young soldier.[4]

Years later, Vuavis, working under the alias "Vidal," began terrorizing Texas ranchers by stealing their horses. Unfortunately for Vidal, he was tracked by one of the best trackers in Texas at that time, Bigfoot Wallace. Creed added his own comments to the story by explaining why the headless body of Vidal did not decompose rapidly, since, after the horse was loosed, he was seen by others out on the Texas hills, including soldiers stationed at Fort Inge, near Uvalde. Creed suggested that a Mexican's diet, which he said was made up of hot peppers and garlic, helped mummify the body and kept it from deteriorating in the hot Texas sun.[5]

The exact date of the crime was never mentioned, only that it took place in 1848. However, since McPeters was mustered into service under Henry E. McCulloch's Company on October 25, 1848, and was not mustered out until December 8, the deed must have been done earlier that year.[6]

It is a fact that Bigfoot Wallace had a grievance against the Mexican army. The original reason he came to Texas from Virginia in 1836 was to avenge the deaths of his cousin and his brother, who were both killed at the Goliad massacre. And since Bigfoot barely survived the ill-fated Mier Expedition and the squalid conditions at Perote Prison, there were more than enough reasons why he wanted to "take pay out of the Mexicans."[7]

Another curious addition to the story is the reference to Captain Mayne Reid's 1865 novel *The Headless Horseman, or a Strange Tale of Texas*. Hunter suggested that Creed's story was an impetus for Reid's own tale, for, as he said, Reid was stationed at Fort Inge at the time. Bigfoot Wallace was also listed as being at Fort Inge in 1850, so, as the story goes, he could have told Reid the legend that he perpetrated.[8]

This is when the story begins to take on a mysterious twist, for Mayne Reid was never stationed at Fort Inge. Yet, in his 1865 novel, he was able to describe the fort as though he had been there.

Mayne Reid, who wrote Westerns much like Zane Grey, was originally from Ireland. He came to the United States early in 1840 and spent the next decade living like a true Texan. His heroics during this time created plenty of fodder for the numerous novels he wrote after his return to England in July 1849.

Although the idea of Fort Inge had already been conceived, it was not inhabited until months after Reid had left Texas. Unless Reid had somehow taken a stagecoach, traveling at break-neck speed across the United States and back down to central Texas, it was nearly impossible for him to have seen the fort. Yet, he was mysteriously able to include the fort in his tale of the headless horseman.[9]

In chapter nine of *The Headless Horseman, or a Strange Tale of Texas*, Reid describes the fort with accuracy, including the "star-spangled banner suspended above [the fort]." He also describes the stockade stabling for two hundred horses, the barracks, the hospital, the commissary, the guardhouse, and so forth. The strangest part about his strange tale is how he could have known such detailed information about the fort without having been there. Virginia Woods, Uvalde County historian, surmises that perhaps Reid had accompanied Bigfoot Wallace on one of his many excursions across the Texas plains, while Bigfoot was carrying the mail to El Paso. Reid had lived in El Paso, so it would have made sense for him to go along for the ride to see old friends and acquaintances, or perhaps do business. Since the beheading of Vidal would have happened not long before Wallace started carrying the mail, the story would have been fresh on his mind. Then he would have bragged about his deed to Reid, who was undoubtedly a most willing listener, regaling his own tales of derring-do, swapping stories with one who was of such a like-mind.[10]

Another thought was that he may have seen the sketches made of the fort, with the "star spangled banner" flying on the hill. But since these detailed sketches were made in 1867, years after his story hit the presses, this again would not be proof. Thomas Cutrer, Reid's biographer for the *Handbook of Texas*, says that

Reid's source for the headless horseman was a South Texas folk-tale.[11]

Unfortunately, Reid's notes that may have contained his inspiration for writing about a headless horseman in south central Texas have been lost either because of the fire that consumed his home or as a result of the planes which bombed the archives in London during World War II. Two of Reid's biographers, Thomas Cutrer and Dr. Joan Steele, refer to Dobie's headless horseman tale as possibly being Reid's inspiration for his tale. Ty Smith, Fort Inge historian, contends that there must be "some nugget or kernel of truth that has sprung from the rumors" concerning Reid being at Fort Inge, but that he had "just not found it."[12]

The next person who was involved with the headless horseman story was James T. De Shields, Texas historian and dry goods salesman. De Shields wrote numerous articles for several publications, including the *Fort Worth Press*. His stories were of the old times in Texas, told by the ones who were there. He would contact various people—Texas Rangers, soldiers in various battles that Texas was involved in, frontiersmen—and would pay them for their contribution. Then he would rewrite their stories, not giving credit where it was due. His first novel, *Cynthia Ann Parker*, won considerable attention, lending him much credence.[13]

J. Warren Hunter initially contacted De Shields in 1906 with hopes that he would buy his Creed Taylor manuscript and turn it into a novel. He had heard that De Shields was looking for information about the Old Timers and wanted to offer him what he had. De Shields bought what has become known as the Hunter Manuscript and over a period of many years, he inserted information or crossed out various words or sentences and added his own interpretations to the original. Twenty-one years after J. Warren Hunter's death, De Shields published *Tall Men with Long Rifles*. This 1935 biography was the story of Creed Taylor's involvement in the Texas Revolution. In De Shields' typical fashion, he did not give credit to Hunter, and, in fact, the title page of the book states,

"As told to the author." Creed had been dead since 1906, so there was no one left to defy him.[14]

Among De Shields' papers and manuscripts, located at the Daughters of the Republic of Texas Library near the Alamo, there is an undated typeset copy of his own version of the headless horseman story. In his version he added a great deal of information not in the original manuscript, and often struck out the name "Wallace," replacing it with "McPeters," if it made the story sound better. He also added Creed Taylor to the story, saying that the three men were each "heavy losers of horses by Vidal's raid. . . ." He further added that the saddle used on the wild mustang was one that was stolen by the bandits. Indeed, his story is more palatable and enjoyable than the original and, again, makes a good story.

In 1924, J. Marvin Hunter, J. Warren Hunter's son and publisher and editor of the *Frontier Times,* published his own headless horseman tale. In this tale, he writes that the horses taken by Vidal and his bandits were Creed Taylor's, and not only were Creed's horses stolen, but also a Mexican's named Flores, who was not given a first name. J. Marvin goes on to retell the story in a much more vivid manner than in the original. This included how Vuavis (who he calls "Vivois" because his father's handwriting was often illegible) had "lingered about San Antonio and Goliad after Santa Anna's defeat at San Jacinto, when he turned out to stealing and became the most noted horse thief in all Southwest Texas." He also changes the date of the story to 1850 since, "[Vidal and his men] had chosen a most opportune time since only a few days previously the Indians had raided the settlements on the Cibolo and the Guadalupe, and in consequence of this raid, nearly every available man in the country had been called out to chastise the Comanches." It just so happened that both Creed and Flores were still at home and could begin their tracking of the thieves.[15]

Perhaps the younger Hunter set the year at 1850 because the fort was inhabited by then and because Bigfoot Wallace was included in the fort's roster for that year. Nonetheless, McPeters is left out of this rendition, and Flores takes over as the silent vindicator.

Hunter also ties in the Mayne Reid connection by saying that his headless horseman novel "was founded on fact, and the parties responsible for the headless rider and his ghostly adventures were well known about San Antonio and throughout Southwest Texas during those days . . ."[16]

He ends his article with direct quotations from Creed Taylor, which was most interesting since this information was not in the original Hunter Manuscript. It could have been possible, however, that J. Marvin had heard the story from either his father or from Creed Taylor himself during the years that he was growing up. He may have even written down what Creed said, keeping the information handy for just the right occasion, though this has not been corroborated.

Although too lengthy to quote verbatim, Creed's language is very colorful and descriptive, again making the story more interesting for the reader. As he gets to the end of the story, Creed says,

> "I heard afterwards, in fact Wallace was my informant, that soldiers at Fort Inge were greatly wrought up on seeing a man without a head, mounted on a superb stallion galloping around the country, scaring the life out of Indians and Mexicans, and frightening scouts and the few settlers out of their wits, and that they finally killed the horse by laying in wait at a watering place and shooting him . . ."[17]

In this rendition, J. Marvin used portions of his father's original manuscript, but again added his own flare for the pen, making the story more interesting. At the end of his article, he inserts that Creed, who "was not given to boasting or exaggeration," was asked if he had gotten his story from reading Mayne Reid's novel. Creed answered that he had never heard of Reid's novel but that he had remembered a "Rid, one of the regulars who was stationed at Fort Inge, but had no acquaintance with him and never knew he had written a book of any kind."[18]

By 1926, J. Frank Dobie was secretary-editor of the Texas Folklore Society. He had published numerous books, including a very popular *Legends of Texas* in 1924. The headless horseman tale is not included in that book, possibly because he had not heard of it yet. But by the time J. Marvin Hunter had published his August 1924 edition of *Frontier Times,* Dobie found it to be most intriguing and decided to include it in his *Tales of Old Time Texas,* copyrighted in 1928. He saw that not only was the story fascinating, but it also included popular characters from the nineteenth century.

Using his own creative bent, Dobie created a tale with lasting effect. He described the surroundings so that the reader could put his imagination right where the action was. For the most part, his telling is an almost duplicate of the Hunter story from *Frontier Times,* except Dobie puts Vidal's body and dangling head specifically upon a mustang, an animal Dobie knew a great deal about. He also may very well have had available Reid's *Headless Horseman* novel, for he quotes the 1886 edition, saying that Reid "added to the legend that he heard growing up." He further suggested that Reid's "phantom horseman of his tale was the patron—the ghostly guard—of the lost mine of the long-abandoned Candelaria Mission on the Nueces, to protect it against profane prospectors." Dobie enjoyed telling the legends of lost mines in Texas.[19]

Dobie also detailed the making of the headless horseman by adding the following:

> Bigfoot Wallace, always daring and eccentric, now made one of his original proposals. In the captured *caballada* was a black mustang stallion that had been herd-broken but that had never felt a cinch under his belly. Bigfoot proposed that he be roped, saddled, and mounted with Vidal's body. . . . The

black mustang was roped, tied up, blindfolded with
a red bandana, and saddled. Then the Texans cut
off Vidal's head and, with chin-strap and thongs,
fastened the horse thief's sombrero firmly to it.
Next, making deft use of buckskin, they laced the
sombreroed head to the horn of the saddle. It was a
Mexican saddle, rawhide-rigged, with a wide, flat
horn. They dressed Vidal's headless body in full
regalia—leggings, spurs, serape—and then . . . fixed
it in the saddle. They tied the dead man's feet in
the stirrups and double-fastened the stirrups to
each other under the mustang's belly so that they
could not fly up. Then, with a wild and terrifying
squeal, he broke away into a run that, as we have
seen, scared up a legend not yet dead.[20]

Dobie ends his exciting tale saying that the three men drove
the horses back to their respective ranches and that they "agreed to
keep still for a while."[21]

Since that time, the tale of the headless horseman has continued to evolve. Contemporary writers such as the late Ed Syers,
Charley Eckhardt, and Zinita Fowler include their own spin of this
gruesome tale of revenge among their tales of Texas ghosts and
legends. Ed Syers, who referred to the headless horseman as "El
Muerto del Rodeo," makes a final addition to Vidal's demise in his
1981 tale. He stated that Vidal's mummified remains were buried
in an unmarked grave at somebody's ranch in Ben Bolt. The headless body of old Vidal rode quite a long way if he was carried from
Uvalde County to Ben Bolt in Jim Wells County.[22]

By 2001, writer Jo-Anne Christensen had demoted El Muerto
from legend to tall tale. She does not include in her tale the names
of the perpetrators or the year Vidal was killed and beheaded. She
instead says that he met his "end when a band of vigilantes caught
up with him and measured out a bit of Wild West justice." She
does say that he can still be seen on the Coastal Plains where "El

Muerto is intent upon perpetrating the eerie illusion that he will not die."[23]

Charley Eckhardt told Ed Syers, he "questions getting a dead man astride a wild mustang." Texas storyteller Tim Tingle says that it's not so much if the story is true but how well the story is told.[24]

Which takes us back to the beginning, for Ol' Vidal is not quite finished with his wild ride across the Texas Plains. As contemporary writer Lee Paul tells it:

> eyewitnesses claimed the horse spouted flames from its nostrils and sent lightning bolts skyward with each clop from its hooves. The eyes in the head under the tattered sombrero were said to be like two fiery coals chipped from the cinders of hell. Some even claimed the specter glowed with an eerie green light and smelled like brimstone as it thundered through the tumbleweeds and desert sage.[25]

Perhaps one of the most curious things about this tale is that when I first began investigating, I was not aware that the eighty-sixth annual meeting of the Texas Folklore Society would be near Creed Taylor's home, which was in Noxville, about thirty-six miles from here. One can still see where his remains lie in a family ceme-tery not far from there.

And what does Taylor's kin say about all this interest in his cre-ation of a headless horseman? Creed's great-great-granddaughter from his first marriage, Mrs. Dovie Hall of Boerne, said there is no doubt as to the veracity of the story. She also says that Creed's grandson by his second marriage, Mr. Lynn Taylor, also agrees that the story is true. Bena Taylor Kirkscey, another direct descendant of Creed's from his first marriage, dislikes that the Hunter Manuscript was altered and that it's "difficult to decide fact from fiction."[26]

One thing that cannot be discounted is the fact that John Bate Berry, Creed Taylor, and John McPeters all lived in Kimble County in their later years. It might be that they tried to outdo each other as they reflected on their tales of younger days.[27]

So is the headless horseman of Texas fact or fiction? That may never be determined. But as John Lienhard recently said on National Public Radio's *Engines of Our Ingenuity,* "I think, what a strange business history is! It's at its best when it still deals with questions—when the truth of things still hovers beyond certainty."[28]

ENDNOTES

1. For more information about the Sutton-Taylor Feud (or the Taylor-Sutton Feud, according to who is talking), read C. L. Sonnichsen's *I'll Die Before I'll Run—The Story of the Great Feuds of Texas* (New York: Devin-Adair, 1962).
2. J. Warren Hunter, *Life of Creed Taylor, Eighty-Three Years on the Frontiers of Texas* (Austin, TX: State Archives, 1901), 252–53; Charles D. Spurlin, *Texas Veterans in the Mexican War* (Nacogdoches, TX: Ericson Books, 1984),137, 178, 190–91; Andrew Jackson Sowell, *Life of "Bigfoot" Wallace, the Great Ranger Captain* (Austin, TX: State House Press, 1989).
3. Sam W. Haynes, *Soldiers of Misfortune: The Somervell and Mier Expeditions* (Austin: University of Texas Press, 1997), 20. Bigfoot Wallace first asked John Duval to write his biography, published in 1870, but the story goes that he didn't care so much for it, so he also asked A. J. Sowell to write it (1899).
4. Hunter, 20.
5. This telling of the story made me curious. Because forensics has always fascinated me, I wanted to know what would have happened at the scene of the crime. So I contacted the El Paso Medical Examiner, Dr. Corrine E. Stern, and asked her the most obvious question: "What would happen if someone got his head cut off and shoved in a sombrero?" I was concerned that his brains would immediately fall out. She consoled me, saying no, if the head was cut off at the neck, the brains would not come out. "The basilar skull protects that from happening. However, as the brain decomposed, which would begin to happen—shortly if the weather was very warm or over a period of a couple of days if it was cooler—the brain matter would come out of a hole in the skull called the foramen magnum (where the spinal cord turns into the brainstem and enters the skull)." I then posed

the question of the Mexican diet, as Creed had stated in his story, asking if it would help mummify the body. She addressed the mummification process saying that, in West Texas, the bodies "tend to mummify because of the dry climate," but that a body can go from "freshly dead to skeleton in a week if the temperature is high enough." E-mail transmission, April 23, 2002, from Dr. Corrine E. Stern, Chief Medical Examiner, El Paso County, Texas, to Lou Ann Herda.

6. Charles D. Spurlin, copyrighted 1984 by the author, and created from *The Compiled Service Records of Volunteer Soldiers Who Served During the Mexican War in Organizations from the State of Texas,* National Archives microcopy number 278.

7. John Crittenden Duval, *The Adventures of Big Foot Wallace, the Texas Ranger and Hunter* (Macon, GA: Burke, 1870). See also Sowell, cited above.

8. Thomas T. Smith, "Fort Inge and Texas Frontier Military Operations, 1849–1869," *Southwestern Historical Quarterly* (July 1992): 2. Thomas "Ty" Smith, military historian, wrote the definitive book on Fort Inge. In an e-mail transmission to Uvalde County historian Virginia Davis on May 7, 2002, Ty writes that Reid is never listed as being present in the Post Returns of Fort Inge.

9. Smith, 1.

10. Thomas Mayne Reid, *The Headless Horseman, or A Strange Tale of Texas* (London: Chapman & Hall, 1865), 48–49. Mention of Bigfoot Wallace being a mail carrier can be read in Sowell's (1989) *Life of Bigfoot Wallace.* I frequently corresponded with and spoke by phone to Virginia Davis, historian with the Uvalde Historical Commission, about Reid and the headless horseman tale. Eventually, my son Taylor Lang and I drove to Uvalde to see where the old fort was and to make her acquaintance. Although the fort is long gone, the flag is still flying. Another interesting fact about Reid is that, while he was in Philadelphia, he befriended Edgar Allan Poe and defended Poe and his honor after his untimely death.

"It was at the base of [the White Mountain] that Mayne Reid drew his inspiration for those famous stories of his that charmed us as boys, and made us long to be Texas Rangers, and destroy Comanches and Mexican desperadoes. He lived in El Paso for a year or more, gathering the material for his marvelous tales." Henderson McCune, "The White Mountain," *Overland Monthly and Out West Magazine* 16 (91): 25.

11. Conversation with Virginia Davis at her home in Uvalde, July 3, 2002. I've seen the sketch of the fort that has the year 1867 written at the bottom. Mrs. Davis also contacted Ty Smith concerning Reid,

and his answer was in an e-mail transmission from Davis to Lou Ann Herda on May 7, 2002.

12. Elizabeth Reid, *Captain Mayne Reid* (London: Greening and Co., 1900), p. 158. Joan Steele, *Captain Mayne Reid* (Boston : Twayne Publishers, 1978), 137. "Reid, Thomas Mayne," The Handbook of Texas Online. *http://www.tsha.utexas.edu/handbook/online/articles/ view/RR/fre24.html* [Accessed Wed Dec 3 18:47:20 US/Central 2003]. E-mail transmission, Davis to Herda, May 7, 2002.

13. "De Shields, James Thomas." The Handbook of Texas Online. *http://www.tsha.utexas.edu/handbook/online/articles/view/DD/fde45. html* [Accessed Sun Aug 18 18:49:36 US/Central 2002]. Also, in a December 2, 1895, letter from former Texas Ranger "Rip" Ford, who was paid to send De Shields information about his service on the Texan frontier, Ford chided De Shields for not giving credit where due. He wrote, "I have signed the article forwarded. It is the right way to do. Any other method would be unjust to a writer. No one would believe you had written all the articles you may publish. Then it is right to let every man be responsible for what he writes. Suppose someone disputes what is said in my article about Col. Hays. Could you reply? Surely not . . ."

14. James T. De Shields, *Tall Men with Long Rifles* (San Antonio, TX: Naylor Co., 1935). In comparing the information about Creed's introduction to Vidal during the Siege of Bexar between *Tall Men* and Hunter's Manuscript, there are many instances where De Shields quotes Hunter verbatim. On p. 61, he uses the exact wording from pages 7 and 18 of the manuscript, recalling portions of Creed's headless horseman as well as Creed's descriptions from the siege. Still, there is nowhere in De Shields' book that mention Hunter's years of gathering information straight from Taylor.

15. J. Marvin Hunter, "The Headless Horseman," *Frontier Times* 1, no. 11 (August 1924), p. 12–13.

16. Ibid., 12.

17. Ibid., 14.

18. Ibid., 14.

19. J. Frank Dobie, *Tales of Old Time Texas* (Austin, TX: University of Texas Press, 1928), 147–49. See also Dobie's *Legends of Texas: Lost Mines and Buried Treasure,* 14th ed. (Austin, TX: University of Texas Press, 1992).

20. Ibid, 154.

21. Ibid., 154.

22. Ed Syers, *Ghost Stories of Texas* (Waco, TX: Texian Press, 1981), 157–58.

23. Jo-Anne Christensen, Ghost Stories of Texas (Auburn, WA: Lone Pine Publishing, 2001), 175.

24. Tingle to Herda in a conversation during the 2001 TFS meeting.

25. *www.theoutlaws.com/ghosts1.htm*

26. Email transmission from *thedove@boernenet.com* (Dovie Tschirthart Hall) to Lou Ann Herda, April 7, 2002. Email transmission from *BenaTKirk@aol.com* (Bena Taylor Kirkscey) to Lou Ann Herda on April 6, 2002.

27. Neither Creed Taylor or Bate Berry is listed among those mustered into service during the Siege of Bexar, as per the *Muster Rolls of the Texas Revolution* (Austin, TX: Daughters of the Texas Republic, 1986). See also O. C. Fisher's account of those who lived in Kimble County in the latter 1800s in *It Occurred in Kimble County and How—The Story of a Texas County* (Houston, TX: Anson Jones Press, 1937).

28. Lienhard, John H. Episode Number 1450: Searching for Cleopatra (online: *www.uh.edu/engines/epi1450.htm* [Accessed Wed Dec 3 18:52:23 US/Central 2003]

Jesse James, twenty-eight years old in Nebraska City, 1875
(State Historical Society of Missouri)

Jess James' grave in Mt. Olivet cemetery, in Kearney, Missouri
(State Historical Society of Missouri)

10

WHO IS BURIED IN JESSE JAMES' GRAVE?

by Tony Clark of Georgetown

In Mt. Olivet Cemetery in Kearney, Missouri, visitors can find a gravestone bearing the name of Jesse James, the Old West's most notorious outlaw. James, the story goes, was slain on April 3, 1882, in St. Joseph, Missouri. He had been living there with his wife and two small children while passing himself off as a cattle buyer named Thomas Howard. Unarmed, he was shot in the back of the head by Robert Ford, a young man Jesse had considered a new recruit for his robber gang. Ford himself was gunned down ten years later in Creede, Colorado.

So history records. However, from time to time people have come forward to declare that the legendary bandit was not killed after all. Even now, more than 120 years after the alleged assassination, at least two camps are claiming that Jesse didn't die in St. Joseph that day.

Interestingly, no one at the time seemed to doubt the report of Jesse's death. Hundreds of people, many of whom knew Jesse, streamed into St. Joseph as the news spread, and they had ample opportunity to view the body—it was packed in ice and left on public display for a few days, first in St. Joseph and then in Kearney, Jesse's hometown.[1] Not one questioned the identification. And certainly no one seemed to doubt the identity of his family members—his mother, Zerelda Samuel; his wife, Zee; and his children, Jesse Edwards James and Mary Susan James. Indeed, the notion that Jesse survived did not come into vogue for decades.

In the meantime, the body was buried on the James farm near Kearney, and Jesse's widow and children lived in relative poverty for a number of years.[2] Some have claimed that the James gang possessed hidden troves of loot from their robberies.[3] If Jesse had lived on and dug up any money, his family seems to have reaped no benefits.

Still, the Jameses got by. In 1902, after Jesse's widow died and was buried in Kansas City, the family had both Jameses exhumed and reburied side by side in the Mount Olivet Cemetery. The outlaw's son eventually became a successful lawyer. Jesse's daughter married and settled into a tranquil existence in Missouri. In 1900, Jesse Edwards James married Stella Frances McGown of Kansas City. Several years later, the couple moved to Los Angeles. Stella eventually made it her mission to try to debunk anyone who sought notoriety by claiming to be the "real" Jesse James. And she found plenty of work.

Some forty years after Jesse James was presumed to have died, a raft of people suddenly started claiming to be the outlaw. On the Arts & Entertainment cable network in 1996, in a show called *In Search of Jesse James,* historian N. David Smith reported that as many as thirty people came forward in the 1920s and 1930s to present themselves as Jesse James.[4] Each had a story that would "explain" how he had escaped death in St. Joseph and lived under assumed names. Most of these elderly claimants were trotted out by various promoters and displayed, for a fee, on theater stages and in sideshows.

One of the earliest known instances involved a man named John James. In late 1931, when Jesse James would have been eighty-four years old, this stranger arrived in Excelsior Springs, Missouri. He talked with a number of oldtimers who had known the James family, apparently gathering information. Then, he proclaimed himself to be the true Jesse James, and not dead after all. He was convincing enough that eighteen elderly citizens said they believed him. At least six signed affidavits to that effect. John James maintained that the man killed in St. Joseph was not Jesse but another outlaw, Charlie Bigelow.[5]

At that point, Stella James got involved. When word reached her of John James's claims, she traveled to Excelsior Springs for a showdown. In her book *In the Shadow of Jesse James,* she tells of the confrontation. She says she found that the chief of police was acting as John James's promoter, and it was he who had obtained the affidavits. With several journalists present, Stella put to John James several questions that the real Jesse surely could have answered. In most cases, the claimant was unable to do so. Two significant pieces of information he lacked had to do with a raid by Pinkerton Agency detectives on the James family farmhouse in 1875. In an explosion that occurred during the attack, Jesse's mother was injured and his half-brother killed. The claimant couldn't say which arm Jesse's mother had lost in the blast, nor could he give the name of the dead child.[6]

Stella described John James as a "pathetic figure" who fumbled question after question. Historian Milton F. Perry, who edited Stella's book, says in a note that sixteen of the eighteen people who had endorsed John James's claim changed their minds after Stella's grilling of him.[7]

Despite this outcome, the man persisted in his impersonation, and a new promoter brought him to California. Flashing the Eureka Springs affidavits, he received considerable attention from news media. He even came to the Jesse Edwards James home and demanded admittance.[8] However, this trip proved to be his undoing.

In tracing the imposter's family history, Stella had found John's sister, Dr. Bessie James Garver, living in Los Angeles. Dr. Garver gave an affidavit declaring that John was not Jesse, and she succeeded in having her brother committed to a mental institution.[9]

However, another character, J. Frank Dalton, soon began receiving attention as he toured the country declaring that he was Jesse James. Dalton apparently had devoted his life to portraying various Western characters. He once toured as one of the outlaw Dalton brothers, until the real Emmett Dalton called his bluff.[10] Other times he presented himself as "Capt. Kit Dalton," a Confederate guerilla fighter who had served (as Jesse James had) with Quantrill's Raiders and Bloody Bill Anderson.[11]

At least two promoters were affiliated with Dalton at various times during his "Jesse James" period. In the late 1940s, under the care of a man named Orvus Lee Houk (sometimes spelled *Howk*), the decrepit old man said he was over one hundred years old, as the real Jesse James would have been by that time. Sometimes the story went that Dalton had employed a stand-in to die for him in St. Joseph.[12] Just what prompted the substitute to accept this dubious honor is not explained.

Other times Dalton claimed the man killed was not he but Charlie Bigelow, the same name dropped by John James. In the latter telling, Dalton said it was Bigelow living with his own family in the St. Joseph house and using the Thomas Howard alias. Dalton personally shot the man, he explained, to provide the corpse needed for his cover story. Bigelow, Dalton reasoned, had been posing as Jesse James when he robbed people, so the rascal had it coming.[13] This is the version given in a remarkable 1975 book entitled *Jesse James Was One of His Names*. The book was written by Del Schrader "with Jesse James III," the name promoter Houk sometimes used. Houk, who declared that he was Dalton's grandson, was the source for much of the information in Schrader's book.[14]

Schrader reports that Dalton used at least seventy-two aliases in his nearly seventy years of living undercover. He also mastered the occult arts, so that he was able to travel freely all over the world, using astral projection (4–8). The author reported that Dalton made numerous fortunes, and that he served in the U.S. Senate under the name of William A. Clark, described as a Montana "copper king" (111).

Dalton also asserted that he was not the only legendary character whose death was erroneously reported. On the list were John

Wilkes Booth, whom Jesse finally had to poison in 1903 (Schrader 138–40); Billy the Kid (228); Butch Cassidy (218–19); and even Bob Ford. Dalton announced that Ford was not murdered in Colorado but had lived to be "my comptroller . . . when I was copper king of the world" (qtd. in Schrader 113).

And Cole Younger, Dalton claimed, never served a day of prison after the James-Younger Gang's disastrous attempt to rob banks in Northfield, Minnesota, even though history says he and his two brothers were captured and spent long stretches in the Stillwater, Minnesota, penitentiary. Cole also lived to a ripe old age, said Dalton, despite the official record that shows he died in 1916 at the age of seventy-two. As Schrader tells it, however, Younger and Dalton last met in 1950, when Cole was 127 years old (264). Wild Bill Hickok, on the other hand, really was killed at the time and place reported—only it was Dalton who shot him (143).

When the Dalton show came to Los Angeles in 1949, Stella Frances James secretly attended a performance. She found that the old man was using the same discredited affidavits originally collected by John James (103).

Dalton also spent time under the wing of Rudy Turilli, who had an interest in the Meramec Caverns tourist attraction in Missouri. Turilli apparently was always on the lookout for ways to publicize this enterprise. The best story I've run across regarding Turilli's promotional tactics comes from historian Perry. In Stella James's book, he says that Turilli "once tried to climb the Empire State Building in a tiger suit."[15] Steve Eng gives a more likely account in the magazine *True West*. He reports that Turilli, to draw attention to the caverns, put on a leopard-skin "cave man" costume and streaked up several *steps* of the Empire State Building. He might have made it all the way to the top had not the police interrupted his progress (19). This promoter also made good use of Dalton, having the old man testify that the James gang often had used Meramec Caverns as a hideout. At one point Turilli sought to have a Missouri court "restore" the name "Jesse James" to Dalton, but the presiding judge would have no part of it.[16] Still, sometime after Dalton died in 1951 and was laid to rest at the alleged age of 107 in Granbury, Texas, a tombstone was placed over his grave bearing the legend "Jesse Woodson James."

J. Frank Dalton's story did not end with his death, however. In fact, it has continued into the present. In the late 1960s, Turilli promised to give $10,000 to anyone who could discredit Dalton's claim. Stella James and her two daughters accepted the challenge, and the case ultimately had to be settled in court. A Missouri jury found in favor of the James women, and an appellate court upheld the judgment.[17]

More recently, other defenders of Dalton's claim have come forward. Houk had claimed to be J. Frank's grandson, and Houk's son now declares himself to be Jesse IV (*In Search*). In the spring of 2000, a faction claiming kinship to Jesse James through Dalton obtained a court order to have the old man's grave exhumed for the purpose of DNA testing. To this group's dismay, however, the body unearthed turned out to be that of a one-armed man, and Dalton was known to possess both his upper appendages.[18] Where this inquiry goes next is anyone's guess.

One might think it too late, well over a century after Jesse's presumed death, for any new claimants to come forward. One would be mistaken. In her 1998 book, *Jesse James Lived and Died in Texas*, Betty Dorsett Duke of Liberty Hill, Texas, presents her great-grandfather, James Lafayette Courtney, as the true Jesse James. Duke bases her claim on family stories, genealogical research, a comparison of photographs of Courtney and his kin with James family pictures, and the fact that Courtney, in his diary, once signed his name "J. James."[19] Duke uses a great deal of circumstantial evidence and conjecture in making her case.

Courtney, she says, moved to Texas in 1871 and bought a farm thirty miles south of Waco in the Blevins community (53–54). He married, had children, and lived under the Courtney identity up to his death in 1943 at age ninety-six (ix).

The supposed death of Jesse in 1882, according to Duke, was actually a cover-up, and the body buried as the outlaw was that of James's cousin, Wood Hite (47). The wife and children at the scene, she believes, were actually Hite's family, and Zee was married to Hite, not Jesse (71). This conclusion protects Courtney, if he was Jesse, from being accused of family abandonment and bigamy. Duke also disputes the DNA evidence from a 1995 exhumation of the supposed Jesse James grave. Experts at the time declared it "99.7 percent" certain that the remains in the Missouri grave are those of the outlaw (*In Search*). Duke, however, suggests that those results came from tests on a tooth that did not actually come from the grave (43–44).

Despite Duke's arguments, some members of the Courtney family do not believe their forebear was Jesse James, and they have challenged Duke's genealogical interpretations and photographic evidence. They also cite documents that indicate Courtney, as a veteran of the Civil War, received a government pension for his Union army service. That Jesse's sympathies lay with the Confederacy is well established. Duke dismisses this fact as just one more instance of Jesse "duping the Yankees" (59).

The other family faction also has had some DNA testing done. It seems to indicate that known descendants of Courtney were related to earlier Courtneys, a finding that calls into question Duke's genealogical research.[20] This testing did not involve the remains of James Lafayette Courtney, however, and Duke believes an exhumation of his grave would be in order so that definitive DNA testing could be done.

In my research, I have found what seem to be two serious problems with Duke's position. Both involve Courtney's daily diaries, portions of which Duke presents in her book. For one thing, although Duke makes reference to the Gad's Hill train robbery in Missouri as a Jesse James holdup (70), the diary places Courtney in Texas the day before and the day after that January 31, 1874, event (157).

Even more troublesome is that Courtney, by his own account, stayed "at home" on September 7, 1876, presumably in Texas, and "worked on . . . seed" (194). Yet it was on that date, historians believe, that Jesse James participated in the single most significant event in the story of the James-Younger gang, the ill-fated raid on Northfield, Minnesota. All participants except the James brothers were killed or captured. Was that some other Jesse James, then, who barely escaped with his life in the bloody shootout? Or was the robbery attempt simply erroneously credited to the fabled outlaw?

Missouri researcher Linda Snyder has looked into the controversy aroused by Duke's book and has put many of her findings on an Internet website. She has posted some fascinating information comparing the traditional story of Jesse James with Duke's version. The comparison seems to favor the historical account. Interested parties definitely should check out this website. Here is the address: http://home.earthlink.net/~ariannayoungblood.

Another worthwhile website that follows the continuing debate is called the "Jesse James Discussion Site Forum." It may be found here: www.delphiforums.com.

So the question of who is buried in Jesse James's Missouri grave, not to mention two more graves in Texas, remains unanswered—or at least it has not been answered to everyone's satisfaction. Perhaps more exhumations and further DNA testing will resolve the issue, but I doubt it. The concerned parties in this highly emotional debate—the Jameses, the Daltons, and the Courtneys—are defending what they believe is their birthright, a substantial part of their very identities. It is unlikely that mere facts can ever change their minds, nor extinguish the fiery longing in their blood.

ENDNOTES

1. Marley Brant, *Jesse James: The Man and the Myth* (New York: Berkley, 1998), 226–30; Phillip W. Steele, *Jesse and Frank James: The Family History* (Gretna, LA: Pelican, 1987), 28.
2. Brant, 230, 234, 236–37.
3. Homer Croy, *Jesse James Was My Neighbor* (New York: Duell, 1949), 253–54.
4. *In Search of Jesse James.* Video. A&E Television Networks, 1996. Call No. AAE 16044.
5. Brant, 263.
6. Brant, 264.
7. Stella Frances James, *In the Shadow of Jesse James,* ed. Milton F. Perry (Thousand Oaks, CA: Revolver Press, Dragon Books, 1989), 138.
8. James, 103.
9. Ibid.
10. Steve Eng, "The Great Outlaw Hoax," *True West,* Feb. 1986: 16–23.
11. Eng, 21–22.
12. Brant, 264.
13. Del Schrader, with Jesse James III, *Jesse James Was One of His Names* (Arcadia, CA: Santa Anita, 1975), 12–16.
14. Schrader, 5–6. Subsequent references are to this book.
15. James, 139.
16. Eng, 20.
17. James, 139; Brant, 264–65.
18. Kent Biffle, "Dig for James' Grave Turns up Body of Wrong Man," *Dallas Morning News,* 30 June 2000.
19. Betty Dorsett Duke, *Jesse James Lived and Died in Texas* (Austin, Eakin, 1998), vi. Subsequent references are to this book.
20. Linda Snyder, *Arianna's Illusions.* Online. http://home.earthlink. net/~ariannayoungblood.

SELECTED BIBLIOGRAPHY

Breihan, Carl W. *The Day Jesse James Was Killed.* New York: Bonanza, 1962.

Curry, Matt. "DNA sought in Jesse James mystery." Associated Press. 30 May 2000.

Drago, Harry Sinclair. *Road Agents and Train Robbers: Half a Century of Western Bandits.* New York: Dodd, 1973.

"James Family History." *Heritage Website.* University of Kansas. Online. http://www.ukans.edu/heritage/families/james.html.

Jesse James Discussion Site Forum. Online. http://delphiforums. com/jesse james/start.

Newmans, Evans. *The True Story of the Notorious Jesse James.* Hicksville, NY: Exposition, 1976.

Settle, William A., Jr. *Jesse James Was His Name.* Columbia: University of Missouri Press, 1966.

Triplett, Frank. *The Life, Times and Treacherous Death of Jesse James.* 1882. Rpt. Stamford, CT: Longmeadow, 1992.

Bob Ford kills Jesse James (Courtesy State Historical Society of Missouri, Columbia)

Charles Banks Williams' sketch of the Pacing White Stallion from Frank Dobie's 1952 publication, *The Mustangs.*

11

A NOTE ON THE PACING WHITE MUSTANG LEGEND

by James T. Bratcher of San Antonio

By 1832, the year Washington Irving reported him in his camp journal that became *A Tour on the Prairies*,[1] stories of a remarkable wild stallion were making the rounds of western campfires. Mustangers had gone after the horse but without success. According to those who had chased him or heard about him in locales as far separated as the Rio Grande Plain to the south and the Canadian Rockies to the north, he was snow white in color, of regal bearing, and with a flowing mane and tail. In some accounts, however, his color varied in a notable detail. Western chronicler Josiah Gregg, and also Mayne Reid, the Irish adventure-novelist who spent time in the West, reported him as having black ears.[2] Neither Gregg nor Reid had seen the horse with his own eyes, nor had Irving. In *Commerce of the Prairies* (1844), Gregg shrewdly guessed that the stallion was "somewhat mythical from the difficulty one finds in fixing the abiding place of [this] equine hero."[3]

Leaving aside Gregg's skepticism for the moment, a second memorable feature, along with the stallion's color, was his unusual gait. This was a pace or rack that remained as smooth as glass even during pursuit. The animal's swift propelling motion, virtually a glide, had thwarted mustangers despite their riding good horses and chasing him as fast as their horses could run. One mustanger had chased him by moonlight: "He moved like a white shadow, and the harder we rode, the more shadowy he looked."[4] The pacer's ability to outdistance *running* horses was uncanny.

Herman Melville wrote of the pacer's serene majesty and "cool milkiness" in chapter 42 of *Moby Dick,* the essay on whiteness. Melville had become acquainted with the horse while doing research for his masterpiece, perhaps encountering him in George Wilkins Kendall's *Narrative of the Texan Santa Fe Expedition* (1844).[5] He attributes the legend, which he cites as a further example of phantom whiteness, to "old trappers and hunters," duplicating Kendall's use of the same words, "trappers and hunters." Kendall had written:

> Many were the stories told in camp that night . . . of a large white horse that had often been seen in the vicinity of the Cross Timbers and near Red River [in northern Texas]. . . . As the camp stories ran, he has never been known to gallop or trot, but paces faster than any horse that has been sent out after him can run; and so game and untiring is the "White Steed of the Prairies," for he is well known to trappers and hunters by that name, that he has tired down no less than three race-nags, sent expressly to catch him, with a Mexican rider well trained to the business of taking wild horses. . . .
>
> Some of the hunters go so far as to say that the White Steed has been known to pace his mile in less than two minutes, and that he could keep up this rate of speed until he had tired down everything in pursuit. Large sums had been offered for his capture, and the attempt had been frequently made; but he still roamed his native prairies in freedom. . . .

A hundred years following Kendall's report, Texas historian and folklorist J. Frank Dobie, who pursued the pacer in library stacks and elsewhere for nearly three decades, provided the fullest treatment in his 1952 book *The Mustangs.*[6] While Dobie's book stands as a monument to the western horse, it overlooks (for some unexplained reason, considering how long he worked with the legend) a central fact about the Pacing White Mustang. The horse had a European counterpart in Celtic "faery" horses. These were noble animals characterized by an exceptional gait (often referred to as "amblers," with ladies as riders) that during the Middle Ages inhabited the same mystical realm that gave us Avalon, King Arthur's enchanted retreat. Usually their body color was white. How the qualities of Celtic fairyland horses came to be transferred to a western mustang, it is impossible to say with certainty. But despite Americans' willingness to accept the Pacing White Mustang as a native-born son of the West, on whose boundless prairies he was unique in history, there are signs he was neither native-born nor unique to the West. Gregg's skepticism was justified.

The story of "Pwyll, Prince of Dyfed," as found in the eleventh-century Welsh collection of tales known as *The Mabinogion,* presents us with a mysterious white pacer (here ridden by a ghostly lady) that pursuers on swift mounts cannot overtake. In the Pwyll story we find faery stag-hounds that are shining white except for having red ears, an oddity that Celtic folklore elsewhere assigns to fairyland horses and that the American white pacer almost shares in reports that give him black ears. In "Pwyll," also, the white pacer is sighted from a mound, as the pacing mustang often was.

"Pwyll" involves a nobleman who visits the Celtic otherworld, a realm of magic and marvels. As strongly suggesting the origin of the American white steed in this mythical dreamland, relevant passages from *The Mabinogion,* as translated from the Welsh by Gwyn Jones and Thomas Jones,[7] are as follows:

> Pwyll arose to take a walk, and made for the top of a mound which was above the court and was called Gorsedd Arberth. "Lord," said one of the court, "it is the peculiarity of the mound that whatever high-born man sits upon it will not go thence without one of two things: wounds or blows, or else his seeing a wonder." . . .

> He sat upon the mound. And as they were sit-
> ting down, they could see a lady on a big fine pale
> white horse . . . coming along the highway that led
> past the mound. The horse had a slow even pace. . . .
> [Pwyll sent a man on foot after the lady.] He fol-
> lowed her as fast as he could on foot, but the
> greater was his speed, all the further she was from
> him.

Pwyll then sent the man on horseback after the lady. At this
point the translated text says, "The more he pricked on his horse,
the further she was from him." The next day, Pwyll sent a second
rider on a swifter horse, but with his similar failure the words are
repeated (and once more recall the American mustanger's words,
even his sentence structure: "The harder we rode, the more shadowy he looked.") On the third day, Pwyll said:

> "Where is the company we were yesterday and the
> day before, at the top of the mound?" "We are here,
> lord," said they. "Let us go to the mound," said he,
> "to sit. And do thou," said he to his groom, "saddle
> my horse well and bring him to the road, and fetch
> with thee my spurs." . . . They came to the mound
> to sit; they had been there but a short while when
> they could see the rider coming by the same road
> . . . and at the same pace. . . . Pwyll mounted his
> horse . . . and let his horse, mettled and prancing,
> take its own speed. And he thought that at the sec-
> ond bound or the third he would come up with
> her. But he was no nearer to her than before. He
> drove his horse to its utmost speed, but he saw that
> it was idle for him to follow her.

Earlier in "Pwyll" we read of enchanted stag-hounds that are
shining white except for having red ears:

And then he [Pwyll] looked at the colour of the
pack, without troubling to look at the stag; and of
all the hounds he had seen in the world, he had
seen no dogs the same colour as these. The colour
that was on them was a brilliant shining white, and
their ears red; and as the exceeding whiteness of the
dogs glittered, so glittered the exceeding redness of
their ears.

R. S. Loomis, in a well-known comparative study that focuses
on Celtic legendry, *Arthurian Tradition and Chrétien de Troyes*,[8]
assures us that red ears (also a red mane) were a mark of the Celtic
faery horse, as well as of hounds. Typically, the horses were white
and possessed of a pacing gait that no galloping horse could match
for speed:

[The Celtic faery horse] was likely to have a white
body, a long red mane, and red ears; . . . we find
unearthly ladies mounted on horses distinguished
by preternatural celerity and smoothness of
motion. The Breton lai [*Lai du Trot*] describes a
cavalcade of lovely ladies issuing from a forest.
"They had palfreys entirely white, which carried
them so gently that if a person sat upon one and if
he did not see the palfrey moving, he would surely
think that it was standing still; and yet they moved
far more fleetly than one would gallop on the tallest
Spanish horse."[9]

As to sighting the pacer from a mound, as in the Pwyll story,
Texas rancher Joe Cruze's family-legend of the Pacing White Mustang names a particular mound from which his grandfather's
vaqueros had watched for the horse. This was at a time not long
"after the fall of the Alamo." A lifelong resident of Hays County,
south of Austin, rancher Cruze contributed his story to a book of

local history published in 1967, *Wimberley's Legacy.*[10] He writes, his words faintly recalling the Pwyll story, which he could not have consciously known:

> There is a high mound north of Creedmore [Creed-moor], Texas, called Pilot Knob. There is where Bill Cruze [the grandfather] kept scouts planted day and night to watch for Indians and outlaws. . . . One day, one of his scouts told him he had seen a snow white horse . . . that acted like a stallion. The scout gave chase to see for sure and the horse hit a pace and single foot and never broke it. . . . Bill Cruze doubted his yarn, but in a week or two, two scouts came up with the same yarn; they had seen the white horse and chased him with the same results. The horse paced away from them, just as he had from the first scouts. Bill Cruze decided to see for himself. He ordered the next man who spotted the horse to notify him. . . .

The Texas family-legend includes a mound, an overlord (the grandfather), retainers ("scouts"), and a dramatic build-up in which eventually the overlord decides he will "see for himself," as when Pwyll called for his horse and spurs. While the shadowy parallels to "Pwyll, Prince of Dyfed" could be mere coincidence, it is tempting to view them as evidence of mythic survival and influence. At long range, the Pwyll story could have conditioned the way Joe Cruze heard and repeated the legend of the Pacing White Mustang. Possibly in the early 1800s or earlier, a Welsh or a Breton (that is, native of Brittany) storyteller sat among the "old trappers and hunters," spinning out his yarn and reintroducing the Celtic pacer—onto fresher pastures—when the talk turned to mustangs. It is something of a stretch to accept the theory, but the supernatural Celtic pacer had to come from the folk mind, and likely so did the phantom mustang who roamed throughout the West.

ENDNOTES

1. Chapter XX records stories Irving listened to on the night of October 21, 1832, while camped with frontiersmen west of the junction of the Cimarron and Arkansas rivers in what is now northeastern Oklahoma.

2. Reid's report took the form of his novel set partly along the Rio Grande, *The War Trail, or the Hunt of the Wild Horse* (New York, 1857). His novel *The Headless Horseman* (1865) draws on a South Texas folktale.

3. Published in New York and London by Wiley & Putnam, Volume II, page 207.

4. Quoted by J. Frank Dobie in *The Mustangs*, page 162 (see note 6 below). Dobie quotes the sentence from a collection of "Frontier Tales" that appeared in *Putnam's Magazine* 8 (1856): 503–7. As the present article suggests in passing, the sentence may hold significance as an archaism.

5. Published in New York and London by Wiley & Putnam, 1844. See Volume I, 88–90.

6. Published in Boston by Little, Brown and Company, 1952. See chapter IX, "The Legend of the Pacing White Mustang," 143–70.

7. Everyman's Library edition, 1963, 9–11; also page 3 for the description of hounds to follow.

8. Published in New York by Columbia University Press, 1949. See pages 105–6.

9. The cavalcade of otherworld ladies, richly dressed and seated sidesaddle on white amblers that a rider can follow but not overtake, turns up in John Gower's fourteenth-century dream-vision poem *Confessio Amantis*, Book IV, "Tale of Rosiphelee."

10. Edited by Williedell Schawe (San Antonio: The Naylor Company, 1967), 17–19. Editor Schawe published the first edition privately in 1963; the 1967 edition is revised. Following page 116 is a photo of Joe Cruze as a young cowboy. *The Mabinogion* would have been as foreign to him as Thomas Aquinas or modernist poetry.

Editor's choice: "Rocky" Rothwell of Cordova, Alaska, was the "he-est" man that I ever met. The first time I noticed him was in a sourdough bar in Ketchikan, Alaska. He had slapped his billfold down on the bar and challenged anybody in that large and densely packed frontier tavern to come up and take it from him— and they could have the first swing! Nobody came. Rocky would drink a water glass of whiskey while he shaved in the morning. Same breed of cat as Old Fat Fullmer!

12

HELL IS FOR HE-MEN!

by James Ward Lee of Fort Worth

Back in Alabama in the 1930s—back when men were men and women were double breasted—our local hero was Fat Fullmer. Old Fat rode a milky blue Indian Chief Motocycle (Hey, that is the correct spelling for Indian motorcycles), and Fat rode it with style. He had saddlebags with more silver than Roy put on poor Trigger's saddle or Gene nailed onto Champion's stirrups. Fat had long leather streamers tied to the handlebar grips, and he wore high boots like an Aggie cheerleader. One time—it must have been 1937 or 1938—Fat rode up in front of the hardware store that his daddy owned and throttled back the Big Indian to a steady gurgle. He leaned the Big Indian over a little and put one of his glorious boots down on the ground and said to the men and boys huddled in front of the hardware store, "Boys, I'll be in Birmingham in fifteen minutes or I'll be in hell."

I thought I would faint at this swagger and strut! This was stuff we saw in the movies and read about in adventure stories. Here was a man defying whatever gods there were in Alabama in 1938. We knew for certain that here was a man. In capital letters, A MAN. Fat had more guts than an army mule. He would ride that "sickle" at 120 miles an hour on those curving mountain roads between Leeds and Birmingham. And fight! Fat would charge hell with a bucket of water. He would fight a buzz saw. And win. Once he got into a fistfight with Jim Ned Grimason at the Hop Rite Inn. Fat took three .32 caliber slugs out of an old 1911 Savage automatic and kept coming. Dr. Clayton dug the bullets out and Fat made a necklace out of them. For all I know, Fat was buried in that necklace of bullets when he died a few years ago. Jim Ned was in the hospital in Birmingham for six weeks.

But that wasn't anything compared to this because old Fat, sitting astride that blue Indian, was throwing down his gauntlet before the Lord God Jehovah. He was daring hell, and that was no small thing in Leeds, Alabama, in 1937 or '38. If anybody ever deserved to be enshrined in the Hellfire and Damnation Mantown Hall of Fame, it was Fat Fullmer of Leeds, Alabama, USA. Once Fat had rocketed through town on his '37 Indian Chief, every other man in Leeds seemed like a pussy to us boys. (Hold it, please. Don't fret. "Pussy" is not what you might think. It has nothing to do with cats—or willows. It is a technical term, which I will define at the proper time.)

Anyway, Fat Fullmer made it to Birmingham that time. And lots of other times. And he burned up the road for several years on that big, milky blue Indian Chief between Leeds and Pell City, Leeds and Anniston, Leeds and Estaboga, Leeds and Villa Rico, Georgia. And when the war broke out Private Fat Fullmer was sent off to India in the Army Air Corps. As he told the story when he got back from the war in "Inja's sunny clime," he and some other hell defiers drank aviation gasoline filtered through light bread. Of course they mixed it with Pet Milk, and that cut the sting.

Hear me one more time: Fat Fullmer was not a pussy. Fat is long dead now, and if all went as he planned it, he is riding his Indian Chief all over hell, which is a lot bigger and more crowded than it was in the Thirties when Fat was riding all over "hell and half of Georgia," as the old folk saying went. God, we admired Fat Fullmer. But way back then we had no idea that he was a throwback to all the world's great hell-bound heroes.

Fat was for us what Prometheus was for the ancient Greeks. Remember how Prometheus defied the gods? Against the express orders of the Olympic establishment he brought fire to mankind. For that, he was bound to a rock and big old raptors and such like pecked at his liver, and if that ain't hell don't ask me what it is. But

Prometheus sort of won because he is the hero of many Greek poems and plays and Shelley's famous 12,000-line poem, which nobody reads today. (Bragging note: I once read it aloud—half of it between Denton, Texas, and Ashdown, Arkansas, and half of it on the way back. Top that, English majors!)

And then there is Sisyphus and that rock. He was put in hell and made to roll a boulder about the size of a 1937 Willys Knight up the hill. Just before he got it to the top, it would break loose and roll back down. Poor old Sisyphus down in hell rolling that rock up the hill and having it roll back down and doing it over and over. He is still rolling it as far as I know. According to Albert Camus, a Frenchman noted for irreverence and deep penetration, Sisyphus was the winner. It is true that the gods took round one, but after centuries and centuries Sisyphus is now ahead on existential points.

And everybody knows more about Milton and that whole *Paradise Lost* business than I do, but this is what I remember: Satan and God tangled it up over turf. God won, and Satan was pastured out in his own domain. But still, he was the devil-in-chief and once was heard to remark, "Better to reign in Hell than to serve in Heaven." He sure didn't want to be an angel in a heaven full of old ladies, babies, and pussies. And Della Reese and that simpering girl with the fake Irish accent? Nossir, Satan and his boys were not cut out for a soft touch with clouds and golden streets and milk and honey. Those were bad guys—meaner than Saddam Hussein, tougher than Rocky III or Terminator II. (Now, it seems, the Terminator has traded in hell for what he calls Cal-ee-fornia.) You may not like everything Satan and his band of blackguards did, but you have got to admire their guts. These guys invented Man-town. Imagine how disgusted they were with milk and honey and ambrosia and whatever the hell else they served in heaven. They ate hog meat and red-eye gravy for breakfast and fire and brimstone for supper. You can't keep a devil from eating pork—or any other unclean animal for that matter. Hey, those devils already have cloven hooves so what's the big deal?

Way after Satan and his bunch had settled the land where there is no sunshine and all you can see is "darkness visible," there wasn't a lot of hell-defying going on up on earth. Some, but not much: Dante and Milton had nearly scared the hell out of everybody. But there was a little hell going on down through the ages: the occasional Black Mass or Witches' Sabbath or some ugly old girls stirring eyes of newts and other tidbits into a chowder and mumbling "double, double, toil and trouble."

Shakespeare has a few people willing to defy hell, but not many. One or two do. Horatio, Hamlet's schoolfellow and another one of those literary guys with no last name, says he will jump in front of Hamlet Sr.'s ghost as it passes over the battlements. He says, "I'll cross it though it blast me." Big talk, but not as big as Hamlet Jr.'s a night or so later. Hamlet sees the ghost of his dead father, and when it beckons him to follow, he sets off after it. Horatio and the guards tell him not to go. They say it might be a vile, devilish ghost and might "tempt him toward the flood." But Hamlet says, "I'll speak to it though hell itself should gape and bid me hold my peace." Bold talk for a guy who can't decide whether "to be or not to be." And don't forget one other Shakespearean tough guy: Macbeth. He says to his nemesis: "Lay on, Macduff, and let him be damned who first cries 'Hold! Enough!'" And he is dead in a few minutes and probably on his way to hell to join all the other bad asses too fierce to even want to be up there with all those nuns and babies and saints and grandmas and Della Reese and little what'shername with the fake Irish accent.

(I might digress for a moment and note that all grandmas, no matter how reprobate they were as girls and young women, turn sanctified in late middle age and all wind up in heaven. I am laying nine to five that Monica Lewinski will wind up with a gray bun at the back of her head making chocolate chip cookies and looking like that old lady in the Hansel and Gretel story. And as Andy Rooney noted, "It seems only yesterday that she was crawling around the White House on her hands and knees.")

But, let me ask you this: Can you imagine The Duke in heaven? No, I think not! The Duke ain't a pussy. A pussy is a man who does work that won't get your hands dirty, work a good-sized woman could do. Coal miners are not pussies, nor are lumberjacks and cowboys and railroad engineers. Willie is being ironic when he tells mothers not to let their babies grow up to be cowboys: "Don't let 'em pick guitars and drive them old trucks/Make 'em be doctors and lawyers and such." Doctors and lawyers and preachers and teachers and lots of other folks who don't get dirty are pussies, but Clint ain't. Nor was Humphrey Bogart. Nor was Ward Bond or lots of others I could name. Benny Hinn is; Pat Robertson is; Regis is; Joe Lieberman is. And probably Garth, but not Willie and Waylon and the boys. Elvis may have been, but Ernest Tubb definitely was not. I know what I am talking about here. I was once a radar pussy in the Navy, and then I taught school for years and years. Try to imagine Ernest Borgnine or Lee Marvin or the late Jack Elam staring at a radar screen or teaching school.

Okay, here's how I got off on this whole business of hell as the last hometown of real he-men. I was mowing my grass one day when it was 105 Fahrenheit in Fort Worth, Texas, and I got to studying about Kipling's poem "Gunga Din." You know the story: it is set in India where "the 'eat would make your bloomin' eyebrows crawl." I was sweating away and my eyebrows were crawling when I remembered that part at the end when Gunga Din is giving a drink of water to the narrator when he "fell behind the fight with a bullet where [his] breastplate should have been." He says, the water Gunga gave him "was crawling and it stunk, but of all the drinks I've drunk, I'm gratefullest to the one from Gunga Din." While the narrator is drinking this disgusting water, some Pakistani or Afghanistani or other "lesser breed without the law," gets off a lucky shot at the "regimental bhisti Gunga Din." Lo and behold, "A bullet came and drilled the beggar clean." Gunga dies, and the narrator says, "So I'll meet him later on in the place where he is gone, where it's always double drill and no canteen. He'll be squattin' on the coals, giving drinks to poor damned souls, and I'll get a swig in hell from Gunga Din."

Well, that set me thinking. Of course the British soldier expected to go to hell and expected "good old grinnin' gruntin' Gunga Din" to go there, too. It is where he-men go; they prefer it to the soft life on Cloud Number Nine with harps twanging away in the background and Della Reese singing "How Great Thou Art" and that little old simpering girl with the fakey accent being all atwitter over some minor sin here on earth. Piddling sins. No serious India sinning like they do out there where "East is East and West is West," out there "west of Suez where the best is like the worst/Where there aren't no Ten Commandments and a man can raise a thirst." So don't talk to Old Kip about deathbed conversions and last minute confessions and milk-and-water angels that sound like they came from Galway Bay. Real men who live their lives in Mantown expect to end up "where there's double drill and no canteen." They want to go there so they can see serious bad asses like Lee Marvin and Lee Van Cleef and Sean Penn.

I know how all those timid people in the Middle Ages—what some call the Middle Evil period—worried about going to hell, and how only a handful of people made pacts with the Devil so they could see Helen of Troy and stuff. It was only after mankind redefined God as Nature way back when Blake was a boy that you got a bunch of he-men challenging the Almighty. Byron was one. He has Manfred and Cain and Don Juan sinning incessantly and daring anybody to do anything about it. And Byron hisownself knew a good sin when he saw it. Dorothy Parker says it succinctly: "Byron walked out with a number of girls."

The poet Blake lauds the devil as pure energy, and if he is right, then hell must be a place of action and swashbuckling romance. Blake says,

> Grown old in love from seven till seven times seven
> I oft have wished for hell for ease from heaven.

Whatever that means.

Blake made the Devil respectable and planned the marriage of heaven and hell. But Blake sometimes wanted to have it both ways. He worries about "Dark Satanic Mills" cropping up all over England's "green and pleasant land." But, hey, that's what the Devil does: He builds "dark Satanic mills." What is supposed to be wrong with that? I am from Birmingham where "dark Satanic mills" fed black and white alike. Percy B. Shelley, whose grandfather was born in Newark, New Jersey, wrote in "Peter Bell" that "Hell is a city much like London—a populous and smoky city." Just like Birmingham. Or Newark, New Jersey. Or Houston. All the devil was doing was promoting industry and energy and profits for big business. Get real. What about our leading he-man, that celebrated compassionate conservative and Christian Methodist. He ran on "a green and pleasant land" ticket and later saw the wisdom of promoting arsenic in the drinking water and building more "dark Satanic mills." And if you can't trust George Jr. I'd like to know who you can trust.

Okay. Let me get back to the story. Time passed. The Middle Evil Period gave way to Enlightenment and other vague periods of life and culture. The Light Brigade happily "rode into the mouth of hell." Huckleberry Finn ponders turning in Jim to the slave traders, but decides to go against the will of God, who was certainly on the side of slavery. Huck decides to help Jim escape and says, "Well, then I'll just go to hell." And remember the shadowy Highwayman in Alfred Noyes's poem. He comes riding, riding, riding, riding and says, "I'll come to thee by moonlight though Hell should bar the way." And old Jesse James from the Stephen Vincent Benet poem:

> He swayed through the coaches with horns and a tail,
> Lit out with the bullion and the registered mail.

Since everybody seems hell bent on going to the nether regions, you wonder what it will be like. Somebody—it should have been

Noel Coward but probably wasn't—said, "The best people may be in Heaven but the best company is in Hell." And Dorothy Parker wrote this little quatrain:

> He whose love is given over well
> Shall see fair Helen's face in Hell,
> But he whose love is thin and wise,
> May view John Knox in Paradise.

I don't know whether I need to identify John Knox, but he was the heavy hitter of the Scottish Presbyterian Church and had a face like a dried prune. Lots of old-timey Presbyterians looked like John Knox. Albert Bigelow Paine, in his biography of Mark Twain, quotes the writer as describing someone by saying "he looks as out of place as a Presbyterian in hell." Nobody in hell is as sour as a Puritan divine; those boys down there are drinking and laughing and whooping and hollering. Nobody in the nether world is butting in where he does not belong. Wendell Phillips says, "A Puritan's idea of hell is a place where everyone has to mind his own business."

But I keep straying from the subject that I announced. How tough guys admire hell and all. General Sherman said, "War is Hell." Old Tecumseh Sherman was tough. Just ask Scarlett O'Hara and them. Talk about little tough guys and you have to remember Audie Murphy, who wrote *To Hell and Back* about being a hero in WWII. Please don't forget Fat Fullmer. Don't forget all his heirs who became Hell's Angels and Banditos and took to wearing Nazi helmets and getting tattoos. Ezra Pound talks about how World War I soldiers walked "eye-deep in hell," and the late William Owens of Pinhook, Texas, and later Nyack, New York, stole that line for a book of his. Old Rudyard Kipling has an anti-marching poem that says, " I have spent six weeks in hell and certify it is not devils, dark, or anything but boots, boots moving up and down again." Hell is surely preferable to all that tramping. Let me say it again: Tough guys revel in hell. The Marines pride themselves on being "Devildogs." And there was the Devil's Brigade in the movie about WWII, which a Texas high school teacher taught as WWEleven.

I just checked my old and tattered *Video Hound* and discovered twenty-three movies on TV with "hell" in the title and fifty-seven with "Devil" stretched across the marquee. You have seen them all—*Devil's Angels* about motorcycle gangs; *Devil's Eight* about a guy who recruits criminals to hunt down moonshiners; and don't forget *Hell's Bloody Devils,* that features motorcycle gangs, Nazis, and the Las Vegas Mob. And there is *Hell's Angels on Wheels,* starring some real Hell's Angels. Let's face it; hell is full of guys like Lee Marvin and Steve McQueen and John Wayne and all those people in *The Dirty Dozen.* Hell is *The Wild Bunch* with William Holden and Ernest Borgnine. Hell is *Hang 'Em High* and *The Outlaw Josey Wales* and Marlon Brando in *The Wild Ones* and *One-Eyed Jacks* and *The Godfather.* Heaven, on the other hand, is Meg Ryan in *Sleepless in Seattle* and *When Harry Met Sally.* Heaven is Doris Day in *Romance on the High Seas* and *The Glass Bottom Boat.* Heaven is anything with that cute little Katy, Texas, girl Renee Zellweger.

If you don't believe me about the popularity of hell nowadays, you could look it up. Google has 4,777,000 sites with "hell" in the title. Not all of them extol its manliness; some are downright scary and right out of Dante's *Inferno.* Check out AmazonDotCom (That's all one word.) and you will find 1672 books with "hell" in the title. I am here to say that hell is very popular nowadays.

Way back, Odysseus, after making a trip to his travel consultant, Achilles, in hell, says he would prefer to be a servant in a rich man's house than a king in hell, but not old Lucifer. He was clear: "To reign is worth ambition though in hell/Better to reign in hell than serve in heaven." So here we are in modern times extolling the virtues of hell and keeping the devil firmly in our minds. The Duke University totemic symbol is the Blue Devil, and New Jersey has a soccer team called "The Devils," and we all know how potent Red Devil Lye is and how good deviled eggs and deviled ham are.

There is even a delectable salsa from Telephone, Texas, called "Hell on the Red." So when old Phil Sheridan said, "If I owned Hell and Texas, I'd rent out Texas and live in Hell," he was not saying that Texas was bad, just that it was second best.

Here is my last word on the subject: Hell is a spaghetti western, and Heaven is a chick-flick.

CORRER DEL PAISANO

TALKING DOG FOR SALE

[Kent Biffle of the *Dallas Morning News* was going to do a story for TFS about smart hound dog tales. This was about as far as he got.]

In Tennessee, a guy sees a sign in front of a house: "Talking Dog for Sale." He rings the bell and the owner tells him the dog is in the backyard. The guy goes into the backyard and sees a black mutt just sitting there.

"You talk?" he asks.

"Yep," the mutt replies.

"So, what's your story?"

The mutt looks up and says, "Well, I discovered this gift pretty young and I wanted to help the government, so I told the CIA about my gift, and in no time they had me jetting from country to country, sitting in rooms with spies and world leaders, because no one figured a dog would be eavesdropping. I was one of their most valuable spies eight years running. The jetting around really tired me out, and I knew I wasn't getting any younger and I wanted to settle down. So I signed up for a job at the airport to do some undercover security work, mostly wandering near suspicious characters and listening in. I uncovered some incredible dealings there and was awarded a batch of medals. Had a wife, a mess of puppies, and now I'm just retired."

The guy is amazed. He goes back in and asks the owner what he wants for the dog.

The owner says, "Ten dollars."

The guy says, "This dog is amazing. Why on earth are you selling him so cheap?"

The owner replies, "He's such a liar. He didn't do any of that stuff."

Clementine Hunter (c. 1887–1988) the artist in 1945
(Courtesy Mildred Bailey Collection, Natchitoches, Louisiana)

13

CLEMENTINE HUNTER: FOLK ARTIST

by Phyllis Bridges of Denton

Folk artist Clementine Hunter lived for just over one hundred years, all of those years in Natchitoches parish in northwestern Louisiana, and most of them on the grounds of Melrose Plantation, where she worked as a field hand in her early years and as a household servant in her later years. Her work as a folk artist, according to Melrose historian Francois Mignon, began in the 1940s after she was over sixty years old.

Clementine Hunter was born in the winter of 1887 on Hidden Hill Plantation near Cloutierville, Louisiana, an area made famous by the bayou tales of author Kate Chopin, whose cotton plantation was very near the place where Clementine Hunter was born and lived out her life. Conditions at Hidden Hill Plantation were so cruel that most observers consider that plantation to be the model for Harriet Beecher Stowe's *Uncle Tom's Cabin*. Significantly, that plantation is today called Little Eva Plantation. As a young girl Clementine left Hidden Hill with her family and relocated later when she was sixteen to Melrose with her family.

Clementine's parents were Creole. Her mother, unmarried at the time of Clementine's birth, was Antoinette Adams. Her father was Janvier (John) Reuben. Her parents were married when she was four years old in the Catholic Church of St. John the Baptist in Cloutierville. Clementine was the oldest of their seven children, four daughters and three sons.

Of her family, Clementine once said, "All my people were Creoles. They say us Creoles got more different kinds of blood than

Baptizing

any other people. When I was growing up all the folks on the lower Cane River were Creoles and spoke nothing but French."[1] The genealogy of Clementine Hunter shows French, Indian, Irish, and African roots, a pattern consistent for the population of the area. Her maternal grandmother Idole, who lived to be 110 years old, came to Louisiana from Virginia as a slave.

Clementine Hunter, who was illiterate all her life, had the opportunity for education as a young girl at the Catholic school in her community. The school was run by French-speaking nuns, who were extremely strict. Although the white and black children at the school were separated by a fence, they nonetheless got into scuffles and fights. Early on, Clementine expressed a disregard for education. Her own words tell the story:

> After about ten, I quit school. Didn't like it at all.
> So I never even learned any of the ABCs. And I
> have made out all right too. All my life I have had a
> strong mother-wit, which is better than stuff you
> learn from books. Leastwise I can say I don't think
> I missed anything by not getting reading and writ-
> ing. It's a heap of folks got book learning running
> out their ears, but I can't say they is smart people.[2]

Her story of how she left school illustrates her "strong mother-wit":

> Sister Benedict was my teacher and she was mean
> and I tell her, I say, "Sister, can I go and get some
> water?" and she say, "Yeah, go ahead and hurry
> back and get to your lesson." And that put her all
> right, and I hurry back. And before she know one
> thing, I had done gone down to the cistern to get
> water and done jumped the fence and gone home.
> Mama would whip me and make me come back
> with her, go back and run off again, never did learn
> nothing. I told Mama I'd rather go in the field and

> work, I'd rather go pick cotton. And I didn't learn
> nothing. I went and pick cotton . . . I didn't learn
> nothing. I didn't want to learn nothing.[3]

So at an early age, Clementine gave up on schooling and took to the fields. She loved to work in the fields and did so until age brought her from outdoor work into the role as laundress and housekeeper and sometimes cook at the main plantation house run by Miss Cammie Henry, owner of Melrose. Essentially Clementine defined herself by her work. In one of her interviews late in life she explained:

> I used to farm, hoe cotton, hoe corn, grow sugar
> cane, pick cotton, done all that. I was about fifteen
> or sixteen when I pick cotton. I would pick now, if
> I could. It was easy to pick. You pull the sack, you
> know, until it get heavy. When it get heavy, you
> empty it, pick some more, empty that.[4]

The ways of the farmhand were familiar to Clementine from girlhood to motherhood. In addition to picking cotton, she helped with the pecan crop, although she did complain of the constant stooping associated with the task.

In 1907 Clementine gave birth to her first child, a son nicknamed Frenchie. His real name was Joseph. Joseph's father was Charlie Dupree, also the father of Clementine's second child, Cora. Clementine and Charlie, fifteen years her senior, were never married. Clementine said they were "just keeping company." In 1914, Charlie died. Ten years later Clementine married Emanuel Hunter, who also worked at Melrose. Of her marriage to Emanuel, Clementine said, "I was scared when I got married . . . But I had a good husband, a good Christian husband and he loved to work and he loved to have something . . . and just like that I'm is right now."[5] Together Emanuel and Clementine lived in the workers' cottages at Melrose. They had five children, two of whom were stillborn and never named. The surviving children were Agnes, King, and Mary. Like her mother before her, Clementine gave birth to seven children in all. She was proud of this accomplishment. Even as a mother of several children, she was obliged to continue working every day. She remembered, "I picked cotton one morning just before I borned one of my babies. I remember how much it was—seventy-eight pounds. Then I went home, called the midwife, and borned my baby. It didn't worry me none. In a few days I was back in the fields."[6]

She tended her children in the field as she picked. Here is the description of her day in the field:

> Put my children under the tree in the field. Pick cotton, 150 pounds, sometimes 200, I pick. All that was fifty cents a hundred, that all they was getting. Fifty cents a hundred and I done dragged my children all in the field. I didn't have no help. Sometime I'd find some of them fast asleep in the weeds. They never die. I raise them all . . . I work hard in my days.[7]

In the 1920s, when she was in her sixties, Clementine Hunter was moved from field work into domestic chores at the plantation. She was expected to tend the vegetable gardens, clean, sew clothes for the children of the household, do laundry and ironing, help with cooking and childcare. She made quilts and baskets, which examined now, show that she was already an artist. She was expected to take work home, usually laundry, at the close of her workday and complete it before the next day's chores. This was the custom of the country at that time.

The change of assignment to the primary residence was a fortuitous event for Clementine Hunter and for the world of folk art. Because the owner of the plantation, Cammie Henry, was greatly interested in art and culture, she invited guest artists to spend extended periods of time in residence at the plantation. They were given staple support so that they could work on their creative endeavors. Writers, painters, musicians, and photographers came and visited at Melrose, usually for several months. One guest stayed for over thirty years. That person was Francois Mignon, usually credited with the discovery of Clementine Hunter's artistic talent. Mignon was a favorite of Cammie Henry, and she chose him to be the historian and archivist of her plantation. Mignon did not leave Melrose until after the Henry family sold the place off and it became a corporate farm, a status that it has today even though the plantation house and outbuildings have been given to the historical society of Natchitoches. Melrose is today a pecan plantation. The buildings are now historical sites open to the public.

When the artist Alberta Kinsey of New Orleans left Melrose after a stay at the plantation, she left behind some tubes of paint in the wastebasket. When Clementine Hunter went to clean the quarters that Alberta Kinsey had occupied, she found the paints and asked whether she could have them. Since they were discards, there was no objection to her taking them. She had paints but not surfaces on which to paint. Francois Mignon, the curator of Miss Cammie's papers, gave Clementine Hunter an old window shade. Her first painting was on that throwaway surface. She painted all night on her first work and showed it to Mignon the next morning. He was amazed at her imagination and flair. From that humble start on castaway materials, Clementine went on to paint over four thousand works. Her works are usually described as primitives, although Alice B. Toklas did not agree with this characterization. Toklas said, "Her painting impressed me. It is really not at all primitive. It is very civilized—as Gertrude Stein said of the African wood carvings that influenced Matisse and particularly Picasso, almost fifty years ago."[8] Some observers and critics used the word "primitive" to mean that Clementine Hunter had no formal training as an artist. Still her work has an undeniable appeal. Many consider Clementine Hunter a reflector of the plantation life which was passing away, a chronicler of twentieth-century country life among the folk. In recording the day-to-day lives of workers on the plantation, Clementine Hunter may be regarded as a pictorial historian of a vanishing culture.

Poor as she was, she could not afford canvas boards. She painted on whatever she found—shingles that had blown off the roof, old snuff bottles, milk bottles, boards, papers—whatever was available. Her paints came mail order from Sears and Roebuck. Mignon and his friend James Register considered Clementine Hunter to be a refreshing primitive artist, and they became her advocates and agents. They worked to get her paintings into exhibits and into the hands of collectors. The few sales did not cover expenses. Clementine continued to work at Melrose as a house servant. She would sell her paintings along with the vegetables she grew at a little stand on the grounds. People in the community became aware of her work and often stopped by her little house to watch her paint. She charged them five cents to watch. Over time the price to watch grew until toward the end of her days at Melrose, she was charging fifty cents for observers. Many of her paintings sold to people in the community for one dollar each. Later the price went to five dollars, then ten. Literally hundreds of Clementine Hunter paintings went for under twenty dollars at the time they were painted. As she became better known through sales and exhibits, the price of the paintings went to a few hundred dollars and then to the thousands. One of her paintings was chosen in 1976 for the United Nations UNICEF calendar, and thus her art went all over the world.

Several area collectors who particularly admired her work began to secure paintings reflecting her various subject matters: work and play of rural Southern folk, religious experiences, and other miscellaneous subjects such as flowers, animals, etc. Many of these collectors were personal friends of Clementine Hunter. Her primary advocates were Thomas Whitehead, Dr. Mildred Hart Bailey (who has willed her collection to the community), and Ann Williams Brittain. It is interesting that Clementine Hunter never saved a single painting for herself. She said that when she was finished painting a work, she was through with it. She seemed to have no sentimental attachment to her work. Her children were not collectors either. Some of her works were sold in the drugstore in Natchitoches, others through James Register in New York and New Orleans. Today a Clementine Hunter major work would bring thousands of dollars. There are some advertised on the internet now for $5000 and up. Clementine Hunter never got this kind of money for her work. She lived within extremely modest means all her life.

In addition to the single works that Clementine Hunter painted and sold or gave away over her thirty-five years as a painter, the artist took on another very important endeavor: the murals for the African House at Melrose. Behind the main house at Melrose plantation, there is a building called the African House, said to be the only example of pure African architecture in the United States. The African House had been built on the plantation by its original owner, a freed slave woman, Therese Coincoin, who apparently remembered the structure of huts in the Congo. The African House had been used for many purposes over the years. It had been a jail, a storage house, a stable. Francois Mignon hit upon the idea of clearing the clutter out of the historic building and asking Clementine Hunter to paint murals for the upper level. She took on the project, and today the priceless murals of Clementine Hunter are permanently affixed to the upper level of the African House. She painted the murals in a makeshift studio on the grounds, and then they were attached to the walls of the African House. There are nine large panels, each four feet by eight feet. The work, done in 1955, took three months of full time effort by Clementine Hunter. These large murals, like her other paintings, reflect the joy and sorrow of plantation life of working folk. There is a baptism scene, a wedding scene, a cotton picking scene, a funeral scene. All of the characteristics that appear in Hunter's other paintings-large subjects, bright colors, exuberant spirits-appear also in the murals.

Clementine Hunter's lifespan coincides with the post-Civil War era of separation of people by color. When she spoke of the separation of schoolchildren by a fence, division by race, she was reflecting the culture that she knew. When a major local exhibit of her work was planned for the community of Natchitoches in 1955 at the college library, Clementine Hunter was not invited. The college did not accept blacks at that time. Because of the courtesy of Ora Williams, a professor of Greek at the college, who was willing to break the rules, Clementine Hunter was sneaked into the exhibit of her own works on a Sunday afternoon when the college was closed so that she could see her paintings on display. Later, in 1986, that same college—Northwestern State University of Louisiana— gave Clementine Hunter, who had never learned her ABCs, an honorary Doctor of Fine Arts degree. She walked into her graduation at the school, by then integrated, at age ninety-nine in full academic regalia. Her simple response to the honor was "Thank you." It must have been a great day for her. It was an even greater day for the community and the college, for the time had come for the simple recognition of talent unfettered by racial considerations.

Clementine Hunter continued painting until the final months of her life. She died of old age on January 1, 1988, surrounded by family and friends. She died in the mobile home to which she had moved after Melrose was sold to the Southdown Land Company. She was buried in a mausoleum adjacent to the country Catholic church, St. John the Baptist, between Natchitoches and Cloutierville. Buried next to her was her lifelong friend and patron Francois Mignon, the historian of Melrose.

Since her passing, the paintings of Clementine Hunter have continued to rise in value. Major art galleries seek her work. The major museums of the country exhibit the paintings. When the Dallas African American Art Museum opened, the inaugural event was an exhibit of Clementine Hunter's work. Mrs. Hunter has been the subject of more than one hundred published articles. She has been a focus of the women's history project at Radcliffe. Institutions of higher learning have paid homage to the illiterate but phenomenally talented folk artist Clementine Hunter. Clementine must have been right when she said she "had made out all right."

ENDNOTES

1. Quoted by James L. Wilson, *Clementine Hunter: American Folk Artist* (Gretna, LA: Pelican, 1988), 20.
2. Wilson, 20.
3. Wilson, 74.
4. Wilson, 110.
5. Wilson, 110.
6. Mary E. Lyons, *Talking with Tebe: Clementine Hunter, Memory Artist* (Boston: Houghton Mifflin, 1998), 27.
7. Lyons, 27.
8. From dust jacket of Wilson.

WORKS CONSULTED

Ford, Oliver. "Francois Mignon: The Man Who Would Be French." *Southern Studies.* Spring 1991, 51–59.

Jones, Anne Hudson. "The Centennial of Clementine Hunter." *Women's Art Journal.* Spring/Summer 1987, 23–27.

Mignon, Francois, and Clementine Hunter. *Melrose Plantation Cookbook.* Natchitoches, LA: np, 1956.

Mignon, Francois. *Plantation Life in Louisiana,* 1950–70. Baton Rouge: Claitor's Pub., 1972.

Miller Hershel. "Clementine Hunter—American Primitive." New Orleans December 1968, 6–11.

Morris, Steven. "The Primitive Art of Clementine Hunter." *Ebony* May 1969, 144–48.

Murphee, Rachel C. "Clementine Hunter, 1887–1998: Artist." http://indigo.lib.lsu.edu, 1996.

Rankin, Allen. "The Hidden Genius of Melrose Plantation." *Reader's Digest* December 1975, 118–22.

Ryan, Robert, and Yvonne Ryan. "Clementine Hunter." *Louisiana Life* Sept/Oct 1981, 32–42.

Cotton-pickin' Time

Henderson Shuffler, Director of the Institute of Texan Cultures, and
O. T. Baker, creator and first director of the Texas Folklife Festival

14

PACKAGED FOLKLORE:
THE TEXAS FOLKLIFE FESTIVAL—
STORYSMITHING AND SHAPESHIFTING

by John L. Davis of Seguin

Many are the definitions of folklore. From the professional side it's what people create and do in terms of traditional beliefs, customs, language uses, survival skills, stories, music, tools, decorations, entertainments, foods, and so forth that informally move across generations in changing patterns. Tradition . . . useful tradition. Today, any group maintaining shared traditions is considered folk. And today, folklore includes material close to its origin, as the definition did not, earlier, allow. Folklore is also an academic field pursued in literate, technological cultures; otherwise, the whole bucket is the province of ethnologists and anthropologists. These remarks mostly follow Richard M. Dorson and Ab Abernethy.

Colloquially, folklore is what grandparents did, or what older people did when young. It is mostly oral or imitative and can be recounted, remembered, or collected, whether it is definitely outdated or still useful. It is often displayed for various reasons, including pride, curiosity, validation, amusement, propaganda, or profit-or all of the above. And this folklore—these traditions that have been preserved through generations—is sometimes packaged for public consumption.

One way to package folklore for public consumption is to hold a folk festival. In this package the folk, whoever they are, are invited to demonstrate what they do in front of a usually paying audience. The invitations include mostly "older" folk activities

Vernon and Norman Soloman playing on The Mall at the American Folklife Festival in 1968

(such as using an aebleskiver pan or a draw knife) or things not often done by the anticipated audience (clogging, pear burning, or hog slaughtering). Usually not included are contemporary crafts like constructing a hamburger or driving a city bus.

Thus, in various ways, folklore can be packaged for consumption like a video of a bullfight or a frozen steak, but it is no longer the whole cow.

And these thoughts were more or less in the minds of the people at the Institute of Texan Cultures when they put together the Texas Folklife Festival as a public event.

There's a great amount of interest today in what is called public and applied folklore. Paraphrasing Steve Siporin (1992), public folklore has always included the concepts of a handler of someone else's culture and the application of the lore in unhistorical ways. In terms of this kind of packaging, folklife festivals and community history days have been around for a long time.

In some respects, the recounting of a myth in, say, classical Greece—with the attendant display of survival skills (running, foods, ceramics, weaponry)—was quite similar to some folk festivals— including commercial vendors. Pausanias catalogued a few, although the central point, admittedly, was not merely to amuse a paying audience.

The Texas Folklife Festival, now an annual event sponsored by the Institute of Texan Cultures, can be seen as an outgrowth of the packaging of folklore that did not begin in the 1930s but was greatly expanded in those years. Of note was the 1936 National Folk Festival, started a couple of years earlier in St. Louis and held in Dallas on the occasion of the Texas Centennial. In terms of the use of graphics, multiethnic content, and public display, the 1936 event was one of many definers of the successes and problems of a folk festival.

Similarly, the Texas Folk Festival is a prime example of packaging, greatly admired by staff, participants, visitors, and professional folklorists. The event has also been damned by various staff, participants, visitors, and professional folklorists. A few individuals have been on both sides of the fence—at the same time.

Thus, the origin and development of the Festival is an instructive and curious story for anyone interested in the care, handling, and feeding of folklore. The event has even spawned folklore of its own in the form of activities and stories. It has been examined by folklorists and journalists, one social psychologist, and even a couple of historians. But its history has not been written, nor the full analysis done. That job would require books, and if attempted, too few people have died to avoid charges of libel.

But here are two details of that story: the Festival as a generator of folklore and certain effects packaged folklore can have on the folk, in about three examples.

In 1968, the Institute of Texan Cultures was invited to cosponsor the Festival of American Folklife in Washington, D.C., with the Smithsonian Institution. Cosponsoring this folklife event meant bringing music, foods, demonstrations, crafts, and such to a new venue. As noted, the idea was not new. Folk festivals had been held, in various forms, for decades.

Many people in Texas were on a roll that year, certainly at the Institute, which had been created over a year earlier to be the Texas pavilion at San Antonio's HemisFair, the world's fair of 1968. The Institute was also established as a permanent humanities research center specializing in the cultures of Texas, then often called ethnic groups.

Washington, including the White House, was well stocked with Texans at the time and amply troubled by race riots. Of course, Lyndon Johnson might have had something to do with the invitation, but Smithsonian officials did see the event as not only a professional gesture but also, perhaps, capable of cooling off a troubled city. Who better to invite to help than the crazy Texans? Besides, the date was July 4.

O. T. Baker of the institute was an organizer if he was anything, and director Henderson Shuffler was a fine manager who could make positive, creative decisions—most of them correct.

And I was a young, naïve, colleague. In many ways, we nearly knew what we were doing. We did seek advice from folklorists to the foggy east, and did have wonderful talent and advisors on deck, including much of the Lomax family, John Henry Faulk, Bill C. Malone, and Ab Abernethy, among others.

Under the pressure of getting the job done quickly, we picked participants from whom we knew, often from Baker's and Shuffler's lists of acquaintances. The assembly of participants is too complex to detail here. Some of these were traditionally taught folk, in terms of music and foods and crafts, among others doing reenactment demonstrations and replica performances. Some fake. At the time, it was all self-defined as folklore.

And this was also the setting for the creation of folklore. As one example, the packaging job generated tall tales just about as efficiently and creatively as if William Alexander Anderson Wallace had been on the marketing staff.

Arnold Griffin, friend of O. T. Baker and Texas rancher and businessman, provided his own trucks and labor to transport loads of raw materials such as logs for woodwork, cooking pots, a blacksmith's forge, and a chunk of Texas the size of a football field. Not a great deal of the earth, of course, but plenty of brush, maguey, prickly pear, and samples of grass to plant in Washington.

The event was held on The Mall which, before we arrived, stretched in pristine form in front of the Smithsonian. The National Park Service took care of that mall. We had three hundred plants. But, no matter, the guardian park rangers had been told to let the Texans dig and plant all they wanted. We did, under the rather unfriendly glare of the rangers and the amazed stare of office workers.

One journalist, who apparently chanced by, was incredulous, until told we were The Texans. "Oh," he said, glancing away in the direction of Lyndon and the White House, "that explains everything." And that became a story.

Even the participants' trips to Washington created narratives that have passed into the storytelling domain. Braniff was in the process of instituting new, direct flights from Texas to the nation's capital largely to take care of migrating politicians and their followers. An initial flight not only carried dignitaries but many of the Texas bunch including Shuffler, the Baca band, KJZT Czech dancers from Corpus Christi, Tigua Indians, and Hondo Crouch, a professional persona creator among his many talents. For departure and arrival publicity, some wore dress as appropriate—the Tiguas, a few of the Czechs, and Hondo in Texas-country garb.

Overall, this was the stuff of story, approaching legend, if not epic. Reed Harp, writing in *Texas Parade* (September 1968) had a lot to do with the creation of story. One of his well-turned descriptions of the journey was "as if the State of Texas were put in a vacuum and sent motor freight to Washington." A delightfully mixed metaphor if ever there was.

Now those were the days when boarding a commercial aircraft was a fairly casual event. Hondo stepped up with what he admitted was a sack of rattlesnakes. This was a small flour sack (later to become a gunnysack) with, indeed, attached rattles. He was waved aboard.

The flight was not uneventful. At one point, the Czech band, spontaneously but part of the package at the time, began a performance at the back of the airplane, thus attracting most passengers. The pilot called for a move of the concert more amidship because he could not trim the craft in flight. When this was suggested as being somewhat unnecessary in terms of flight control—which it isn't—the fact quickly was added to the story that the pilot simply couldn't hear the music well enough.

Then, somewhat before landing, Hondo ceremoniously crawled the length of the plane's aisle looking for an escaped rattlesnake. Now Hondo, in rural garb, was strange enough to pique curiosity, but two conditions made the search memorable. First, Hondo was amazingly articulate in explaining what he was doing to those under whose seat he searched and, second, not all passengers on the flight were a part of the Texan crowd.

Henderson Shuffler (sixth from left) and the Texas delegation on their way to Washington, D. C., and the American Folklife Festival in 1968

Eventually the stewardesses (no stewards, then) restored order and the joke was explained. Still, the pilot radioed ahead asking that security meet the airplane on arrival.

This story was subsequently embroidered on by a host of tellers including, but not confined to, O. T. Baker, Guich Koock, Ace Reid, Bill Brett, myself, and certainly Hondo. Amazing were the variants as they sprouted in Texas. The story has even received a bit of attention by students of folklore.

By comparison, here's an original version by Reed Harp in *Texas Parade* (September 1968) . . . without narrative analyses or motif comparisons:

> And Hondo Crouch came tripping through the terminal in his customary slouch hat and Levis with a pillowcase full of chewing tobacco and rattlesnake skins over his shoulder. Four big rattles protruded from his sack. He didn't blink an eye. But the crowd gave him plenty of room.
>
> Flight 107, Braniff International turned into a hoop-tee-do. People were standing up, walking around, singing, playing instruments and having a blast as the big jet roared across country. The excitement never let up during the flight. Harmonicas moaned an appropriate background to the tall tales being swapped that night on Flight 107.

For further comparison, here's Henderson Shuffler's later words in a thank-you letter sent to certain participants and friends—and to people he thought might just help support such an event in Texas: "The Secret Service has been in a fluttering dither ever since they found one of Hondo's rattlesnakes in the President's bathtub and a Tigua tomahawk in Ladybird's favorite flowerbed." This is creation of Texas myth on a drive-through basis but, even with the stereotyping, it has a delightful side.

The East Texas String Ensemble at the Texas Folklife Festival

And the Washington event was a success. By one count, 500,000 people attended and the city remained peaceful—while the Texans lived up to legendary status. And the event became the Texas Folklife Festival.

Rather expectedly, in retrospect, various Texans who were in Washington for the 1968 event, high-placed and otherwise, asked "Why don't you do this in Texas?" So we did, although planning took three years for the event to open on home turf.

And the Festival (as well as the national event) was soon confronted by a specific (if not peculiar) generation of folklorists who pointed out that to present folklore at a festival was taking the activities out of context—and therefore rendering them inauthentic. But worse, by providing a package-performance venue for the folk we were also destroying lives—or at least changing lives. Although these charges, in several variants, were delivered in the jargon of professional folklore, we were accused of falsifying folklore and playing God—or Satan. As had others, long before us.

Both charges are true. Certainly, inviting and bringing in a traditional storyteller or chair caner, clogger or baklava maker to a public event was, indeed, taking the folklore out of context. Certainly—to that degree at a minimum—what is displayed is not what happens at home.

And in providing a venue for a demonstration or performance, we were in fact a Satan in the garden. Perhaps with different motives, but with no less power to effect shape shifting. The Festival has hosted a couple of traditional storytellers who immediately decided they were ready for Hollywood. We invited chair caners whose private business (conveniently advertised through the event) remarkably blossomed as compared to the chair caner in the next county who wasn't invited. The Festival offered a venue to purveyors of folk medicine who, suddenly offered an audience, felt validated and confirmed in their claims about the beneficence of mesquite wine, prickly ash, powdered snake tongue, and reconstituted armadillo milk.

In addition to legitimate ethnic community participation, the Festival was approached by a few purely social or commercial groups who claimed to be able to professionally replicate the folk dances of the sturdy Norse, the cautious Japanese, or the happy Bolzenians. In most cases, research avoided these replicas.

And research efforts at the Institute heavily overlapped the content of the Festival, but in doing so, the Festival was said to have not only packaged folklore, but perhaps to have created ethnic groups. In some ways, this is also true.

The obvious examples are the Texas Wends, the Lusatian Serbs, and other Slavic Europeans. While numerically powerful groups, such as the Germans, taken as a whole, manage to superficially preserve some rapidly changing Old World customs, small groups, especially when under economic stress, cannot.

The Wends were faced with harsh conditions in their new land, nowadays near Serbin in Lee County. During hard times in a new place, so-called folk costume, ceremonial dancing, even traditional foods and a native language are secondary considerations in life. Not that pride of origin and a desire to preserve a way of life disappear. But when acculturation to new conditions becomes survival, non-essential ceremony and skills inefficient in a new setting fade or disappear until a later and more affluent generation takes pride in honoring, reviving, and sometimes selling the "old ways."

For the Wends in a new homeland, a lot of the old country had been left behind. Some thirty years ago field researchers found discarded Sorbian-language books and few artifacts deemed of much value by locals. But some customs, some items had been kept— among them, wedding dresses. The Wendish wedding dress was black, to some minds representing a woman's hardship in marriage— a strikingly rational view. Dresses turned gray, then disappeared into the white of "everybody else"—like much Wendish custom— although a few stories and customs remained in older heads.

Still, a few early workers—some from their own ranks—had written about the Texas Wends. Some Wends prospered and thus had discretionary time and money on their hands. This makes preservation, or at least replication, possible. The Wendish Cultural Club was born, along with ideas for a local festival and museum.

The Institute supported some of the fieldwork in the settlement area, in part for an exhibit at the Institute. Sylvia Ann Grider did competent folklore and historical research—and finished a book published in 1982 by the Institute. During all of this, participation in the Texas Folklife Festival had been offered and planned.

Wendish research efforts in support of festival participation made available European foods, costume, dances, music, and much never done in Texas or even brought along. These replications became part of the self-definition of the Texas Wends in their annual Wendish Fest near Serbin and for parts of some of the exhibits at the Serbin museum. The Wends do not claim all this material was ever a part of the Texas group experience, but as presented to outsiders at the Texas Folklife Festival and at Serbin, that can be the impression.

And is this folklore? Of course it is. Some not exactly as traditionally linear as elder folklorists would define, but much of what the folk do is folklore. Even the activity of participating in a codified, public event becomes traditional craft, whether at Serbin in Lee County or in downtown San Antonio.

The Wends are, with all the change, replication, self-definition, and genuine preservation, a community. Rather than call the Institute's role one of "creation," I prefer the word "encouragement." To others, this is tinkering with reality.

Some time ago, most folklorists redefined performance to include backyard, in-context situations (even admitting they were changing lives while in the backyard, recording and interviewing). And demonstrations at folk festivals were legitimized in a different sense.

The latter is certainly packaged folklore but is still folklore.

15

SAME SONG, SECOND VERSE COULD BE BETTER, BUT IT'S GONNA BE WORSE!

by Jean Granberry Schnitz of Boerne

In 1945 in Alice, Texas, my best friend's twin brother drove his sister and me crazy singing this parody to the tune of "Mary Had a Little Lamb":

> Rabbit ain't got no tail at all,
> Tail at all, tail at all,
> Rabbit ain't got no tail at all,
> Just a powder puff.

Then he chanted loudly:

> **Same song, second verse,**
> **Could be better, but it's gonna be worse!**

Next time through, it was, "Same song, third verse," and so on. By the time he got to "Same song, twenty-seventh verse . . . ," we were chasing him around.

Some historians say that music developed when savages learned to pattern their yelling into recognizable sounds and phrases. As language developed, those who carried news from place to place learned to "sing" the news to tunes familiar to the people so it would be easier to remember and to reflect new happenings.[1] If that is so, then recycling tunes to new sets of words is almost as old as music.

Whether for profit or fun, putting new words with old tunes—and vice versa—has become a way to preserve folklore, which can be passed on from generation to generation and group to group. The subjects of the new lyrics tend to be subjects that reflect the daily lives of people. The tunes are always popular tunes of the times. "Music is an art whose material consists of sounds organized in time. Through the various types of patterns in which these sounds can be arranged, music can serve as a medium for the expression of ideas and emotions."[2] Songs are essentially poems set to music—with patterns of meter and rhyme capable of fitting several tunes. All types of music, including classical, sacred, folk, popular, country—whatever—are subject to recycling. The changing of words and lyrics can be accomplished by variations, or by parodies. Variations include minor—or major—changes in the tune or the lyrics and tend to leave the basic content of the song the same. With most folk tunes, variations are quite common, particularly when music was passed on without having been written down. John A. and Alan Lomax in *American Ballads and Folk Songs* put it this way:

> Worse than thieves are ballad collectors, for when they capture and imprison in cold type a folk song, at the same time they kill it. Its change and growth are not so likely to continue after a fixed model for comparison exists. . . . There is thus an element of sadness in imprisoning a folk song in type. . . . The printed form becomes a standard, and a fixed standard. So long as the song is passed from one to another by "word of mouth," its material is fluid, frequent changes occurring both in words and in the music.[3]

According to one dictionary, to parody is to mimic, "to make fun of another's style by imitating it with comic effect or to attempt a serious imitation . . . a take-off, a travesty."[4] Parodies are easy to recognize, because they have recognizable melodies but not the original words. Perhaps "recycling" is a better description than either parody or variation.

During the late 1930s, and throughout the 1940s and 1950s, singing was part of just about any group situation, especially family, school, summer camps, service clubs, and church groups. It was a favorite activity to sing familiar tunes with new sets of words, and an ongoing project to come up with new words. Most of these parodies were more fun to sing than the original words. Texas public schoolteachers did a great job of teaching schoolchildren the correct version of the words and music. At Mitchell School in Victoria in the early 1940s, I remember Mrs. Josephine Waller sitting on a high stool looking over the top of the piano and playing as we children sang dozens of classical and semi-classical songs that children were supposed to know. She taught us no parodies, only the correct version of many songs.

Linda Scudder Payne of Nacogdoches remembers:

> We were always making up special parodies about whatever took our fancy while we were in school [at Graford near Mineral Wells]. We took school bus trips rather regularly, and singing passed the time. I remember one rather awful song we sang about our coach to the tune of "Kaw-Liga." Most of these originals were one-time, spur-of-the-minute things that meant something only to us, and were soon forgotten (one of life's mercies!).[5]

I have sung many of these parody verses for more than sixty years without knowing some of them are actually in print. I found the source of some of them in a dog-eared old songbook my mother used to accompany singing for Rotary Clubs and other Civic organizations across South Texas. It was *Sociability Songs,* published by Rodeheaver Hall-Mack Co., probably in the early 1940s.

Some songs had words that I was forbidden to sing since they were considered "naughty" by my parents. But we sang them anyway—slyly making sure we were not observed. By today's standards, the words were not that bad, but singing them could result in having our mouths washed out with soap. I clearly recall the taste of soap.

Research revealed that one of my favorites was in John Jacob Niles' *Songs My Mother Never Taught Me,* published in 1929, and appeared as "The Hearse Song" in *American Ballads and Folk Songs,* collected by John A. and Alan Lomax in 1934. This came from the Lomax version:

> Did you ever think as the hearse rolls by
> That the next trip they take they'll be laying you by,
> With your boots a-swinging' from the back of a roan
> And the undertaker inscribin' your stone. . . . etc.[6]

Nobody I know ever saw this song in print, but we sang it like this:

> Did you ever think as the hearse rolls by
> That you may be the next to die?
> Ah-um! Ah-um!
>
> They'll put you down in the soft warm dirt,
> And cover you up, but it sure won't hurt.
> Ah-um! Ah-um!
>
> Oh, your eyes fall in, your teeth fall out,
> And nobody's there to hear you shout.
> Ah-um! Ah-um!
>
> Oh, the worms crawl in, and the worms crawl out,
> They crawl all over your chin and snout,
> Ah-um! Ah-um!

At the 1999 meeting of the Texas Folklore Society, Sierra and Acayla Haile and the other children sang a more modern—and more gross—version of this same song.

Many parodies exist for older American popular songs like "Yankee Doodle" and others. Many songs about Texas and cowboy songs are predominately parodies, as I discussed in a separate paper in Nacogdoches in 2000.

Many popular Civil War tunes have been parodied. Time and space prevent my presenting a complete list, but one of the most popular is "John Brown's Body"—itself a parody. Quoting Maymie R. Krythe in *Sampler of American Folk Songs*:

> The tune of "John Brown's Body" and of "The Battle Hymn of the Republic" has had a long and unusual history; not all sources agree as to its origin. However, some say it began about 1856 in the South as a humble Methodist camp-meeting song, often sung by Negroes with religious words. It was said that William Steffe, of Richmond, Virginia, a composer of Sunday-school songs, was asked, in the 1850s to go to Georgia to lead the singing at a camp meeting. The young man was much surprised on his arrival to find there were no song books for the gatherings. Steffe asked how he could get the participants to sing. He was told just to make up words as he went along. . . . This is what he tried in his first song:

> Say, brothers, will you meet us?
> Say, brothers, will you meet us?
> Say, brothers, will you meet us?
> On Canaan's happy shore?
> Glory, glory, hallelujah,
> Glory, glory, hallelujah,
> Glory, glory, hallelujah,
> Forever, ever more.[7]

This was soon parodied into a version called "John Brown's Body." Then, as told by Margaret Bradford Boni from *The Fireside Book of Folk Songs*:

> In 1861, Julia Ward Howe, on a visit to some army camps, heard the soldiers singing a grim chant, "John Brown's Body," to the tune of a camp-meeting hymn, "Say Brothers, Will You Meet Us?" Deeply moved by the scene, she later wrote for the fine, sturdy tune the words of the "Battle Hymn," one of the most stirring poems to come out of the Civil War. It became the marching song of the Northern armies, and undoubtedly one of the best of all marching songs. "John Brown's Body," however, still remains popular.[8]

But in the early 1940s I and my friends sang another version, complete with varying hand and body motions:

> John Brown's baby had a cold upon its chest,
>   (Repeat 3 times)
> And they rubbed it with camphorated oil.

My favorite parody of "Battle Hymn of the Republic" has been around at least sixty years that I know of:

> I wear my pink pajamas in the summer when it's hot,
> I wear my warm red flannels in the winter when it's not,
> And sometimes in the springtime and sometimes in the fall,
> I jump between the covers with nothing on at all.
>
> **Chorus:** Glory, Glory, Hallelujah!
> Glory, Glory, What's it to ya'?
> Glory, Glory, What's it to ya'
> If I jump between the covers with nothing on at all?

We sang this verse sometimes:

> One grasshopper hopped right over another grasshopper's
>   back, (4 times)
>
> **Chorus:** They were only playing leapfrog, (3 times)
> When one grasshopper hopped right over another
>   grasshopper's back.

Another Civil War Song ("Listen to the Mockingbird") was parodied thus (and sung at the Texas Folklife Festival in 2000 by some of
the Civil War re-enactors). Parrott shells were developed by Robert
Parker Parrott and were used at Vicksburg by the Union army.

> Oh, do you well remember, remember, remember?
> It was in the siege of Vicksburg,
> And the Parrott shells were whistling through the air.
>
> **Chorus:** Listen to the Parrott shells,
> Listen to the Parrott shells,
> Oh, the Parrott shells are whistling through the air,
> Listen to the Parrott shells
> Listen to the Parrott shells,
> Oh, the Parrott shells are whistling through the air.[9]

It is an obvious parody—meant to be funny or make fun—
when a song from the 1890s such as "Daisy Bell" gets an added
verse not written by the original author, Harry Dacre.[10] I suspect
this parody had been around for a long time before I and my
friends sang it.

> Harry, Harry, here is your answer true,
> I'm not crazy all for the love of you,
> There won't be any marriage,
> If you can't afford a carriage,

'Cause I'll be switched if I'll get hitched
On a bicycle built for two.

Other versions are more emphatic:

'Cause I'll be damned if I'll be crammed
On a bicycle built for two.

"In the Shade of the Old Apple Tree," with words by Harry
Williams and music by Egbert Van Alstyne, was composed in 1905
after the writers strolled through New York's Central Park and
were unable to find an apple tree such as they had enjoyed during
their boyhood in the Midwest.[11] I never did learn the correct
words, as I sang:

'Neath the Crust of the Old Apple Pie
There is something for you and for I,
It may be a pin that the cook just dropped in,
Or it may be a dear little fly.
It may be an old rusty nail
Or a piece of a pussy cat's tail,
But, whatever it be, it's for you and for me,
'Neath the crust of an old apple pie.[12]

As long ago as I can remember I have sung these two sets of
words to the tune of the pre-World War I song, "There's a Long,
Long Trail" (words by Stoddard King and music by Zo Elliott,
who meant it to be a sentimental song to be sung at a fraternity
banquet before WWI started[13]):

Version I:

There's a long, long nail a'grinding
Up through the sole of my shoe,
And it's ground its way into my foot

For a whole mile or two.
There's a long, long hike before me,
And the time I'm dreaming about,
Is the time when I can sit me down,
And pull that long nail out.[14]

Version II:

It's a short, short life we live here,
So let us laugh while we may,
With a smile for every moment
Of the whole bright day.
What's the use of being gloomy,
Or what's the use of our tears,
When we know a mummy's had no fun
For the last three thousand years?[15]

To the tune of "Auld Lang Syne," we preferred to sing:

The fish it never cackles 'bout
Its million eggs or so,
The hen is quite a different bird,
One egg—and hear her crow.
The fish we spurn,
But crown the hen,
Which leads me to surmise,
Don't hide your light,
But blow your horn,
It pays to advertise.[16]

This was one of my favorites of the many parodies of "Mary Had a Little Lamb":

Mary had a swarm of bees, swarm of bees, swarm of bees,
Mary had a swarm of bees,

And they to save their lives
Went everywhere that Mary went, Mary went, Mary went,
Went everywhere that Mary went,
For Mary had the hives.

Classical tunes were not immune to the "treatment":

Toreador—Hey!
Don't spit on the floor
Use the cuspidor,
That's what they're for.

Classical, you say?

Oh, the girls in France do the hula, hula dance
And the clothes they wear would freeze a polar bear—

We sang:

Here comes the bride—big, fat and wide . . .

My children sang:

Happy birthday to you, you live in a zoo . . .
You look like a monkey and you act like one, too.

My irreverent grandson sang:

Jingle bells, shotgun shells,
Grandma laid an egg . . .

To the tune of "America" my friends and I sang:

My Country 'tis of thee,
I came from Germany,

My name is Fritz.
Give me some cigarettes,
Give me a keg of beer,
And we'll be jolly friends, forevermore.

To the tune of "The Star Spangled Banner" we sang:

Oh, say can you see
Any bedbugs on me?
If you do, pick a few
So we'll have bedbug stew.

To the tune of "Into the Air, Army Air Corps," my Cub Scouts in the 1960s sang:

Into the air, Junior Birdmen,
Into the air, upside down . . .

At the Bandera Storytellers meeting in May of 1999, Bob Reeder sang a parody to "A Spanish Cavalier":

A Spanish cavalier
Sat on a keg of beer
And smoked him a great big cigar, dear,
And the smell of his feet,
Killed a neighbor down the street,
And now he's in the jail behind the bars, dear.

That same Spanish cavalier
Sat in the electric chair
And smoked that same big, black cigar, dear
And the smell of his shoes
Blowed out the electric fuse,
And now he's as free as you and I, dear.[17]

Linda Scudder Payne's favorite parody is sung to the tune of "When You Wore a Tulip":

> When you drove a Buick, a big yellow Buick,
> And I drove a little red Ford,
> Oh, ho-oh you tried to crowd me,
> Yes, you zoomed right by me,
> But your insults I ignored, I ignored.
> Then you stuck in a mud hole, a big, slippery mud hole,
> Your engine it raced and roared.
> Oh-ho, then I pulled your Buick, your big yellow Buick,
> At the tail of my little red Ford!

Still another of Linda Payne's favorites is sung to the tune of "After the Ball," a song from the 1890s by Charles K. Harris:[18]

> After the ball was over,
> Nellie took out her glass eye,
> Put her false teeth in some water,
> Threw her blonde wig on the floor,
> Stood her cork leg in the corner,
> Her hearing aid hung on the door.
> The rest of poor Nellie went "bye-bye"
> After the ball.

Spike Jones and his orchestra performed many popular parodies in the 1940s and 1950s, including a great musical parody of "Glow Worm." My favorite was a parody of the Stephen Foster song "Jeannie with the Light Brown Hair"—which he called, "Brownie with the Light Blue Jeans." Somebody (maybe Spike Jones) in the 1940s or 1950s parodied "Glow Worm" like this:

> Shine, little glow worm, Turn the key on.
> You are equipped with tail light neon,
> When you gotta glow, you gotta glow,

Glow, little glow worm, glow.

To the tune of "My Bonnie Lies over the Ocean," my friends and I sang this gem:

My Bonnie has tuberculosis,
My Bonnie has only one lung,
Her eyes are worm-eaten and sightless,
Her teeth are worn down to the gum.

Chorus: Bring back, bring back,
Oh bring back my Bonnie to me, to me,
Bring back, bring back,
Oh, bring back my Bonnie to me.

One night as I lay on my pillow,
One night as I lay on my bed,
I stuck my feet out of the window,
Next morning my neighbors were dead.

Chorus: Bring back, bring back,
Oh, bring back my neighbors to me, to me,
Bring back, bring back,
Oh, bring back my neighbors to me.

I found some other verses that we sometimes sang, but had almost forgotten:

My Bonnie leaned over the gas tank,
The height of its contents to see,
I lighted a match to assist her,
Oh, bring back my Bonnie to me.

My breakfast lies over the ocean,
My luncheon lies over the rail,

My dinner is still in commotion,
Won't someone please bring me a pail?[19]

This version was pretty popular during the 1940s and 1950s:

My mother makes beer in the bathtub,
My father makes synthetic gin,
My sister makes fudge for a quarter,
My God, how the money rolls in!

I tried making beer in the bathtub,
I tried making synthetic gin,
I tried making fudge for a living,
Now look at the shape I am in.[20]

Lew Schnitz sang it this way:

My father makes counterfeit money,
My mother makes synthetic gin,
My sister's a Zeta Tau Alpha,
My God, how the money rolls in![21]

"My Bonnie Lies Over the Ocean" has become a personal favorite of mine as a vehicle for parody and poetry. Its tune and meter just beg for parody! To date I have written dozens of parody verses for various occasions to this tune. Coming in second place for my poetry-writing purposes is "Red River Valley," also with dozens of parody verses.

"Clementine" lends itself to parody. This is the version we sang some 60 years ago:

I found a peanut, found a peanut,
Found a peanut just now.
I just now found a peanut,
Found a peanut just now.

Cracked it open, cracked it open,
Cracked it open just now,
I just now cracked it open,
Cracked it open just now.

Additional verses:

It was rotten, it was rotten, etc.
Ate it anyhow, ate it anyhow, etc.
Got sick, got sick, etc.
Went to the doctor, went to the doctor, etc.
Had to operate, had to operate, etc.
Died anyhow, died anyhow, etc.
Went to heaven, went to heaven, etc.
Kicked me out, kicked me out, etc.
I found a peanut, found a peanut, etc.
Etc. (*ad nauseum*).

Since the songs of World War I were popular long after the war, the parodies were numerous! To the tune of "K-K-K-Katy":

K-K-K-K P,
Terrible K P,
It's the only j-j-j-job that I abhor!
When the m-moon shines over the guardhouse,
I'll be mopping up the k-k-k-kitchen floor.

More than four pages of verses to the World War I song regularly called "Hinky Dinky, Parley-Voo?" are included by John and Alan Lomax in American Ballads and Folk Songs. Lomax states: "There is in print a private, not mailable, collection of more than six hundred stanzas concerning the famous mademoiselle."[22] Many of the verses Lomax attributed to John Jacob Niles' Songs *My Mother Never Taught Me*. My mother did not teach me this version:

The first Marine, he found the bean, Parley-vous,
The second Marine, he cooked the bean, Parley-vous,
The third Marine, he ate the bean,
And blew a hole in a submarine,
Hinky-dinky parley-vous.

Lew Schnitz remembers that his young teachers in Sutherland Springs during World War II sang the following verse expressing jealousy for the cadets on the fast track to being pilots at nearby Randolph Field at San Antonio:

Cadet got into the barber's chair, Parley-vous,
Cadet got into the barber's chair, Parley-vous,
Cadet got into the barber's chair,
Instead of a wolf,
He's a teddy bear,
Hinky-dinky parley-vous.[23]

Linda Scudder Payne sang this version:

Farmer, have you a daughter fair, Parley-vous,
Farmer have you a daughter fair, Parley-vous,
Farmer have you a daughter fair,
Who washes the family's underwear?
Hinky-dinky parley-vous.

Another World War I vintage tune was sung by Ira Scudder to the tune of "'Til We Meet Again":

Where the roast is turning,
And the toast is burning,
Though the boys are far away,
They dream of home.
There's a silver lining
Thro' the dark clouds shining.

So, turn the roast,
And scrape the toast
'Fore the boys get home.[24]

We sang several versions of "Halls of Montezuma" but that
has been adapted by children of the 2000s like Sierra and Acayla
Haile:

> From the halls of Montezuma to the shores of Spitwad
> Bay,
> We will fight our teachers' battles with spitwads made of
> clay,
> We will fight for lunch and recess
> And to keep our desk a mess.
> We are proud to claim the title of "Teacher's Number One
> Pest."[25]

Summer camps have been popular among Texas children for
many years, and parodies are definitely popular at these camps
because people already know the tunes and the words can be
adapted to whatever situation. The same is true for various scout
activities. Activity directors at the Presbyterian Westminster Encamp-
ment in Kerrville led the singing of these words to the tune of
"Alouette" in the early 1940s:

> All you et-a, think of all you et-a
> All you et-a, think of all you et,
> **Leader:** Think of all the soup you et,
> **All:** Think of all the soup you et,
> **Leader:** Soup you et.
> **All:** Soup you et. Oh.
> Repeat, adding new item.
> (Each verse added something, repeating from the
> beginning each time, for example: Meat you et, salad
> you et, potatoes you et, corn you et, soup you et . . .)

Sixty years ago these words sung to the tune of "Are You Sleeping?" were funny, but no longer! They're much too true to be funny now!

> Rheumatism, rheumatism,
> How it pains, how it pains,
> Up and down the system,
> Up and down the system
> When it rains, when it rains.

> Perfect posture, perfect posture!
> Do not slump, do not slump,
> You must grow up handsome,
> You must grow up handsome,
> Hide that hump! Hide that hump!

Nancy Harrison remembered singing (to the tune of "If You're Happy and You Know It, Clap Your Hands," which is the same as "I Was Born About Ten Thousand Years Ago"):

> Get your elbows off the table, Mr. Best,
> Get your elbows off the table, Mr. Best,
> We have seen you once or twice,
> And it really isn't nice,
> Get your elbows off the table, Mr. Best.[26]

At camp, and at other gatherings, we ALWAYS tacked this parody onto the traditional words of "Show Me the Way to Go Home":

> Direct me to my domicile
> I'm fatigued and I want to retire
> I partook a little intoxicant about 60 minutes previous
> And it ascended to my cerebellum.
> Wherever I may perambulate,
> Over terra, aqua, or atmospheric vapor,

You will always detect me warbling this melody,
Direct me to my domi,
Direct me to my domi,
Direct me to my domicile.

Another favorite is "Good Night, Irene," with many versions. My favorite verses:

When Irene goes off to dreamland,
She rolls up the hair on her head,
She pins it all up in curlers
And hangs it on the foot of her bed.

Sometimes she sleeps in pajamas,
Sometimes she sleeps in her gown,
But when they're both in the laundry,
Irene is the talk of the town.

Another favorite camp song was sung to the tune of "Stars and Stripes Forever":

Be kind to your web footed friends,
For a duck may be somebody's mother,
Be kind to your friends in the swamp,
Where the weather is always damp.
Now you may think that this is the end—well, it is.

Parodies were also popular at adult meetings such as Lions Club and Rotary Club during the 1930s and 1940s—and beyond. Meetings were frequently started with a singing session. My mother played piano for several service clubs during the years, and the paper clips and markings on the songbooks indicate that parodies were quite popular.

Winnie Sandel of Huntsville and I sang this parody to the tune of "The Girl I Left Behind Me" in Refugio, Texas, in the early

1960s, but I suspect this parody had been around quite a long time before that:

> Oh, the liquor was spilled on the barroom floor
> When the bar was closed for the night,
> When out of a hole in the wall came a mouse,
> And he sat in the pale moonlight.
> Well, he lapped up the liquor on the barroom floor,
> And back on his haunches he sat,
> And all night you could hear him roar:
> "Bring on the dad gum cat!"

I found this verse (and a slightly different version of the above) in *The Beer Bust Song Book*:

> From behind the bar came a big black cat,
> And he gobbled up the little mouse.
> So the moral of this story is:
> Don't ever take a drink on the house.[27]

One of the most popular parodies of the 1960s was written by folk singer Tom Glaser after he heard children parodying some of the songs he sang at his children's concerts. This was a parody of "On Top of Old Smoky," which was very popular in the early 1950s and was itself a parody of one of the variations to "The Little Mohea."[28] Reba Short's research found it in an old Kentucky Mountain songbook.[29] There is also more than one version of "On Top of Old Smoky." "On Top of Spaghetti" got such an enormous response the first time Glaser sang it at a concert that when he recorded it in 1963, it promptly went to the Number One spot on the hit charts, surrounded by rock 'n roll records. Since then the song has been heard in unexpected places. It is now used to help teach remedial reading because it holds the children's attention so successfully. "I never intended anything like that," Glaser admits, "But kids still find it as hilarious as ever."

On top of spaghetti all covered with cheese,
I lost my poor meatball when somebody sneezed.
It rolled off the table and onto the floor,
And then my poor meatball, it rolled out of the door.

It rolled in the garden and under a bush,
And then my poor meatball was nothing but mush,
The mush was as tasty as tasty could be,
And early next summer it grew into a tree.

The tree was all covered with beautiful moss,
It grew lovely meatballs and tomato sauce
So if you eat spaghetti all covered with cheese
Hold onto your meatballs and don't ever sneeze.[30]

A shipwreck in the 1860s inspired "The Ship That Never Returned." The same tune was used in 1903 to tell about a train wreck in "The Wreck of the Old 97."[31] Then in the 1960s the tune was appropriated to tell about a man who never returned ("The MTA Song");

Well, let me tell you of the story of the man named
   Charlie,
On a tragic and fateful day.
He put ten cents in his pocket, kissed his wife and family,
Went to ride on the M.T.A.

Chorus: Well, did he ever return,
No, he never returned,
And his fate is still unlearned.
He may ride forever 'neath the streets of Boston,
He's the man who never returned.[32]

"Froggie Went A-Courtin'" has a long history, dating back to 1549, 1580, and 1611. In *Singin' Texas*, Abernethy includes this information along with a version he learned in grade school, which is pretty close to the version I learned when I was in grade school.[33] We sang this version of "Froggie Went A-Courtin'" in the 1960s, but I don't know where it came from.

> Froggie went a courtin' and he did go, Uh, huh.
> Froggie went a courtin' and he did go, Uh, huh,
> Froggie went a courtin' and he did go
> To the Coconut Grove for the midnight show, Uh, huh.
>   Uh, huh, Uh, huh.
>
> He sidled up to Mollie Mouse's side, Uh, huh.
>   (Repeat twice more)
> He said, "Miss Mousie, will you be my bride," Uh, huh,
>   Uh, huh, Uh, huh.
>
> Not without my Uncle Rat's consent, Uh, Uh.
>   (Repeat twice more)
> I wouldn't marry the president. Uh, Uh, no, sir, Uh, Uh.
>
> So long, Clyde, you better hit the road, Uh, Uh.
>   (Repeat twice more.)
> You ain't no frog, you're a horned toad. Uh, uh, Uh, Uh,
>   Uh, Uh.

Much early church music was borrowed from secular songs. Edmund Lorenz's history of church music describes it as follows: "In 1540 appeared in Antwerp a collection of spiritual songs with 152 folk melodies. . . . About the same time Marot issued his metrical paraphrases of the Psalms set to hunting and dancing tunes. . . . From this it may be seen how prevalent was the fashion of transferring secular tunes to sacred uses."[34]

Ehret and Evans in *The International Book of Christmas Carols* write,

The first Christmas hymns were probably sung to the melodies of Jewish temple hymns and psalms. . . . Carols were a very different breed from the hymns. They derived from secular, pagan sources. . . . As the church struggled against the influences of pagan customs, she sternly barred carols from sacred services. But outside the church, Nativity carols appeared in increasing quantities and flourished. Nearly all were simple folk songs that sprang from the hearts of humble country people.[35]

A study of the tune names or metrical indices of almost any hymn book will indicate the prevalence of using and re-using the popular hymn tunes. In the *Methodist Hymnal,* for instance, some tunes are recycled as many as five and six times, and it is very common to see a tune appear more than once—or to see the same words appear with alternate tunes. This could be the subject of a separate paper, called "Same Song, Third Verse."

Some of the parodies of hymns will never make it into a hymn book. Lew Schnitz sang this one to the tune of "At the Cross":

At the bar, at the bar where I smoked my first cigar
And the nickels and the dimes rolled away,
It was there by chance that I tore my Sunday pants,
And now I have to wear them every day.[36]

A more recent addition to my list of parodies is one that was sung at Mountain View, Arkansas, at the folk center there in the summer of 2001. It is sung to the tune of "Just a Closer Walk with Thee."

Chorus:
Just a bowl of butter beans
Pass the cornbread, if you please

I don't want no collard greens
Just a bowl of them good old butter beans.

Verses:
Just a slice of country ham
Mashed potatoes, strawberry jam
I'd trade my brand new pair of jeans
For a bowl of them good old butter beans

See that big old country lad
He's made everybody mad
They don't love him by no means
'Cause he ate up all those butter beans

See that gal a'standin' thar,
With blue eyes and yaller hair
She's not pregnant as it seems
She just ate a big bowl of butter beans.

It seems to be more of a robbery than a parody that the religious folk tune, known during the 1930s as "Great Speckled Bird" first became "I'm Thinking Tonight of My Blue Eyes." (Same song, second verse.) Then in the 1940s the same tune was sung by Hank Thompson with the words of "I Didn't Know God Made Honky Tonk Angels." (Same song, third verse.) Along came Kitty Wells, who sang, "It Wasn't God Who Made Honky Tonk Angels." (Same song, fourth verse!)

During the 1940s and 1950s we were singing school songs that we didn't know were parodies. For example, our favorite Raymondville High School fight song was sung to the tune of the Notre Dame fight song. Though these words were not popular with the school administration, it was sung anyway. Years later, I realized that half the schools in South Texas—and probably all over the United States—were singing the same song, adapted for their school's name and initials:

Beer, beer for Raymondville High,
Bring on the whiskey; bring on the rye,
Send those freshmen out for gin
And don't let a sober senior in.
We never stagger, we never fall,
We sober up on wood alcohol,
All ye sons of R H S,
We're out on the drunk again.

"The Eyes of Texas" was itself a parody of "I've Been Working on the Railroad." It was written by John Lang Sinclair in 1903.[37] The tune is popular for parodies.

While this one is not a "school song" *per se,* it was sung in 1948 on the campus of Raymondville High School. During the noon hour, about ten to twenty girls (a large percentage of the entire student body) would link arms and do a form of line dance to the tune of "Ta Rah Rah Rah Boom De Ay":

We are the gopher girls,
We always go fer boys,
They never go fer us,
We only go fer them.
We are the beaver girls,
We'll always be fer boys,
They'll never be fer us,
We'll always be fer them. **Repeat.**

My sister-in-law, Dauris Granberry, sang this parody to the tune of "Washington and Lee Swing"—which was also parodied by "Betty Coed" (or was it the other way around?):

You take the legs from some old table;
You take the arms from some old chair,
And take the neck from some old bottle,
And from a horse go pull some hair,

> You can put them all together,
> With the aid of paste and glue,
> And I'll get more lovin' from that gosh darn dummy,
> Than I'll ever get from you.

Rarely a day goes by that I do not hear on the radio or television a parody of some tune or other. For instance, Ford has a commercial parodying "God Bless Texas" by saying "Ford is the Best in Texas." Wal-Mart has a version of "Rawhide" with the familiar sound effects, including a yellow smiley face wearing a Stetson and nodding in time to the music. Wal-Mart has another to the tune of "Put on a Happy Face."

I once heard a Fruit of the Loom commercial to the tune of "Turkey in the Straw," and also a Velveeta commercial to the tune of "I'm a Yankee Doodle Dandy." If you listen for parodies in television commercials, I can guarantee you will find them!

Parodies have always been popular vehicles for political songs. This has been a fact throughout history, but space will not allow inclusion of very many of these. There is an entire book full of nothing but parodies about the Kennedy family. I found a parody in the San Antonio *Express-News* entitled, "The Feats of the Mayor," sung to the tune of "The Streets of Laredo."[38]

Proof that parodies are still popular can be found in these examples that were used during the Republican National Convention on August 3, 2000. Tune: "The Eyes of Texas Are Upon You":

> The eyes of Texas are upon Bush
> And Dick Cheney, too,
> We're going to kick Al Gore's tush,
> The Democrats are through!
>
> **Chorus:**
> Can't you hear the Texans cheering
> On that January morn

When our President is sworn in?
George W, blow your horn![39]

On Friday, August 4, the headline read, "'Yellow Rose' is a crowd-pleaser." This was sung to the tune of "The Yellow Rose of Texas":

> George Double-ya from Texas
> Is here to save the day
> Our nation needs a Texan
> To steer our country's way,
> With Secretary Cheney
> And Laura by his side,
> We'll finally have a president
> For whom we can take pride.
> (Words to both parodies by Sherry Sylvester)[40]

By far the funniest thing I saw on television during the presidential election aftermath was the image of a bearded hippie-type holding a candidate's placard and singing a parody to "Blowin' In the Wind" that ended,

> The answer, my friend, is on CNN;
> The answer is on CNN.[41]

On November 21, 2000, Dr. Laura Schlessinger read a parody of "Hokey-Pokey" that ended:

> You put the stylus in, you pull the stylus out,
> You make a dimpled chad or else
> You let the chads fall out . . .
> You do the hokey-pokey and you turn it all around,
> That's what it's all about.

On *Saturday Night Live,* November 18, 2000, two characters wearing Bush and Gore masks sang a parody of Sonny and Cher's "I've Got You, Babe" that was really funny.

An article in the *San Antonio Express-News* pointed out the many parodies that were being bandied about during the election crisis, but they also pointed out the value of keeping a sense of humor about a bad situation. After September 11, 2001, numerous parodies were written about a very non-humorous situation. So many parodies were played on the radios and television that WOAI radio spent several afternoons playing and talking about the various parodies that were proliferating.[42] My favorite—to the 1960s tune of "Oh, Donna," started out: "Osama. Osama."

Parodies are indeed alive and well in 2002! In fact, the most recent addition to this collection of parodies appeared in Dear Abby's column on March 10, 2002, with a version of "My Favorite Things" attributed to Julie Andrews' concert for AARP:

> Maalox and nose drops and needles for knitting,
> Walkers and handrails and new dental fittings,
> Bundles of magazines tied up in string,
> These are a few of my favorite things.
>
> Cadillacs, cataracts, hearing aids, glasses,
> Polident, Fixodent, false teeth in glasses,
> Pacemakers, golf carts and porches with swings,
> These are a few of my favorite things.
>
> When the pipes leak,
> When the bones creak
> When the knees go bad
> I simply remember my favorite things,
> And then I don't feel so bad.
>
> Hot tea and crumpets, and corn pads for bunions,
> No spicy hot food or food cooked with onions,

Bathrobes and heating pads, hot meals they bring.
These are a few of my favorite things.

Back pain, confused brains, and no fear of sinnin',
Thin bones and fractures and hair that is thinnin',
More of the pleasures advancing age bring,
When we remember our favorite things.

When the joints ache, when the hips break,
When the eyes grow dim,
I simply remember the great life I've had
And then I don't feel . . . so baaaad![43]

Parodies have served many purposes through the years. They have entertained and educated, thrilled and disgusted, challenged and enchanted people of all ages for many generations. They have reflected attitudes, ideas, and traditions that contribute to our folklore. As we have seen, the art of singing and composing parodies is alive and well. If you pay attention, you will find that almost every day television commercials reveal a new version of some old song, or something appears in the newspaper that is a parody. If you bring up the subject just about anywhere, you will find that everybody knows a parody—or two or ten—and will likely sing for you on the spot!

What would the Texas Folklore Society hoots be without Lu Mitchell's entertaining parodies? She performs with remarkable skill and talent, writing her own material about timely subjects such as "I Want to Be a White House Intern" (to the tune of "I Want to Be a Cowboy's Sweetheart"), "Back in the Stirrups Again," ("Back in the Saddle Again"), "Shall We Gather at the Dumpster?" ("Shall We Gather at the River") and many others. My favorite is to the tune of "Bendemeer's Stream":

She's a little ol' lady with hair snowy white
But the FBI's hot on her trail tonight.

She's down in Brazil with the janitor, Hank,
And the loot from the Googlesburg National Bank.[44]

Enter the Internet! Searching for the keyword "parodies" results in hundreds—even thousands—of opportunities to read, see, and hear parodies varying from humorous children's verses and funny commercials to raunchy adult parodies—and everything in between! On one website, I found musical parodies in abundance—most very entertaining. The commercials and reverse commercials are pretty funny, too. Gone are the days when parodies had to wait for years to be passed on from one person to another and from one generation to another! I can tell you this, though: They are parodying modern tunes and not "Mademoiselle from Armentiers."

END NOTES

1. Marion Bauer, "Folk Music—a General Survey," *International Cyclopedia of Music and Musicians,* 9th Ed. (New York: Dodd, Mead & Company, 1964), 714.
2. Martin Bernstein and Martin Picker, *An Introduction to Music* (Englewood Cliffs, NJ: Prentice-Hall, 1972), 1.
3. John Lomax and Alan Lomax, *American Ballads and Folk Songs* (New York: The Macmillan Company, 1968), xxxv.
4. *The American Heritage Dictionary of the English Language,* ed. William Morris (Boston: Houghton Mifflin Company, 1973).
5. Linda Scudder Payne, e-mail to author, 2000.
6. Lomax, *American Ballads,* 556, 557.
7. Maymie R. Krythe, ed., *Sampler of American Songs* (New York: Harper & Row, 1969), 116–17.
8. Margaret Bradford Boni, ed., *Fireside Book of Folk Songs* (New York: Simon & Schuster, 1947), 220.
9. Texas Folklife Festival Hoot at the barn, June 3, 2000, as sung by Dennis and his brother.
10. Carl Van Doren, *The Fireside Book of Favorite American Folk Songs* (New York: Simon and Schuster, no year), 19–22.
11. *Reader's Digest Family Songbook,* W. A. Birnie, Editor (Pleasantville, NY: The Reader's Digest Association, 1969), 192.
12. *Sociability Songs* (nc: Rodeheaver Hall-Mack Co, approx. 1934), 125.
13. *Reader's Digest Family Songbook,* 36–37.
14. *Sociability Songs,* 125.

15. *Sociability Songs,* 125.
16. *Sociability Songs,* 125.
17. Bob Reeder, as sung at Bandera, Texas, May, 1999.
18. Van Doren, 35–40.
19. Frank Lynn, *The Beer Bust Song Book or Pictures to Look at While Others Are Singing* (San Francisco: Fearon Publishers, 1963), 47.
20. Lynn, 23.
21. Lew Schnitz, interview with author, 1997 and 2000.
22. Lomax, 557–70.
23. Lew Schnitz, personal interview with author, 1997.
24. Linda Scudder Payne, e-mail to author, 2000.
25. Acayla and Sierra Haile, recorded at Texas Folklore Society Meeting, 1999.
26. Nancy Harrison, personal interview with author, 1998.
27. Lynn, 12.
28. *Fireside Book of Folk Songs.*
29. John Jacob Niles, *Songs of the Hill Folk* (nc: G. Schirmer, Inc., ca. 1934), 2–3.
30. *Reader's Digest Festival of Popular Songs* (Pleasantville, NY: The Reader's Digest Association, no year), 284.
31. William L. Simon, ed., *The Reader's Digest Country and Western Songbook* (Pleasantville, NY: The Reader's Digest Association, 1983), 214.
32. Jacqueline Steiner and Bess Hawes, "The M.T.A. Song," The Atlantic Music Corp.
33. F. E. Abernethy, *Singin' Texas* (Dallas, TX: E-Heart Press 1983), 18.
34. Edmund S. Lorenz, *Church Music* (New York: Fleming H. Revell, 1923).
35. Walter Ehret and George K. Evans, *The International Book of Christmas Carols* (New York: Walton Music Corporation, no year), 4–5.
36. Lew Schnitz, personal interview with author, 1960.
37. *San Antonio Express-News,* July 1, 1999.
38. *San Antonio Express-News,* April 27, 2000.
39. *San Antonio Express-News,* August 3, 2000, p. 11A.
40. *San Antonio Express-News,* August 4, 2000, p. 12A.
41. CNN, November 17, 2000.
42. WOAI radio, San Antonio, Texas, late November 2001.
43. "Dear Abby," *San Antonio Express News,* March 10, 2002.
44. Lu Mitchell, from performances at Texas Folklore Society meetings.

Some real bronc-bustin', snake-stompin' cowboy boots, from a calendar

(Photos by Georgia Caraway)

Wooden Scotty dog postcard with hand-painted details

16

TEXAS KITSCH AND OTHER COLLECTIBLES

by Georgia Caraway of Denton

A lot of people may not understand the importance of the State of Texas in the overall scheme of the universe—or why someone would choose to present a paper on collecting only Texas items. It is hard to conceive of a book explaining "How to Speak Iowan," or a battle cry "Remember the Brooklyn Bridge!" Texas, however, has been the topic of thousands of books, and national television programs such as Dallas and Walker, Texas Ranger have spread the word—perhaps somewhat warped—of the uniqueness of this Special Corner of Heaven. Equally as important, visitors to Texas have taken home tens of thousands of collectible items—some real "kitsch"!—to further spread the word about this state's far-reaching fame.

I began collecting Texana—not kitsch—while I was working on my master's degree in Texas Studies at the University of North Texas. Texas Studies was a short-lived program that Jim Lee created during the chauvinistic excitement of the Texas Sesquicentennial. My degree means I devoted a large part of my life to the formal study of things Texan. I know of "no whar but Texas" where you could get a master's degree based on the history and literature of a state.

My collection of Texana began in a sane fashion—not kitschy—with collecting books about Texas that were required reading for my degree. I decided that I would only collect first-edition hardbacks written by Texas-born authors—a bonus would be if it sported an author's autograph. As my appetite grew, my quest expanded. I had about two hundred editions, but it was getting more difficult and more expensive to find collectible books locally. So I began to scour flea markets, garage sales, antique shows, and bookstores near and far for rare and not-so-rare editions. And I lowered my standards to any book written by a Texas author or about Texas. My husband sarcastically suggested that my definition of a Texas author was anyone who visited Texas and wrote a book before he or she returned to his or her state of permanent residence. I assured him that my criterion was much stricter—the author had to cross the Texas border, write a book, and eat at a Dairy Queen before returning to his or her home state.

When the number of volumes in my collection reached more than one thousand, and the bookshelves were filling more rapidly than we could build more, I decided to diversify. Again my standards suffered. I began to search for Texas kitsch.

Kitsch is art and literature with little or no aesthetic or commercial value. It comes in every size, on every type of material—pottery, barbwire, red and white corncobs—anything that the creative kitsch mind could use to create something tacky but marketable. There are thousands of Texana kitsch items on paper—recipe booklets from the Centennial and Texas State Fair advertising Texas food and fiber products, photographs of Texas people, and Texas postcards, among others.

Texas postcards are a collecting field in kitsch unto themselves. The only rule that governs their inclusion is that the subject be specific to Texas. Texas kitsch is flooded with cards showing the Texas Centennial, Texas attractions such as the Alamo and cacti in the El Paso area, advertisements for businesses such as the Arthur A. Everts jewelry firm and El Fenix in Dallas, the bath houses of Marlin and Mineral Wells, Carnegie libraries and historical governmental buildings like City Hall in San Antonio and Waco, and real photos of the 254 historic courthouses. True lovers of postcard kitsch put them in large hardback memory books and lay them out on the coffee table in the livingroom.

A friend of mine in Denton collects only postcards about Denton. He especially cares about the two universities: Texas Woman's University, known in the past as Girls Industrial College, College of Industrial Arts, and Texas State College for Women; and the University of North Texas, once called North Texas Normal and North Texas State Teachers College. He has more than one hundred TWU cards and fifty UNT cards. Note: collectors of kitsch are never reluctant about showing their trophies.

Looking through his cards, one sometimes finds that the messages are more interesting than the cards. One from the penitentiary in Huntsville reads, "Please don't think this my stopping place."

Cards depicting scenes from towns and cities are especially important, particularly early scenics, local industries, or editorial messages such as a card showing the billboard from Hondo—"Welcome. This is God's Country; Please Don't Drive Through It Like Hell. Hondo, Texas."

Texas is famous for its brags about everything from wildlife to produce. There is the famous Texas Jackalope, usually with a cowboy on board. Or longhorns with outrageous horn spans. Or the outsized potato from Marble Falls or the giant tomato from Jacksonville. Some kitsch collectors specialize only in Texas Brag cards.

Another special kitschy postcard is the three-dimensional souvenir card, with a string tag attached for the greeting and mailing address. A surviving popular example is a charming, wooden Scotty dog with hand-painted details with a pyrographic message that reads, "Having a dog gone good time in Dallas Texas." His eye is a thumbtack. Can you imagine anything like that surviving today's mechanized Post Office equipment? The one-and-a-half-cent stamp on my Scotty tells the knowledgeable collector that this is a pre-1925 piece. Postage for postcards changed from one cent to two cents in 1925. The extra half-penny was for the additional weight.

The bluebonnet, the Texas state flower, can be found on dozens of photographic postcards. The bluebonnet can also be found on some Texas pottery. William Meyer and Franz Schultz established Meyer Pottery in Atascosa in 1887. They made jugs, churns, mugs, poultry fountains, ant traps, and in the forties and fifties they fired hundreds of the bluebonnet-decorated souvenir pieces for serious kitsch art collectors. Texas kitsch art is also a good source for finding amateur paintings of bluebonnets from the 1940s and 1950s. Matching hand-painted inexpensive wooden frames usually surrounded these paintings.

In some cases on these little paintings, instead of the bluebonnet, we have another Texas icon—the Alamo. The Alamo is perhaps the most famous of the Texas landmarks, known throughout the world for the heroism of its defenders and for the mission's distinctly recognizable architectural shape. Thousands of examples of items can be found with the Alamo's façade painted, inscribed, printed, or etched on them. One popular item was a painted velvet Alamo pillow cover before I converted it into a beauty of a purse. You can imagine the comments I got about this purse when I carried it in my home state of Pennsylvania. The Alamo is famous even in foreign lands.

A world of kitsch and fine art came out of the Texas Centennial. A. Harris of Dallas contracted with Imperial Glass Company in 1936 to produce a glass platter of the Alamo for the Texas Centennial for exclusive distribution through their store. When the Centennial year was over, the mold was destroyed so that no other copies could be made. Other Centennial Imperial Glass pieces offered included a matching glass creamer and sugar bowl.

The Texas Centennial Exposition ran for 178 days, from June 6 to November 30, 1936. The celebration marked the hundred-year anniversary of Texas's independence from Mexico. Dallas campaigned to hold the celebration there and the city's offer to put up $10,000,000 was accepted. With some federal, state, and private donor money, about $25,000,000 was raised. Fifty buildings were erected in Dallas's State Fair Park, with the Hall of State being the centerpiece. These art deco buildings of the 1930s might be what one would call "architectural kitsch," unobtainable by your average kitsch collector.

Ceramic versions of "Old Rip" by the House of Webster, Eastland, Texas

Thousands of different items were made for the Centennial, many of them are cross collectibles into other categories: post-cards, salt and pepper shakers, ashtrays, jewelry, Czechoslovakian plates illustrating Texas themes, a replica of a Colt .45 six-shooter, parasols, dishes and bowls adorned with bluebonnets, sheet music for "Come on Down to Texas," walking sticks, sunbonnets, license plates, mason jars, doorstops, Swanky Swigs, playing cards, hats, miniature buildings, calendars, pincushion shoes, pottery and souvenir spoons to name just a few.

Souvenir spoons are universal collectibles in the realm of kitsch art. Texas spoons from nearly every town and hamlet have been produced in sterling and silverplate. The spoons, in demitasse size, advertise businesses as well as the towns of their location. The Arthur A. Everts jewelry firm, as well as the Texas Centennial, circulated souvenir spoons during the Centennial year.

Personal apparel also is popular among kitsch collectors. Enid Collins designed wooden box purses and canvas and leather purses from her factory in Medina, Texas, from 1958 until 1970 when she sold her company, Collins of Texas, to Tandy Corporation of Fort Worth. She was famous for her gaudy designs using braids and plastic beads and gemstones. Although I have more than sixty of these bags, the Roadrunner purses are my favorites. They come in a medley of shapes, sizes, and colors and are pure kitsch.

Other clothing items include bronc-bustin', snake-stompin' cowboy boots, Texas ties, and scarves. The 1950 book by John Randolph *Texas Brags* (Hufsmith, Texas, 1950) inspired the themes and humor found on the popular Texas-map scarf. The Texan's view of the vastness and importance of Texas as compared to the rest of the states is clearly illustrated by having Texas cover one-half of the United States map. The scarf depicts Texas as having the most cantankerous coyotes, the most hellacious javelinas, the prickliest pears, the jumpinest jackrabbits, most rambunctious roadrunners, and the peskiest prairie dogs. And one popular scarf shows San Angelo as famous for "The Hairiest Goats (Mohair than

Goats)." Every Texas kitsch collection must have a drawer of these artistic scarves and hankies.

Household items play an important part in collecting Texas kitsch. The braggadocio, puns, and jokes found on Chamber-of-Commerce-inspired scarves and hankies can be found on table-cloths and napkins. One need never to be far away from one's kitsch collection, even at dinnertime. Souvenir plates are very popular among Texas kitsch collectors. Texas souvenir plates are produced for nearly every tourist stop as fundraisers for women's service clubs. The Vernon Kiln Company of California produced most of the more serious plates. They are beautifully rendered and of high quality pottery. On the other hand, most of the garish plates distributed by civic history organizations follow the same designs as the tablecloth and scarves or pillowcases and are collectably tacky.

Pottery manufacturing was a serious industry from the earliest times of Texas settlement. The weight of pottery churns, jugs, and other household utilitarian pottery prevented settlers from bringing pottery produced in the north and east in wagons to Texas. Texas potters did bring their pottery-making skills with them.

Horton Ceramics of Eastland (1852 to 1954) was the predecessor to the House of Webster Ceramics in Eastland. House of Webster produces about 200,000 pieces of pottery per year to be used by the House of Webster food gift company of Rogers, Arkansas. Much of the production is Texas kitsch. Dozens of pottery designs such as churns, telephones, apples, thimbles, and beehives are produced to contain their homemade preserves, apple butter, and honey.

But perhaps the most famous kitsch art from the House of Webster is the ceramic replica of the legendary horned toad, "Old Rip." The legend goes that when the Eastland County Courthouse was dedicated in 1897, a Texas horned toad was placed in the cornerstone. When the courthouse was razed in 1928, thirty-one years later, the cornerstone was reopened, the horned toad twitched and woke up. The name "Old Rip," based on Washington Irving's Rip Van Winkle, was resurrected. Old Rip was sent on a national promotional tour and even visited President Calvin Coolidge in Washington, D. C. When Old Rip came home, he caught pneumonia and died. His body was sent to a taxidermist and his remains were placed in a casket in the rotunda of the new Eastland County Courthouse. House of Webster Ceramics began making these horned toads as giveaways for school children and tourists who visited their manufacturing plant. I have received several of these ceramic horned toads as gifts. They come in different colors and shades, but all have the name "OLD RIP" emblazoned on their chest.

While searching the Internet for more examples of Old Rip as an example of Texas kitsch, I was amused to note that ceramic Old Rips are sold all over the United States. My most recent replica came from Fort Worth for a two-dollar investment. Most Texas examples cost between two and five dollars. However, invariably if Old Rip resides in California, he commands twenty to twenty-five dollars. Just because it's kitsch doesn't mean it's cheap! Maybe the entrepreneurs in California have added on import costs—or just maybe they are beginning to learn what everyone here was born knowing—that Texas is indeed the center of the universe and outsiders have to pay accordingly.

Enid Collins roadrunner purses from the 1960s

The Upshaws of County Line, Nacogdoches—Monel and Leota Upshaw and their thirteen children, descendents of freedmen who established County Line, or the Upshaw Community, in the 1870s
(Photo by Richard Orton of Austin from his exhibit "The Upshaws of County Line")

17

TEXAS FREEDMEN'S SETTLEMENTS
IN THE NEW SOUTH

by Thad Sitton of Austin

For the last year, James H. Conrad and I have been engaged in research about Texas freedmen's settlements. These were independent black rural communities usually established within twenty years after the end of slavery. We currently know of several hundred of these dispersed rural communities, few of which were ever incorporated, or platted, or even properly listed on county maps. These were "unofficial" places by their very nature—some so much so that the high sheriff and the census man only rarely intruded in their affairs.[1]

Southerners called such places "settlements," whether black people or white people lived in them. Settlements have been neglected, or misunderstood, by Southern rural historians, Frank Owsley once argued in his book, *Plain Folk of the Old South* (1949). Even in the heydays of such settlements, a traveler might pass through one without even noticing that a community was there. Infrastructure was slight, and it might be scattered about at different locations in the dispersed community. Almost always there was a church, or churches, and a school; almost always there was a grist mill and a cane mill on someone's place to produce the community's survival staples of cornmeal and cane syrup; rather often, there was a small cotton gin, sometimes of the multiple-use category that also ground corn and sawed limber. And sometimes there was a community post office, though perhaps with a name change. As a general rule, when the larger white society intruded on a freedmen's settlement with a post office, railroad depot, or major sawmill, the black community got a new name, whether it wanted one or not.

Communities often renamed themselves for internal reasons or used more than one name at the same time. Considering how unofficial they were, no wonder that many freedmen's settlements ended up with multiple names—that in Cherokee County "Hog Jaw" became "Sweet Union" and "Andy" became "Cuney." In Goliad County, one community became successively known as The Colony, Perdido, Centerville, Ira, and Cologne, the name used in *The New Handbook of Texas*.[2]

In any case, the names alone almost justify the hunt for freedmen's settlements. Several of the state's "Bethlehems" are freedmen's settlements, and all three of its "Nazareths." Scattered across the eastern half of Texas are Green Hill, Yellow Prairie, Red Branch, Black Branch, Weeping Mary, Board Bottom, Jerusalem, Freedmen's Ridge, Egypt, Frog, Elm Slough, and my personal favorite name, Lost Ball.

Some important patterns of social history show up in the names. The common use of place names from the Bible and the word "chapel" emphasizes how many settlements began with establishment of rural churches. The words "sand," "creek," "branch," "slough," and "bottom" are common components of settlement place names, suggesting locations on less-than-ideal cotton soils in sand hills and flood-prone creek and river bottoms, a generalization supported by a close study of the map. Even more interesting, the word "colony" also commonly occurs in settlement names—for example, Peyton Colony, Saint John's Colony, Grant's Colony, and so on—and it is reasonable to ask what community founders thought was being colonized? The wilderness? White rural society? Both at the same time? I think both at the same time.

The names come and go from our master list as additional information arrives, and no wonder: it was complicated out there in the postbellum Texas countryside, and we labor not to call a fish a fowl. Perhaps after moving around for a brief while to test their newfound freedom, many former slaves signed on as wage-hands or sharecroppers with their former masters, or with neighbors of their former masters, and sometimes these sharecropper communities grew large enough to take names. Other freed persons moved into satellite communities adjacent to, or very close by, existing white towns, and these "quarters" also took names. Often in the beginning, before the white towns grew around them and converted them into neighborhoods, some of these urban quarters were geographically separated from their parent communities and somewhat resembled the independent black settlements of the remote countryside. For example, at Clarksville, now a mixed-race neighborhood of west central Austin, well within the ring of city development, freedmen once had run their own affairs in church and school, separated by a buffer of wooded hills and bad roads from Anglo Austin. At least some of Clarksville's early residents chose to remain aloof from white society, relying instead upon small cotton patches, big gardens, and a menagerie of domestic livestock to make a living. Some of Austin's dot-com executives now dwell in $600,000 homes where poor black families once ranged chickens in the yards and rooter hogs in the creek bottoms.[3]

Although plenty of betwixt-and-between places existed to confuse the historian, it is fair to generalize that freed people moved into three general sorts of communities after emancipation: sharecropper quarters, town quarters, and independent freedmen's settlements, where some or most of the settlers were landowners. My discussion focuses on this third sort of place. Furthermore, it seems high time to do so. Despite their historical importance, and for reasons I don't entirely understand, freedmen's settlements have been woefully neglected in the historiography of the New South.

If you try to answer the simple question, "What happened to African Americans after emancipation?" and turn to the literature, you will find a good many works of scholarship analyzing the swift transformation of freedmen into cotton rent farmers, principally sharecroppers. You will note some studies (though surprisingly few) detailing the migration of freed people into newly-formed "colored quarters" of white towns. And, if you search closely, you will find some accounts of the long-range "exodus" of Southern blacks to the new African-American developer towns of Oklahoma and Kansas, this movement peaking as Democratic "Redemption" loomed on the horizon during the late 1870s. But the story of the internal exodus of former slaves to found remote, independent, landowner communities is yet to be told.[4]

Where can you go to read a book-length history of such a freedmen's settlement? I know of only three alternatives and all from out-of-state: William Montell's *The Saga of Coe Ridge,* Janet Sharp Hermann's *The Pursuit of a Dream,* and Elizabeth Rauh Bethel's *Promiseland: A Century of Life in a Negro Community.* Published by Temple University Press in 1981, Bethel's intimate and detailed study of a South Carolina freedmen's settlement is by far the most important of these three books. In Texas, Ron Traylor recently completed a master's thesis study of Barrett's settlement in Harris County.[5] Finally, the wonderful oral autobiography of the late Reverend C. C. White, *No Quittin' Sense,* edited by Ada Morehead Holland, sheds fascinating light on several Texas freedmen's communities, including Robinson's settlement, a few miles east of Nacogdoches.

At this point I'd like to discuss some of my ideas about the social patterns of the origins and essential nature of Texas freedmen's settlements. But so remote, unofficial, and undocumented were most freedmen's settlements that generalizations about them may end up always remaining somewhat "beyond the data," especially since so much of the settlements' oral history long since has disappeared into the grave.

To understand the origins of the settlements, you have to try to understand the circumstances of freed people during Reconstruction. Historians James Smallwood, Barry Crouch, Laurence Rice, and others have contributed greatly to our recent knowledge of this period, but even more important for me as a white person interpreting black history have been the several hundred personal accounts of slavery, emancipation, and the decades thereafter recorded in the ten-volume WPA Texas slave narratives edited by George Rawick. To read these accounts is to come as close as anyone can to standing in the freedmen's shoes.[6]

Circumstances were harsh; options were limited. Most Texas slaves owned nothing beyond the clothing on their backs at the time they learned they were free, and many felt they had no choice but to remain for a time with their former owners in some arrangement of wage-hand or sharecropper peonage. The alternative was to be "turned loose like a bunch of damn hogs in the woods," one man said. The dream of landowner independence, of "40 acres and a mule" provided by the conquering federal government, died very quickly. For many people, the devil they knew seemed preferable to the devil they didn't, at least for a time, though a remarkable number of freedmen reported that things changed very little immediately after emancipation. At one large cotton plantation along the Brazos River, disciplinary beatings familiar under slavery continued into the sharecropper-era, though some reforms had taken place. Now, at least, nobody was nailed by his ears face-first to a tree all night for punishment, as had been the custom.[7]

Ex-slaves interviewed during 1937 not infrequently asserted that black people in some ways had been better off during slavery than at present, and in context this seems not so much a favorable opinion of slavery as a bitter commentary on the apartheid society that replaced it. Sharecropping remained a hard row to hoe for many, right down to World War II. Asked what he had done since emancipation, one man told his interviewer: "I was sharecropper. And, White Man, that was when slavery really began."[8]

Gradually, during the first decade after emancipation, freedmen accumulated property, resources, and knowledge of white society and moved away to what they hoped would be improved circumstances on other white men's farms, to employment in town, and to their own land, as squatters and landowners. During Reconstruction, the white society they moved into was incredibly dangerous. Barry Crouch, James Smallwood, and other recent historians have mined the correspondence of Freedmen Bureau sub-agents during the years from 1866 to 1870 to describe just how danger-ous. Crouch estimated that at least one percent of black males in Texas age fourteen to forty-five were murdered during Recon-struction. Bureau agents relayed many reports of numerous freed-men bodies discovered in their areas, with federal troops seemingly incapable of stopping the carnage. Students and teachers were attacked on their way to Bureau schools, and blacks were beaten or shot for failing to show proper deference to whites or for just act-ing like they were free by walking the roads or plowing their own fields.

Some white-on-black violence seemed aimed at subjugating blacks economically and socially and at enforcing the new apartheid. Other violence seemed gratuitous, random, and spur-of-the-moment, fueled by bitterness over loss of the war and loss of human property and emboldened by the refusal of local courts to take action to protect freedmen. An ex-slave from the Hempstead area interviewed by John Henry Faulk in 1941 reported that freed-men had to be careful about sitting on their front porches in the late evening, since passers-by on the road occasionally took recre-ational pot-shots at them. At some places, outlaws, such as Cullen Davis of Harrison County or the man black people called "Dixie" in Freestone County, murdered so many freedmen and KKK-like organizations became so active in raiding homesteads after dark, that farm families commonly abandoned their houses at dusk for a night in the nearby woods. You hear of this practice of leaving home after dark to take cover from many localities, including Nacogdoches County.[9] "White capping," the generic term blacks used for these nocturnal, terroristic, Klan-like activities, took place all across Texas.

That much is not speculation-unpleasant as it may be to con-template, conflicting as it does with obsolete earlier interpretations of what happened to black Texans during Reconstruction. But what I have to say from this point becomes more speculative.

A minority of freedmen continued the quest for forty acres and a mule long after they recognized they would have to get these things for themselves. The only true escape from white violence, economic exploitation, and social domination was landownership in an all-black community physically isolated from whites, these people believed. This impulse to seek independence from whites and self-exclusion from white society gave rise to the freedmen's settlements. Some people who felt this way left for the new black developer towns in Oklahoma and Kansas, but most relocated only a few miles to some unclaimed local wilderness of swampy bottoms or sand hills.

Anglo-American Southerners often were well aware of freedmen's migration into patches of local wilderness to make a living by hunting, fishing, foraging, and small-farming, and they usually didn't like it. For one thing, it meant a loss of needed agricultural labor. One traveler wrote to his wife after crossing the Trinity bottoms in 1875: "All the improvements worth noting are on the prairie, but a 'free nigger patch,' with demoralized log-hut, occasionally appears in the low wooded bottoms, where that class mostly live." Was this man witnessing the origins of a new freedmen's settlement?

The rise of black landownership and the increase in freedmen's settlements seem closely linked. Although exact dates of origins often are difficult to establish, most freedmen's settlements began between 1870 and 1900. During that same time, Texas freedmen farmers owning their own land rose from 1.8 percent of all black farmers in 1870 to 31 percent in 1900—a very great achievement, considering the social and economic factors that worked against black land acquisition.[10]

Most of this astonishing increase in farm ownership took place in the two decades between 1870 and 1890, during which time black Texas owner-operators increased by almost 1400 percent, nearly doubling the rate of increase in Florida, the next-highest Southern state. Twenty-six percent of black Texas farmers worked their own land by 1890.[11]

All this black land purchase had required hard dealings against long odds. To buy land, an African-American farmer needed the money or credit to purchase the land, a white landowner willing to sell it to him, and the tacit agreement of whites in the area to allow him to occupy it. Once a black person broke through these barriers into landownership in a locality, others tended to follow him; once someone had "colonized," families gravitated to the colony. Not surprisingly, the Texas counties having the largest number of freedmen's settlements also had the largest percentages of black landowners.

As the disapproving Trinity bottom traveler noted, the impulse for isolation, avoidance of whites, autonomy, and landownership showed up immediately after emancipation when some freedmen moved into areas of unclaimed land as squatters. These squatter lands typically were pockets of wilderness on infertile or often-flooded soils that antebellum cotton agriculture had bypassed—sand hills, pine barrens, post oak belts, and creek and river bottoms. There was a lot of this sort of unsettled land available in 1870, and for a decade or so thereafter. Despite Frederick Jackson Turner's theory to the contrary, the moving line of the Southern frontier had left behind many internal "frontiers," where poor settlers continued to pioneer the wilderness for generations.

As in the case of Lewis's Bend in Refugio County and Evergreen in Titus County, some freedmen's settlements remained squatter communities until their depopulation in the mid-20th century.[12] Land could be purchased for a small price, or preempted from the state, but to what advantage, many thought. If you had the use of the land already, why buy it and pay taxes on it? Furthermore, many people were Southern stockmen ranging hogs and cattle in the open woods, and this traditional use right on other men's property made land ownership almost unnecessary. The hogs with your mark in their ears sufficiently staked out your "hog claim." Let somebody else pay the land taxes.

Land squatting by blacks and whites was far more commonly done and easily accomplished than historians have recognized. In 1887, a scandalized newcomer to southeastern Texas wrote, "The people have been in the habit of using every man's property as their own for so many years that they have come to believe that the land has no owners."[13]

Many other settlements began several years after emancipation, after a freedman, or freedmen, somehow accumulated enough money for land purchase. Strong black leaders with mysterious resources showed up at the origins of many freedmen's settlements, then other people moved in to build a community around them. The pioneer landowner rented to later-comers, sold land to them, and generally functioned as community patron and benefactor. Perhaps the patron profited from the later-comers, but it was also in his self-interest to facilitate the formation of community. It was lonely out there in the white countryside. Very often, the landowner-based settlements chose the same semi-wilderness settings as the squatter settlements—uncleared forests, sand hills, and river bottoms—areas remote from whites where land was cheap.

As in the case of squatter settlements, many landowner settlements were situated along county lines. Was this because streams, with their affordable, or unclaimed, bottomlands, often formed the boundaries between counties, and because land values generally declined with distance from centrally located courthouse towns? Were county lines also good places to hide out and assume a low profile? Some whites disapproved of black landownership and independent black settlements.

Family members, typically a band of siblings, formed the core pioneers at many settlements. This was true of the County Line (Upshaw) settlement along the Angelina River in western Nacogdoches County, founded by the teenaged Upshaw brothers, Guss, Jim, and Felix, just after emancipation. The Upshaws squatted on wilderness land, then purchased it (perhaps with the aid of their former owner). Other black people purchased land from the Upshaws or became land squatters in the vicinity. Guss and Jim in particular served as community stalwarts for a half century—jacks-of-all-trade who blacksmithed, ground corn, sawmilled, and built hundreds of necessary material things (including even cotton wagons) from scratch.[14]

Other settlements clustered around a church congregation that pioneered the new land as a group. Early settlers often cooperated in building first-generation log cabins, clearing land, and fencing cultivated fields. Then they cooperated to build the new community's most important infrastructure—first, the brush arbor, then, the church itself. Such churches also functioned as schools and principal community centers.

White assistance is discernible at the origins of many freedmen communities. How could this be otherwise, when it was so hard for a black person to obtain land? Often, this assistance came from the former slaveholders who sold freedmen land, arranged for them to purchase it from other whites, deeded it to them outright, or simply allowed them squatters' rights on it. A mixture of altruistic and self-serving motives may be assumed, including the need to locate and stabilize a nearby source of willing agricultural labor, a need for cash after wartime losses of capital, feelings of paternalism and responsibility for former slaves, personal friendships with certain freed persons, and blood relationships with certain freed persons.

Ugly as it was, brutal as it could be, slavery also was the time of a great intimacy between black people and white people in the South, and no one who reads the slave narratives can fail to pay attention to what the former slaves have to say about this. Personal relationships formed during slavery facilitated the origins of many freedmen's settlements, no doubt about it.[15]

So much for origins. What of the long track of the freedmen's settlements down through time? They remained remote, located at the end of country roads that county commissioners somehow never got around to paving, and most black residents liked it that way. A general caution persisted regarding contacts with unfamiliar white people, and a certain "protective coloration" was maintained. A black farmer who could well afford to paint his house or buy a Model T Ford, might choose not to do so for social reasons. A black man from a settlement visiting the courthouse town on Saturday might choose to dress not in his best Sunday outfit but in everyday work clothes, overalls and straw hat, so as not to attract unpleasant attention.

Many settlements remained hardscrabble places, where people made a living by small farming, large gardens, chickens in the yard, and hogs and cows on the open range (whatever the official stock law proclaimed). Frugality and recycling were the iron dictums of the Texas countryside, but never more acutely so than at these places. Three anecdotes to illustrate this (which I can duplicate from white sources, incidentally, all except for the detail about the baling wire): C. C. White recalled that people in his community couldn't afford matches and so kept a succession of stumps burning from which to light household fires; each stump would last the better part of a week. Alice Wilkins remembered that when her family ran out of salt they processed dirt from the smokehouse floor through the lye hopper to make, as she said, "a grey kind of salt." At the Flat Prairie Settlement of Washington County, Grover Williams's grandmother commonly made Grover and his brothers "jumper jackets" from worn-out cotton sack ducking, the button-holes fastened with baling wire.

Hunting, fishing, and foraging for wild plant foods remained important for settlement inhabitants long after such things had become recreational activities for people in the towns. Sheriff's deputies, census takers, county tax officials, and medical doctors only occasionally intruded into the affairs of such places, which self-policed themselves, birthed their children with midwives, buried their own dead, and practiced a high measure of community help-out. Some rural whites resented the clannishness and real or presumed "uppityness" of African Americans in such settlements, and they might go over to harass them when liquored up on Saturday nights. This could be dangerous, however. Blacks in freedmen's settlements were more inclined to fight back.[16]

An economic marginality from soil infertility and small farm size often forced quests for other sources of cash and sometimes for outside employments. In the agricultural down-times of the yearly round, settlement people chopped ties for the railroad, sold firewood in town, peddled farm produce in town, gathered pine knots for the woods crews of lumber companies, made charcoal, and distilled whisky. For traditional and practical reasons, as well as because of a sometimes-grinding poverty, nineteenth-century crafts, skills, and techniques of making-do survived longest at the settlements. The last old man in an area who knew how to make white oak baskets, rive pieux-board fences, or plow with an ox usually resided in the freedmen's settlement. Some community members, often younger people and increasing over time, periodically took jobs from whites as tenant farmers, woods-crew and sawmill workers, pulpwood haulers, stockmen, fence builders, and domestic help, but they maintained their community ties.

Community decline began sometime before midcentury, caused by multiple blows from circumstances far beyond local control. First came the ravages of the boll weevil, then the drastic fall of cotton prices during the Great Depression (aided and abetted by government programs that favored larger farmers over small ones), then World War II, which drew so many young people away from the countryside, never to return. Then, finally, came the bitter loss of community schools due to the divisive reform programs of consolidation and integration, leaving the churches and the graveyards as the only surviving community institutions—the first and now the last. By the year 2000, only at Juneteenth and community reunion day does the church parking lot fill with cars and the church pews with people, and the passerby sees how many souls still remain focused on this small rural place beside the county road.

Long-gone Anglo-American settlements have their reunions, too, but something seems different here. Our general notion of black people abandoning the hated countryside for increased freedom and improved opportunities in town is true enough, but it doesn't fit the counter-current history of the freedmen's settlements. These were marked places, rare communities where black people ran their own shows. "Freedom colonies," some older residents had called them. When a settlement held its Juneteenth in years past, African Americans from other rural communities and the town quarters often showed up. Schools at freedmen's settlements tended to expand their grades upwards over time, with children from neighboring common school districts being bussed in to these "magnet schools" to continue their education. A remarkable number of settlement schools became eleven-grade rural high schools sponsored by Rosenwald Fund money, available during the early 1920s. Community support remained strong, and these schools often lasted into the 1960s, long after the Gilmer-Aikin Law made things very difficult for any rural school to survive.

The freedmen's settlements once were valued places—sometimes almost legendary places—in the consciousness of black people, and they haven't been forgotten. You can see this at reunion day, when the church parking lot fills up with cars with out-of-county and out-of-state license plates. And you can see this at County Line in Nacogdoches County, St. John's Colony in Caldwell County, and other places where some people are returning after decades to life in the countryside.

ENDNOTES

1. Our full story of Texas freedmen's settlements will be published by University of Texas Press in late 2004 and is tentatively entitled, *"Freedom Colonies": Independent Black Texans in the Time of Jim Crow.*
2. Over two hundred black landowner communities are listed and discussed in *The New Handbook of Texas,* including Cologne, County Line (as "Upshaw, Texas"), Sweet Union, St. John's Colony, Peyton Colony, Cuney, Barrett's Settlement, and other communities mentioned in this essay.
3. Michelle M. Mears, "African-American Settlement Patterns in Austin, Texas, 1865–1928." (Master's thesis, Baylor University, 2001).
4. See the "Exodus of 1879" listing in *The New Handbook.* Strange as it may seem (and it seems very strange), not a single scholarly article on freedmen's settlements had appeared in the pages of the *Southwestern Historical Quarterly* or the *Journal of Southern History* by the end of 2003.

5. Ronald D. Traylor, "Harrison Barrett: A Freedmen in Post-Civil War Texas." (Master's thesis, University of Houston, 1999).

6. See, in particular: James Smallwood, *Time of Hope, Time of Despair* (Port Washington: Kennikat Press, 1981); Barry Crouch, *The Freedmen's Bureau and Black Texans* (Austin: University of Texas Press, 1992); George P. Rawick (ed.), *The American Slave: A Composite Autobiography:* Series 2, (Vol. 2–10) *Texas Narratives* (Westport: Greenwood, 1972–1973).

7. The story of ear nailing comes from a former bondsman whose narrative appears in Rawick (ed.), *The American Slave: Texas Narratives,* p. 1581, as do other details in this paragraph.

8. Eli Coleman in Rawick (ed.), *The American Slave: Texas Narratives,* 3:851.

9. Smallwood, *Time of Hope,* 127.

10. Loren Schweninger, *Black Property Owners in the South, 1790–1915* (Urbana: University of Illinois Press, 1990), 162–65.

11. Ibid.

12. The story of these places is told by Deborah Brown and Katharine Gust, *Between the Creeks: Recollections of Northeast Texas* (Austin: Encino Press, 1976) and by Louise O'Conner in *Cryin' for Daylight: A Ranching Culture in the Texas Coastal Bend* (Austin: Wexford Publishing, 1989) and *Tales from the San'tone Bottom: A Cultural History* (Austin: Wexford Publishing, 1998).

13. John A. Caplen, "Camp Big Thicket: Life in the Piney Woods, 1887." In *Tales From the Big Thicket,* edited by Francis E. Abernethy (Austin: University of Texas Press, 1966), 112.

14. Researched by Richard Orton. The Upshaw brothers and their County Line community receives recurrent discussion in our book to be published by the University of Texas Press (see note 1).

15. As historical marker files at the Texas Historical Commission in Austin attest, philanthropic former slave owners played important roles in the origins of the Cedar Branch, Hall's Bluff, and Fodice communities of Houston County and were probably involved at other places in the county.

16. For an account of a racist attack on a freedmen's settlement and the community's self defense, see Monte Aker's chilling *Flames After Midnight: Murder, Vengeance, and the Desolation of a Texas Community* (Austin: University of Texas Press, 1999), 122–33.

Richard Orton, Austin photographer, with the Upshaw family at the opening of Orton's show, "The Upshaws of County Line"

Pat Barton frying up a mess of channel cat for the delectation of his friends

Pat Barton, Bill Clark, Gene Barbin, and the editor at the Hatchett's Ferry fish camp

18

TOBY'S HOUND

by Pat Barton (1934–2001) of Nacogdoches

⌒

[Pat Barton's exit left a large hole in our lives. We hunted and fished together, and we camped and cooked and explored the woods and water together—and we listened to Pat tell stories and generally entertain everybody within earshot. Or we listened to him deliver a long, uninterruptible lecture on some esoteric aspect of mathematics, his profession which he dearly loved. Whether he was telling stories or being arithmetically erudite, Pat was the center, the binder of our group, and we always listened.

"We" are "Wink" Barbin, Bill Clark, and the editor, and we send our fond regards and sweet remembrances to Pat with this story that he told at our Angelina River fish camp at Little Sanchez or at Hatchett's Ferry or at the log cabin on his Beech Creek farm. Pat told so many stories that we can't keep track of them, but we can still hear them in our minds. Needless to say, Pat's stories lose a large dimension when they move from the spoken word around a campfire to the computer-written word in an academic publication.

When any two of us get together, Pat is always close in our midst, grinning and talking and making us happy—all of this in the sadness of our loss.—*Abernethy*]

One time we were 'coon hunting with Mr. Rawlinson up on Beech Creek. His nephew Toby was along with us, and some country boys from Sacul had brought some dogs that we didn't know very well. I could tell Mr. Rawlinson wasn't too pleased with these unknown dogs. He was particular about running his dogs with any others that might be less cultured than his own famous well fed, highly refined 'coon dogs. With him it was a matter of pride and worthiness as well as concern that some ill-mannered 'coon dog might cause his dogs to suffer confusion or possibly even embarrassment. Sure enough, before the night was over it got them into a controversy.

About midnight we had a big fire on a sandy bank of Beech Creek, warming our hands and backs and lighting up the lower limbs of a big old beech tree towering above us. We had had a couple of good races and got two good 'coons. We were enjoying a pleasant rest by the fire and a pot of coffee when the hounds opened up again about three or four bends down the creek toward the river. Something was wrong though.

The Sacul boys' dogs struck the trail first and pretty soon Mr. Rawlinson's big dogs chimed in, but he didn't think they sounded right at all. I thought that even I could detect a certain tentativeness and lack of enthusiasm in their baying. Mr. Rawlinson immediately blamed it on the Sacul dogs. Said they had led his dogs into trailing some trashy 'possum or rabbit or deer.

They all started in to bickering about it when Toby spoke up. He claimed he had a way to find out for sure what they were running. He walked to the back of his truck and let down a pen door. Reaching in, he pulled out an old-looking dog with one ear nearly gone. We watched surprised as he knelt down and said something in the old dog's good ear. I could nearly swear I saw that old dog nod his head ever so slightly as Toby whispered to him a good fifteen seconds or longer. Toby then gathered the dog up in his arms, and walking out to the edge of the firelight, he pitched him out into the darkness toward the distant baying hounds. Watching this, everybody fell silent occupied with his own thoughts about Toby and his one-eared dog.

Half an hour later we were rinsing out the coffee pot and kicking dirt on the fire when Toby's dog came trotting back in amongst us. Toby dropped down on one knee and the old dog stuck his muzzle right up in Toby's ear. They carried on this whispering act for half a minute or so, this time Toby doing the nodding. Finally Toby arose, looking grave.

One of the Sacul boys with profound anguish in expression and voice blurted out, "Well? WELL? What in the HAIL did he say?"

IV

THE FAMILY SAGA

(Continued)

LINDA M. ROACH

19

PASSING THE LIGHT: HOW FAMILY STORIES SHAPE OUR LIVES

by Jan Epton Seale of McAllen

Several short stories: What do they have in common?

1) A neighbor's grandchild came over to play in the yard. Mark is a beautiful fair child with light blue eyes and pale blond hair. When Mark fell and skinned his knee, he began to cry piteously. I went over to inspect the damage. After Mark showed me the nearly invisible wound, he stopped crying, looked up at me with those gorgeous pale blue peepers, and said, "I'm really delicate, you know."

2) Whenever a friend combs her hair, she says her mother's voice just at her shoulder murmurs, "You can't make a silk purse out of sow's ear." My friend says she's learned to say back, "Exactly what *can* be made out of sow's ear?" Or, "But I never wanted to be a silk purse!"

3) Sara is six. At bedtime, she insists on cleaning the lint from between her toes. Her mother says, "That's your Aunt Nancy exactly—picky, picky, picky."

These stories illustrate the power of family stories over us, even small stories—not only narratives, but admonitions, observations, adages, comparisons, accusations, and compliments.

Russell Baker, in his award-winning autobiography *Growing Up,* reminisces about this force in his young life:

> If my homework was done, I could sit with them
> and listen until ten o-clock struck. . . . I loved the
> sense of family warmth that radiated through those
> long kitchen nights of talk. . . . Usually I listened
> uncritically, for around that table, under the
> unshaded light bulb, I was receiving an education
> in the world and how to think about it. What I
> absorbed most deeply was not information but atti-
> tudes, ways of looking at the world that were to
> stay with me for many years.[1]

We are always hungry for stories because we are trying to
figure out our lives. Have others been in this or that situation?
What, then, have they done about it? We are shaping ourselves as
we live our lives, and we can never get too much information.

Certainly there are family stories told for pure entertainment
value, but family stories in particular are inordinately useful. They
teach the values, strengths, weaknesses, and expectations of those
listening to them. And we pick and choose from the stories as our
needs signal.

We are born bearing stories over which we have little control:
how we were wanted or unwanted, how hard our birth was, what
Uncle John said when he saw us. And we are added to the family
lore. What we do in childhood becomes stories. All this, while we
in turn begin to absorb the information presented to us that we
may not even conceive of as "story," but simply as "the way things
are"—events in our neighborhood, our parents complaining about
or praising at the supper table, the daily rituals of eating, sleeping,
and working.

As we grow, we begin to act as filters for the stories we hear.
We reflect on what we have heard, and we start to develop the ability to choose the stories we like, those we want to be part of, and
to reject or simply not hear those we dislike.

A writing student of mine told a family story she had learned
only recently. It was a tragic tale of how her great-grandfather had

shot and killed her great-grandmother. The woman died in the arms of her daughter, my student's grandmother. Ginger added at the end, "My grandmother was a good writer. She wrote all this down, describing it in detail with a lot of drama. My mother gave me the papers when I was home last time."

Ginger, the young, talented writer in my class, might choose to remember the story for the fact that she had in her veins the blood of a murderer. Or, she could take from the story the fact that she is the descendant of a writer. She too might fulfill her dream of being a writer, partly because she chooses that genetic boost.

Family stories have a descriptive and a prescriptive nature. Thus, we may conclude that 1) we are living our lives out to a large degree by the formulas of our family stories; they shape us powerfully and always will; and 2) the stories we tell, and the way we tell them, can powerfully shape those who come after us. Or, as Daniel Taylor, in *The Healing Power of Stories,* puts it, "There is an ongoing tension between living as our stories dictate as opposed to dictating the stories we live."[2]

The stories of our family's background and origin act as history lessons and guides to the nature of particular families. Family origin stories serve to bind us together: "That's the McKinneys for you;" "You can't help it if you're a Bernbaum;" "We Gomezes don't do it that way." They give us a sense of belonging, however many warts and freckles our family has, and they make sure we huddle together and move forward. In other words, family origin stories support Darwin's notions of survival of the fittest. Did your family survive through skilled mercantilism, hardscrabble farming, a fabulous stroke of luck, or sheer grit and determination? What stories do you put forward to support one or the other of these theories?

Nearly every family origin story will contain a famous ancestor. My friend in the Rio Grande Valley, from eight generations of Hispanics living north of the Rio Grande, tells me he is directly descended from Cortés. In his case, he has impressive documentation to substantiate it. Students in my autobiography classes volunteer famous ancestor stories right and left. "They say we're from the family of Marie Antoinette." "My great-great-great grandfather invented cricket." "Pancho Villa had several wives you know, and who knows how many lovers; . . . I'm from one of those relationships."

We like to claim kinship to presidents, kings and queens, notorious gangsters, inventors, and famous entertainers. My female cousins and I, when we want to claim a little wildness, like to remember that Sally Rand, the famous burlesque entertainer, was our grandmother's second cousin.

We may smile as we think of these stories that connect our families with greatness of some sort, but the stories function usefully as well. They serve to tell our young, "You too can be great. After all, you inherited the same traits."

Family stories are so powerful that adopted children often adopt the history of their adopted family. No matter that there is no bloodline to follow. It's as if the spiritual and emotional bloodlines of adopted child and adopted family have been fused. Studies have shown that college students who knew their origins, or who had origins to claim, generally did better in life, were happier and more successful.

And wives often know their husbands' family stories better than the husbands do. I have wives in my writing classes who enroll in order to tell their husbands' family stories. This may be a natural talent of women, to be the story-keepers, the scrapbook makers, the connectors in the family. But it may also be a genetic predisposition by the mother to tie in to what is most interesting, relevant, and strong in a family whose children are at least half of that clan.

Another kind of origin story is the birthing story. What children are told about their births may powerfully influence their self-concept. Elizabeth Stone, in her book *Black Sheep & Kissing Cousins,* gives a very full discussion of the influence of birthing stories on the lives of those who are told the story of when they appeared in the world.[3]

A few birth stories seem to be the defining moment in the psyche of a person's life. Years ago, a student in an autobiography class wrote of her birth in a farmhouse on the Kansas prairie about 1930. Here is her account:

> I was brought forth with instruments and handed to Grandma. "Put it aside; it won't live."
>
> Grandma didn't. She took charge of me. She stayed with us for days.
>
> The next day Dr. Wilson drove 24 miles to see Mother and noted, "It's still alive."
>
> Grandma asked for a formula.
>
> Dr. Wilson took her aside and said, "No, No, Mrs. Hanks; it won't be here tomorrow."
>
> Grandma, determined I not die of starvation, soaked bread in water, dipped a clean cloth in this water and squeezed drop after drop into my mouth.
>
> The next day Dr. Wilson looked at me and shook his head. He gave Grandma a formula and medicine dropper. He cautioned everyone not to get their hopes up for if I did live, I probably wouldn't be "right."
>
> The instruments that saved Mother had left their mark on me. My head was misshapen, an ear nearly off, one eye almost out of the socket, the lid was torn on the other one. My mouth was pulled to one side, the top lip twisted, my jaw was crushed, and I was tongue-tied and couldn't cry. I had five deep gashes in my head. One arm was broken at the elbow.

Can you imagine the bonding between the child and the grandmother, and how the story of her birth has informed her entire life? Every writing she did in the class after this initial one thanked God in astonishment and wonder for her existence. The grandmother, both by her actions and her sharing the story, truly passed the light.

What about family stories on the subject of love? Do you approve of falling in love at first sight, or will a love that is supposed to last forever be one that carefully grows from perhaps a modest friendship, to a deepening appreciation for the traits of the beloved? And then, does that love need a long courtship, or may the star-struck lovers immediately proceed to the justice of the peace? The stories of circumspect courting, virgins at the altar, and vows of fidelity are often now heard and viewed as merely quaint by young people today.

My maternal grandmother, with whom I was very close, gave me a great gift. She passed the light of her courtship and wedding on to me in her story of it. This story is incorporated in a longer poem I wrote about her life, a poem which continues to be warmly received, no doubt because people are reminded of their own favorite grandparent. Below is an excerpt dealing with her and my grandfather's wedding night:

> I see her great astounding Victorian body—
> six-foot-tall bride with a sober hand
> resting on Grandfather's sitting-down shoulder.
> The wedding—a Sunday night after revival meeting,
> a trip 3 miles in a buggy home to her house,
> a sister going upstairs with her
> to help with a white nightgown,
> wide pink satin ribbon woven down the front,
> how she trembled when her sister left her
> at the top of the stairs,
> how she righted herself with a small smile
> when Grandpa, ascending, said,
> "Why Pearl, you look so pretty!"
> (She wouldn't tell me more.
> He had been dead fifteen years that afternoon.)[4]

Divorce may be treated casually in one family and seriously in another. For young people still marrying—and the Sunday social pages show that the practice has not died away by a long shot—they may reflect on their families, perhaps even the example of their parents staying together, and be genuinely dismayed by the prospects of divorcing. Others agree that weddings are kind of fun, and if "things" don't work out, they'll not get too uptight about "splitting the blanket," which term, they may or may not use, depending upon their family stories. "First comes love, then comes marriage, then comes Susie pushing a baby carriage!" Have you heard it lately? Will the girls in your family be learning it as a jump rope chant, and as the order of love?

Importantly shaping some families are stories of fortune and money. Did Uncle Minyard make his money honestly? If he didn't, is honesty the reason he lost it all? Why did our side of the family not enjoy the same affluence as the other? Was it plain bad luck, or bad judgment, or foolish living? When it comes to family stories, everything depends more on the uses made of them than on their plots or consequences.

Concerning politics, did your family help elect the successful and popular leaders of the community and nation? Or did your ancestors show their freedom by organizing protests or supporting unpopular candidates and causes? Was there a renegade Democrat or Republican in the family, one who was ostracized or beleaguered on family occasions?

And how do your family stories reflect attitudes toward health and illness? Have you been told so many times about your perilous childhood illnesses that even now, you hesitate to join an exercise class? Do you stay on your feet, regardless of how you feel, because your grandfather milked the cows in wintertime even though he had influenza? Do you let your child stay home from school with a stomachache, or do you remember that that was your ploy for skipping school, and thus take a tough approach to his infirmity?

Almost every family has one or two neurotic people who have made the stories of their health the focal point of their lives. Often these people live out their lives savoring the effects of a childhood illness or accident. And their healthy siblings may not forget the parental neglect resulting from the attention the sick child received.

With its savage treatment in the past, mental illness often lingers in the shadows of family stories. Taboo stories of sanitarium treatment, nervous breakdown, shock treatment, and bizarre behavior—these narratives, if they ever surface, often come as a surprise to a family. Nevertheless, they're important to know, in light of what has been discovered both about the hereditary nature of some of these mental disorders, and their ready detection and effective treatment through new means.

Sometimes suicide is a part of mental illness, but by no means always. Is there a family attitude toward suicide? Perhaps it is that one should not consider it under any circumstances. Or are there frequent instances of it to be pondered, with such examples not to be replicated?

What stories of anger and violence come from your family? Was anger expressed in verbal or physical abuse? Or was it by pouting, sarcasm, and coldness? Was your great-grandmother redheaded and temperamental? Did you children tiptoe around, seek out private hidey-holes to avoid the wrath of your mother or father? How were family arguments solved?

These traditions will in part determine how you handle anger. If you loathed your father's anger, you may have vowed not to be that way. If you idolized him, thinking he could do no wrong, such as did Frank McCourt in *Angela's Ashes,* you may feel your own explosive anger is justified in adulthood.

Does your family lore contain stories of race or racism? More oppressed peoples will likely have more stories centering on race— stories that shore up the self-esteem of family members by touting the pre-eminent qualities of the race, as in the writing of Zora Neale Hurston, or by showing how family members were coura- geous in the face of racism.

A story about race can take whatever turn the teller desires it to take. For example, my friend Alonzo told a story about attending a relative's funeral in San Antonio, taking along his sister and aunt. The deceased was of mixed parentage. At the meal following the funeral, the Anglos arrived first and clustered at one table while the Hispanics, of which Alonzo, his sister and aunt were a part, took the remaining table when they arrived. The Anglos did not seek to mingle with the out-of-towner Hispanics. My friend thought nothing of it, enjoying the company of those at his table, but he reported that his sister and aunt interpreted the seating arrangement as a racial slight and discussed it all the way home.

Are men's and women's roles quite set in your family, or are they flexible? In one family, the script is written that by the boy's tenth birthday, he will have gone hunting or fishing with the men. Why? "Because we've always done it that way."

If we observe the openness of gay and lesbian identity today, perhaps we should also look at our own family stories, where homosexuals existed gamely under such genteel names as "gay bachelors," "maiden ladies," "old maids," "dandies," and "fops." Maybe it is not that we have more homosexuals now, but that our family stories have quit hiding, either by taboo, or semantically, their normal presence in the population. What is the message of your family to the gay members of it? Are they ostracized, or appreciated for their often very valuable contributions to society?

Daniel Taylor, in *The Healing Power of Stories,* observes, "Middle age makes storytellers of us all."[5] While we are alive, Taylor says, we have the opportunity to be both the characters in the stories and the co-creators. Gratefully, there has been in the last thirty years or so, a revival of interest in memoirs, in writing autobiographies, and lately, in diversifying from the written page into storytelling on audio and videotapes. Now thousands of older people are recording their memoirs in some way, many at the request of their children.

Stories of the older and old have value because these folk have lived through so much. Their ways have been tried and found true. Or tried, and found wanting, with the consequences. The old are eager to tell their stories. In every age there have been remarkable stories from the old, but I think the stories of our old today are particularly interesting and needful, in part, because of the fantastic changes that have taken place during the past century, the time of their lives.

Robert Akeret, in his book *Family Tales, Family Wisdom*, suggests seven areas where elder stories are particularly worthwhile for families:

1. locating meaning and appreciating mystery of life
   (*"I feel I was placed on this earth to. . . ."*)
2. understanding life forces
   (*"I had no way of knowing what was ahead for me."*)
3. personal values, esp. those over an entire lifetime
   (*"The orange in the toe of my Christmas stocking was the best gift of all."*)
4. dealing with life-changes: living high and low, turning points, crises
   (*"We lost everything we had, including the cow and mules."*)
5. personal identity and social connectedness; self-knowledge
   (*"It was at that brush arbor revival meeting that I knew . . ."*)
6. life and death consciousness; cycle of life
   (*"I have outlived all but two of my seven children."*)
7. roots and traditions, origins, customs, symbols
   (*"My father always said . . .)*[6]

Of these important messages about life, Taylor says that "Writers and storytellers are responsible not to poison the lives of their hearers with toxic stories. If stories have the power to enlighten and heal us, they must, by definition, have the power to mislead and harm us. Nazi Germany told itself powerful and compelling stories, but they were stories of death. If our storytellers fail us, the people perish."[7]

In telling stories from your past, remember that the past, as well as the future, is subject to change. Your interpretation of what happened in your life will be changing as long as you live.

From time to time, re-examine your stories. Do you see an event in a different light now? Do you have new information? Has a new meaning occurred to you? Have you had a change in attitude toward money, religion, politics, or gender definition?

A student in one of my classes wrote about a time when she and her new husband were saying goodbye to his parents when her husband had to report for active duty in WW II. At the time, the young bride and her mother-in-law were on chilly terms. As they said goodbye, the older woman's mouth twisted into a bitter shape, and for years, the daughter-in-law assumed the facial gesture was a goodbye smirk at her. Only recently had she come to the realization that the older woman's face was contorted in grief and love for her son who might never return.

Telling our stories and allowing others to tell theirs may heal us. Our stories connect us with others: we share and feel ourselves a part of the ancient circle around the campfire. Without our stories, we are patternless. The world needs our stories to remind them of values and choices, to explain experience, to show wonder, the power of free will, and, as Joseph Campbell put it, simply "the rapture of being alive." We achieve a kind of balance when we tell our stories and when we receive those of others. By articulating in words the events, thoughts, actions, meditations, interpretations of our pasts, we come to understand our present, and we benefit the future of those we love.

The Kiowa writer Scott Momaday tells of being taken as a small boy by his father to visit his great-grandmother. She took Scott's hands in hers and wept softly as she pronounced her blessing on him. Momaday writes of the incident, "That was a wonderful and beautiful thing that happened in my life. There, on that warm, distant afternoon: an old woman and a child, holding hands across the generations. There is great good in such a remembrance; I cannot imagine that it might have been lost upon me."[8]

So let us pass the stories of light, not the darkness of toxic stories, by telling our stories often and well. Let us trust that our stories will fall on ears that can take them and shape them for the best use in furthering the human spirit.

Let us hold hands across the generations.

ENDNOTES:

1. Quoted by Elizabeth Stone in *Black Sheep & Kissing Cousins* (New York: Times Books/Random House, 1988), 109.
2. Daniel Taylor, *The Healing Power of Stories* (New York: Doubleday, 1996), p.76.
3. *Black Sheep & Kissing Cousins,* Chapter 8, "Legacies."
4. "Pearl Bell Pittman," first published in *Southwest,* eds. Karl and Jan Kopp (Albuquerque: Red Earth Press, 1977), 97–99.
5. Ibid., p. vii.
6. Robert U. Akeret, *Family Tales, Family Wisdom* (New York: William Morrow, 1991), 39.
7. Taylor, 119.
8. N. Scott Momaday, *The Names: A Memoir* (New York: Harper, 1976), 65, as quoted in Taylor, 155–56.

OTHER WORKS CONSULTED

Benedek, Emily. "Looking for a Story to Tell." *Utne Reader.* September/ October 1997, 49-51ff.

Henderson, Sallirae. *A Life Complete.* New York: Scribner, 2000.

Leibovitz, Maury and Linda Solomon, eds. *Legacies.* New York: Herper-Perennial, 1993.

Linn, Denise. *Sacred Legacies.* New York: Ballantine Wellspring, 1998.

Kearl, Michael C. "An Investigation into Collective Historical Knowledge and Implication of its Ignorance." *Texas Journal* 23 (Texas Council on the Humanities).

Martz, Sandra and Shirley Coe. *Generation to Generation.* Watsonville, CA: Papier-Mache Press, 1998.

Pickett, Keri. *Love in the 90s.* New York: Warner Books, 1995.

Pipher, Mary. *Another Country.* New York: Riverhead Books, 1999.

Polster, Erving. *Every Person's Life Is Worth A Novel.* New York: W. W. Norton, 1987.

Sander, Scott Russell. "Most Human Art: Ten reasons why we'll always need a good story." From *Georgia Review,* reprinted in *Utne Reader,* September/October 1997, 54–56.

Stillman, Peter R. *Families Writing.* Cincinnati, OH: Writer's Digest Books, 1989.

Vandagriff, G. G. *Voices in Your Blood.* Kansas City: Andrew and McMeel, 1993.

Claude Ellis and Violet McCormick, who met the risk and challenge of settling Scurry County and survived by perseverance and hard work, 1930

20

TWO TALES OF MY FAMILY:
TWO TALES OF WHO I AM

by Charlie McCormick of Radnor, Pennsylvania

The wind can blow across West Texas at speeds of up to fifty miles per hour as it rushes across the empty space to wherever the wind must go. As it makes its hurried journey, the wind scatters dust, tumbleweeds, and the occasional traveler throughout the landscape. Every now and then, though, a cactus or ravine will catch and hold an object from this blowing stream, and settle its capture into the thin, West Texas topsoil. At least, I thought, that is what must have caused my grandfather to root here.

I knew that Grandad—as we kids called him—had started in the North, in Oklahoma, and ended up in no place in particular. The place had a name, Snyder, but not much more than that. It was just a forgotten little county seat in a forgotten little county that must have seemed, rather than pleasant, a little more tolerable than where my granddad had come from. Why he left home at all remains a mystery, as must every young man's journey from "there" to "here," but he found a "here" in West Texas that appealed to him for some reason so he stayed awhile. Make no mistake, the land had and has its own charm; it's not easy to see, but it's there. It is found in the soft hills and rough animals, in the white cliffs of the Caprock, and in the sound of the wind as it whips through the mesquite. Its charm is found in its dare of vast spaces. Grandad took this dare, and one day, from either desire or necessity, he decided to stay. In fact, he did one better than just staying: he thrived—which shouldn't be confused with getting rich or becoming powerful. It means simply that he grew roots and found in the land enough sustenance to survive. To be fair, he found more than enough; it was enough even to send for his girl, my Granny, back home in Oklahoma. They married when she arrived in Scurry County. Her new home must have appeared a little bleak at first, but like most women living in Texas in the early 1900s, she proved to be as tough as the land into which she had been transplanted. And my granddad's flower, Violet, thrived too.

Together, Granny and Grandad made life in a hard land bearable and even beautiful. She gave birth to and tended six children while taking care of the rural grocery store and gas station my grandparents opened, and he worked as the iceman in the area, making deliveries to those who needed the cold. They must have dreamed of more, though. For awhile, it must have seemed if their dreams were to be forever eclipsed by bawling babies, fighting brothers, and a truck that was too old to run. In time, however, the babies grew up, the brothers quit fighting (at least each other), and-even though the truck still wouldn't run-the grocery store's business began to pick up, for civilization and opportunity were getting closer. So were my grandparents' dreams.

The boom in their small grocery store and gas station business was attributable to one of the most significant discoveries in the Big Country: the Scurry County Canyon Reef Oil Field. As far as oilfields go, it turned out to be one of the great ones, making this once quiet little county the largest oil-producing county in the nation. With the discovery of this subterranean Aladdin's lamp came the wildcatters and treasure-hunters who fixed their eyes on a filthy prize they called oil. These seekers of wealth came from near and far, often finding that which they sought, and their fortune revived the hopes and dreams of those like Grandad who were already in the area and were now susceptible to the lure of success, given the sudden surge in their local business traffic.

Unfortunately, drilling for oil was (and remains) expensive. My grandparents and their neighbors were not able promoters nor had they friends with the money to finance a drilling operation, but they had always found opportunity to save what little money they could earn. (Whatever else Scurry County might have offered, its cultural, artistic, and stylistic activities were not going to break a man or woman.) So, reaching deep into the tin can they kept at the back of the top shelf or searching into the mattress they slept on every night, my grandparents and their neighbors pulled out their life-savings and debated whether they should risk it all and possibly strike, or risk it all and have to start again from scratch.

My grandparents took the risk and struck, and their lives were changed forever.

I know that their decision to risk it all changed my life too. This defining moment in my grandparents' life forged my legacy and sent my life down a path it otherwise would not have traveled. Had they decided not to take a chance, I would not have had the opportunities I did. I might have had worthwhile experiences anyway, but they would not be the same ones that I have come to assume are the experiences that have made me who I am.

It took me a long while to make the connections between the life I was living and the risks my grandparents took, and until I did, I never spoke of it at length with my father. Not too long ago, however, as I was thinking over these things, I asked my father to tell me the story of his parents, and I listened closely to what he said. This is what he told me:

> Daddy left Oklahoma with his family when he was a young man, and they moved to New Mexico. It wasn't long before they starved out there and began the long trip back home. On their way back, they stopped in Scurry County and leased a farm that didn't do all too well. But Daddy decided to stay anyway. He got lonely out here and sent for your Granny who was still back in Willis, Oklahoma. They leased a farm out west of town and did some dry-land cotton farming, but that never really did too good. Let's see—I guess Daddy's break came

when he got a chance to buy a grocery store and filling station, the one that use to be out on Highway 180. He left Mother in charge of that and us boys while he sold what everyone needed—ice and kerosene.

Daddy was able to lease a farm in the early part of the boom that did pretty good—at least good enough for him to be able to move his filling station to town and begin his own small business. He owned a little land about that time as well that he got some offers to drill on, but instead of selling the land's mineral rights to the drillers, he kept them. Most everybody else sold their mineral rights because it was a quick way to make a buck back then. Although his tactic didn't make him rich, he got about eight percent on the oil produced. And that was only because he was in the pay. A waitress that worked for him at his truck stop had some land right next to his, and she always told us that if she would have been in the pay too, she wouldn't have to be working as a waitress. It kind of made us all feel a little funny about going in there.

By the mid to late '40s, Daddy had made a real business of his filling station. He just seemed able to tend to his business like other people tended to their person. For a man that could hardly read, he could sure make a decision. Working hard was just part of who he was. Daddy retired by the mid '60s.

Not quite the story I was expecting. In fact, I was disenchanted with my family's story after I heard my father's rendering of it. I wanted my version's claim to Granny and Grandad's risk, challenge, and adventure, not his tale's emphasis on perseverance and hard work. I was also disappointed by my seeming lack of skill in remembering my family's tale. How often had I heard a relative tell this story? Why did I remember it differently from my father? I wanted to know the truth of my grandparents' lives because I felt my own life was implicated in that truth.

I know that the disenchantment I felt at hearing—really listening to—my father's tale of the family is selfish because it does not take into account that my father also shares a stake in our family saga, and he tells the tale, therefore, as authentically as he can. His version might not be any more factual than my version, but its authenticity obviously seems genuine to him.

But if we cannot even agree as to what the story is, why bother telling a family tale? If we are doomed to inaccuracies and untruths, then why not simply tell folktales and fairytales all the time with richly developed characters in exotic locales? Here is my answer: Something has been passed from my grandparents to me. It is partly biological, but not entirely a matter of genes. My potential—as well as the color of my eyes—is a gift, an inheritance, from my ancestors. When I can name this gift, when I can claim it by giving it a narrative form, the potential becomes mine. If I can name my grandparents' risk, if I can own their courage through the stories I tell, then that courage is part of my inheritance as their heir. It is part of who I am. My father's story about the family is different from my own because I know now that my father has claimed his gift from them too. If his parents could persevere and achieve a lifetime of hard work, then my father must have the potential to do the same.

My grandparents' gifts of their life stories are of the most selfless kind. They allow me—as well as my father—to manipulate their lives. With that sort of power and personal investment, I would do well to be cautious. Perhaps that is why I did not want to get their story wrong. I did not want to abuse my grandparents' selflessness. I am less concerned about imprecision now, though. Their gift was the characters, the images, and the plots. They never promised the themes. And they certainly never promised to become the brand new characters I created who wear their faces and answer to their names. That is the nature of their gift. And it gives me a peace of mind to know it.

This is also the nature of their gift to me: it does not reach a conclusion. Today, I can only see and hear part of the story—a story of risk, adventure, and success. Tomorrow, a new set of circumstances in my life and the need for a new identity may find me telling the story my father told of his parents' sorrow, defeat, quietness, perseverance, and simplicity. This will not make the former tale of my grandparents false nor give a more accurate account of my grandparents' history, but it will most certainly reflect a change in myself—a young man who is just beginning to see the extent to which he resembles his father and grandfather.

❧

The wind can blow across West Texas with gusts of up to fifty miles per hour. When it does, it collects the stories that we have released from the cages of our mouths and hearts and lifts them up out of our control, spins them around, mixes them up, arranges them anew, and lets them float gently back to the ground. When we stumble across them (as we always do), we pick up and pocket that arrangement which suits us best at the moment, which we consider, perhaps, the most attractive. Whether or not the facts are correct is of secondary importance. What is primary is the ability to re-think and re-tell a resonant story of where we came from and, therefore, who we are and who we might be. After all, our best truths have always been fiction. But we folklorists have known that for a long time.

CORRER DEL PAISANO

SLAVES
by Mary Ann Long Ferguson

I must stop long enough to tell this story before going on with our new home. In Mississippi I had had only a personal maid that my father had given me when I married and later a nurse maid for the children, but Mr. Ferguson did not believe in owning slaves so they were left behind. Mr. Ferguson had gone to a slave auction with his father once when just a child. His father had just bought a slave woman and her teen-aged daughter was the next to go on the block. A man who was dreaded by all the slaves was bidding on her, and the mother fell at Grandpa Ferguson's feet begging him to buy her daughter so she wouldn't be mistreated. He did buy her, although he had to give $1,000.00 for her, but this scene lived on in Mr. Ferguson's heart, and he vowed never to own a slave. Many people back in Mississippi had already freed their slaves before we left there because they were beginning to see the wrong in it.

Ralph Ramos, radio and television personality, professional football and hockey player, wrestler, U. S. Marine in WWII, and a student of East Texas history and folklore

21

RED KELLY'S GRANDMOTHER

by Ralph Ramos of the *Beaumont Enterprise*
and *Beaumont Journal*

Copyright 1975, The Beaumont Enterprise.
Reprinted with permission.

~ ~

[I came across this old May 10, 1973, *Beaumont Enterprise* clipping when I was cleaning out my files. I had kept it because I knew Red Kelly casually, and the story by photographer-journalist Ralph Ramos included other folks that I knew about. And I knew and admired and read Ralph Ramos and kept a lot of his clippings. Ralph got in the newspaper business when he was a kid selling papers in Ohio in the 19-teens and stayed in it and radio and television all of his life. During the Thirties and Forties he also played professional football and hockey (Texas Ice Rangers), was a pro wrestler, was the Buckskin Rodeo manager, and was a U. S. Marine during World War II. Ralph had lived long and intensely when I met him in the late 1950s, and we came together in our interest in East Texas history and folklore. I admired Ralph as a man and as a mover among and writer about the people of East Texas. Yankee though he was, he loved the people and the stories of East Texas. So I do this in remembrance of him.—*Abernethy*]

On the other side of Red Kelly's family were the Martins.

His grandmother, Mary Martin, was left a widow with five daughters and a son on their plantation-like place in northern Tyler County's Billum's Creek area. She was quick to get a reputation, as one oldtimer put it, "having more sense than any other woman in Tyler County."

When her husband died he left her 25 or 30 head of cattle. A fellow named George Kirkwood came by to buy. Mrs. Martin told Kirkwood to get her the agreed amount of money and he'd get the cattle. A few days later Kirkwood returned proffering a check. Mrs. Martin's response, "No checks, bring me money." Kirkwood retreated and returned with money.

Her reputation for sharpness continued to grow into legend. She sold a season's shearing of wool to a neighborhood minister who conveniently forgot to pay.

One day, sitting in his church, Mrs. Martin listened to his fiery preaching on salvation. He waved his arms and shouted over his congregation, "What must I do to be saved?"

Mrs. Martin calmly rose from her pew and shouted back, "Pay me for my wool!"

And, there was the time when a man stopped at her kitchen door pleading for a bite to eat. "Certainly," said Mrs. Martin, "just chop me some firewood first."

"I'm too weak to cut wood."

So, Mrs. Martin fed him and said, "Now cut the wood."

"Now," said the moocher, "I'm too tired and sleepy. I need to rest a minute then I'll get up and go."

Mrs. Martin reached over behind the kitchen door and came up with a rifle which she aimed at the moocher, saying in a tone there was no mistaking, "Now you cut that fire wood or I'll shoot you right between the galluses."

[Grandma Martin got her wood cut.]

Copyright 1975, The Beaumont Enterprise. Reprinted with permission.

CORRER DEL PAISANO

BURYING PA GARDNER

Samuel Greenwood Gardner died in 1931 in Banty, Bryan County, Oklahoma. His grandsons, Greenwood Gardner of Oklahoma City and John Gardner of Denison, tell the story in an interview in July 20, 2000.

Pa stepped into the creek behind the house when he was going after the cows. He got wet up to his knees but kept going to bring the cows up to the house. The next evening he got a cold and it went into pneumonia and he died.

To the left of the breezeway in front is the bedroom in which Pa Gardner died. It was cold and Granny had piles of quilts in the room for Pa. Granny came out of the room one morning and said, "He's gone." Then she went to the kitchen where she had cooked him a pan of oatmeal. She took it to the back yard and scraped it onto the ground for the chickens.

"I was real tight with Pa," said John. "I was about three and he would give me a penny when he had one. I was holding his hand when he died."

The day after Pa died wagons and buggies were parked in front of the house to go to take Pa to the cemetery. Greenwood didn't get to go to the funeral. So from the porch he watched them drive off in a line to go to bury Pa.

John went to the funeral. They put Pa in a wagon, in a wooden box, that maybe Daddy [Leroy Gardner, Pa's son] had made. John rode in a buggy and the mud was so bad that the man driving the buggy had to get off to pull the horse along and to lighten the load. John got to stay on the buggy because he was little. Trip Fuller came behind the wagons and played the banjo part of the way, off and on, to the cemetery.

A FAMILY FULL OF SCARS

by George Ewing of Abilene

My mother's poverty after her father died never wiped out her Old South aristocratic tastes, but when I was two or three, the meager evidence we had of this heritage was her one sterling silver baby spoon and a many-faceted sugar bowl.

"That's *cut* glass!" she used to explain, but the only significance of *cut* that I got from that was the half-inch white scar in the middle of my brother Henry's thick black left eyebrow. I knew the story by heart. When he was just a little fellow tugging at the skirt of our pretty teenage cousin Ruth, she had accidentally knocked the sugar bowl off the icebox, and it bounced off Henry's upturned face, splitting the eyebrow to the bone and providing an identifying feature he would wear to the grave.

Henry's lifestyle seemed to attract injury. After he started to school in Bishop, Texas, at recess one day when he was running full speed with his eyes on the boys chasing him, he glanced ahead and saw his path cluttered with little girls. Unable to stop—and certainly unwilling to hurt the friends of Mardelle McKenzie, whom he loved with all his heart—he turned and dived headfirst into a brick wall. He was sent home with a lump in the center of his forehead the size of half an orange and both eyes swelled shut. Those eyes turned so black he was the envy of all the tough boys of the neighborhood, and the knot never disappeared completely from his forehead.

When Henry was about ten or eleven and we had moved to Edinburg, we became Tarzan fans. The Lower Rio Grande Valley didn't produce the type of vines we saw Tarzan swinging on, but we could make do with a twenty-foot tow chain hung on a big mesquite out near the garage. We were aping it up pretty well until Henry decided that if I would swing the chain up toward him, he could dive from the garage roof and grab it. The plan worked pretty well until he discovered he couldn't hang on without sliding down the chain. His Tarzan yell turned to a howl when the big hook on the end stopped his slide—but ripped a three-inch gash in his belly from crotch to abdomen. We got him unhooked with no trouble, but when he ran into the back door, holding himself together with both hands, he realized that he could not possibly expose himself to the two church-going women friends of my mother who were sewing in the livingroom.

"Mother! Come here," he called from the diningroom.

"What is it, Henry? Come in here." She was obviously too busy to get up.

"I can't! You come in here!"

"Well, why can't you?" Mother was getting a little annoyed.

"Well, I hurt myself! I can't come!"

This brought her to her feet and into the diningroom, where one glance at the blood running through his fingers and down his leg triggered one of the screams she was famous for, and that brought the other two, shouting advice, to the side of the blushing boy. It all worked out in his favor, though; he was rushed to the doctor, had "stitches taken" to get his parts back together, and got to lie up in bed glorying in the attention he got from visiting and envious friends. None of us had ever had stitches. In later years, however, we used to keep each other in stitches telling of Henry and the screaming woman.

Some months later, Henry was walking in his Sunday, slick, leather-soled shoes on the top of a church building Pappy's crew had just finished framing, when his feet slipped, and he bounced through three sets of two-by-ten ceiling joists on the way to the ground thirty feet below. He came crawling out from under the building, flat on his stomach, just as Pappy and one of the elders came around the corner engaging in a serious discussion of the blueprints. Henry looked up at the astonished men, gave one long groan, and passed out. Since no one had seen him fall, no one knew what was going on. He came to before the hastily called doctor finished examining him, and was diagnosed as having his breath knocked out and a few ribs cracked. Once more he and his taped-up chest were the center of attention for a few days.

When he was sixteen, and a bunch of us were going swimming one night, Henry, who had never swum in this big canal before, beat us all to the bank and dove in, putting a long gash in his head on a pipe a few feet under the water. But I guess that wasn't any dumber than the time when, a few years later, just before he flunked out at Texas A&M (is that possible?), one night he was cruising the streets with a bunch of other Aggies in an old jalopy. He was on the running board when he decided he would show off by climbing around to the other side of the car by way of the rear bumpers, only to discover, too late, that these had been removed. He stepped into the dark spot where the bumper should have been—and ended up sitting in the street, unable to walk with two sprained ankles.

Henry would have known that the dumb-injury family stories didn't start with him. When he was a pre-schooler he was visiting kinfolks in Cleburne and was fascinated by the way Uncle Jack Jordan, a groceryman, could deftly tie knots in the twine string around the brown paper bags used for everything in those days—even though Uncle Jack had only a thumb and one finger on his right hand!

"What happened to your fingers, Uncle Jack?" little Henry asked.

"Wore them off playing the Jew's harp." This was Uncle Jack's usual reply, but now and then he would tell the real story. As a boy, he and his brother were playing with an ax at the chopping block. Jack would lay his hand on the block; his brother would swing the ax, stopping it just above the hand; Jack would jerk his hand away, and the brother would complete the swing.

"After we did it a few times," Uncle Jack said, "I thought, 'He always stops before he hits me,' and he thought, 'He always moves his hand,' so the next time he didn't stop, and I didn't move." I never heard what they did with the three fingers on the chopping block.

Maybe Henry just inherited a careless-injury tendency. Pappy told us of the time when he was a boy leaning on his .22 rifle, with the muzzle on the top of his shoe, when the gun discharged and blew off his big toe. One of my aunts authenticated this story and added that his mother sewed it back on with her needle and some cotton thread. Then too, my grandpa, visiting us about the time I was born (that would make him about seventy-one) in Robstown, during a flood when the cow pen was under two feet of water, offered to tend to the animal. He didn't think about how many boards with nails in them might be lying around a building contractor's house. When he got back to the porch, he had a short plank on each water-and-manure-soaked shoe, held on by sixteen-penny nails completely through each foot. After he managed to get them pulled out and washed his feet, since this was in the days before tetanus, Grandpa avoided "lockjaw" by soaking both feet in coal oil from the barrel on the back porch that held the fuel for our up-to-the-minute stove.

We would not have expected Grandpa to go to a doctor. He had lost his faith in that profession some thirty years earlier when he was having some earaches, went to a physician who poked around in his ears and left him stone deaf for the remaining fifty years of his life. This wasn't the only discouraging medical experience in my family's story file. Uncle Robert told me of the time he came from Cleburne to Robstown to build a house for a rancher near there. When he checked into the hotel, he had a sore throat and asked that the local doctor be called to prescribe something for it. Without so much as washing his hands, the doctor began to probe with his fingers and a flat stick in Uncle Robert's mouth, discussing, as he did so, a call to a Hispanic's house he had just made.

"Why, that girl's got smallpox. Got *all* the symptoms! Textbook case—but they wouldn't believe me!"

Well, he made a believer out of Uncle Robert; in a few days he, too, was flat on his back with smallpox, and the hotel owner was flabbergasted at the idea of his other customers finding out about it, so he had the patient moved out by night down the back fire escape and taken to a shed out on the ranch where he was to build the house. There, for a couple of weeks or more, he was left to nurse himself back to health, aided only by the doctor, who now convinced he might pass the disease on to someone else, would come by now and then, shout some instructions from the road some fifty yards from the shed, and maybe leave some medicine on the gatepost. My uncle told it as if he was the butt of a good joke.

Another uncle, Alec, gave up on doctors when he was in an army hospital in France during World War I, terribly ill with influenza. One day, the soldier in the cot on his right was carried out dead, and the next day the one on his left took the same trip. Uncle Alec figured he was scheduled for the next day and thought, "If I'm going to die, I just as well do it somewhere more pleasant than this stinking hospital tent!" So he got his 220-pound frame out of bed, found his uniform where the nurses had stashed it, put it on, and walked out, no one daring to try to stop him. He was well in a few days. I heard the story many times back in the Twenties, but when I asked Uncle Alec about it sixty years later, he added what my family would agree was the clincher: "There's no doubt in my mind; it was my mother's prayers that did it—and she changed my whole life."

It may have been not so much a mistrust of doctors as a faith in home remedies that caused my family to get along with a minimum of professional help. (I was sixteen the first time I went to a doctor—and that was only because I fell over a wheelbarrow at school, cutting my shin to the bone on a cotter pin, and the teacher made me go.) Pappy liked to tell when he and my cousin Luke, both young carpenters, went to visit Aunt Janie, who had a houseful of children by that time. They mentioned that they had both got lice at the cheap boardinghouse where they had been staying.

Tiny Aunt Janie reacted, "Don't come in the gate! You're not bringing lice in *my* house or to *my* kids! Stay right where you are! We'll fix those lice! Get your clothes off! I'll get a tub and water."

I guess it must have been some distance to the next house, for Pappy told how they had to undress, bathe, and shampoo with homemade lye soap in the front yard, dry off, and sleep on the porch that night tied in cotton sacks dusted with sulfur powder—but they had no trouble with lice.

Home remedies seemed to work better for my kinfolk than they did for some. Once I was telling a boy that tarantulas were not poisonous enough to be afraid of; they wouldn't hurt anyone.

"Not hurt anyone! Are you crazy? My father, when he was a boy, almost died of a tarantula bite!" This was contrary to my experience with the big old gentle spiders, so I asked more about it.

"Oh, it probably would have killed him, except that his daddy grabbed him as soon as he killed the spider, jerked his pocketknife out, cut the bite on Dad's thumb open about an inch, spit tobacco juice into the hole and rubbed it in. Dad's hand swelled way up, and he was awful sick a few days, but the poison and pus drained out. It left a bad scar—*but he live over it!*"

My family's medical practice was more successful. When Uncle Alec, playing first base in a sandlot ball game, got his rather long nose in the way of a batted ball, it healed without professional help but had a rather sharp nose angle to the right for several years. But then one day he was playing third base, and a ball hit his nose from the other direction, putting the end about where it was originally, and leaving only a slight S-curve in the upper portion to remind us of his athletic career.

More remarkable was Pappy's remedy for a leg injury. He needed to get a brand new pine door ready to hang by trimming it down to fit the opening with his razor-sharp drawknife. He put his knee up against the end of the door to give himself more pull on the knife, when it slipped, and the blade went completely through his kneecap! He quickly grabbed the knee, pulled the cut's edges together, and thought, "If I go to a doctor, he'll open this cut and clean it out—and all the fluid under the kneecap will drain out, and I'll probably have a stiff leg the rest of my life. The knife was freshly sharpened and clean. The new wood was clean. There's probably no infection in the cut." So he held it shut with one hand, hopped around on one foot until he found some scantlings to make a splint, tied his leg straight so it couldn't bend, then cut away the pants around the knee with his pocketknife, rubbed some carbolized Vaseline (a long-time family all-purpose disinfectant) on the wound, wrapped a bandage of clean rags about it, and went on with his work. It not only healed rapidly, it left only a barely visible hairline scar and a completely functional knee that gave no trouble the rest of his life.

Pappy always saw logic in what he was doing. As the oldest of the four boys in Grandpa's "younger" family, he felt responsible for a younger brother whose arm was broken on the school play-ground. Reasoning that the lad might faint if he didn't stay active, Pappy and his other brothers made the injured one run all the two or three miles home where their mother set the arm and put it in a sling. Apparently, the exercise didn't hurt anything; the arm healed, and gave my family a good story I heard many times.

Even the treatments that did not result in perfect healing were thought to have worked to the advantage of the injured. As a tod-dler around the turn of the century, Uncle Joe, Grandma's last child, fell into a bed of coals in the fireplace, horribly burning both hands and feet. This is the only story that hints that Grandma could let her emotions control her. She panicked, grabbed the baby, smeared hog lard over all the burned skin that was just hang-ing from his fingers and toes, and began to bind them up together with rags.

"No, Mama, don't do that!" screamed her oldest daughter, Fannie, who was a mother herself by this time, and just happened to be at the house. "The fingers will all grow together! He won't be able to use them!" Fannie grabbed Joe away from her mother, took off the wrappings, and carefully greased and bandaged each finger and toe separately.

The wounds healed, but not without terrible scarring. The toes bent under his feet—but years later this would keep him from being sent to the front in World War I and gave him an early discharge, which his mother, who died of the 1918 flu, saw as an answer to one of her last prayers. The scar tissue on his hands also kept his fingers from straightening more than about half way, but the right hand's curve could hold the hammer or saw that made him a carpenter and cabinet builder who could work on any job and be hired immediately by any contractor who had ever seen his work. The left hand was even more remarkable. Every scarred finger was curved exactly right to fit the neck of a violin (fiddle, he called it) and could make the old waltzes sing so pathetically that I found tears in my eyes the first time I heard Uncle Joe play. He was by far the best country fiddler I ever heard; he could listen to the classical violinist Fritz Kreisler on the radio and by ear come awfully close to duplicating the performance.

Uncle Alec's burning was far less dramatic, but recounting it got a lot of laughs at family reunions. When he was about eighteen and seated for breakfast, Grandma accidentally dropped a big pot of boiling coffee on the table and the entire contents into Uncle Alec's lap.

"Take off your pants! Take off your pants!" Grandma was yelling—but his somewhat prudish sixteen-year-old sister (who in later years was a missionary to Japan) was pointing at the door and screaming,

"But go in yonder! Go in yonder!"

Alec was also featured in one of the stories in which injuries were the embarrassing result of trying to show off prowess. He was foreman on a construction job when he saw two carpenters pecking away at nailing blocks up under the overhang of a roof, a difficult job, since the work is overhead and the hammer swings against gravity. Alec knew he could do better.

"Here! Let me show you how—you've got to get a good swing!" He grabbed a block with the big nail started in it, held it up in the proper place, gave the hammer a magnificent full-arm swing, drove the nail deep into the wood—and lifted a one-inch flap of skin from the base of his thumb that was holding the block. Stepping back and trying to hide the gushing blood, he explained, "See? That's the way to drive those nails!" but the other carpenters just grinned and continued in their own inept way.

My stable, wise, older Uncle Robert was nearly as embarrassed when he watched with exasperation three laborers on his job ineffectively trying to take a fence post out of the ground.

"Look! Do it this way!" Uncle Robert grabbed the post and pushed it back and forth in the muddy ground a few times to loosen it. Then he crouched with the post between his thighs, hugged it up against his chest, gave a tremendous heave upward, lifted it from the ground—and broke three ribs!

"See? You have to pull straight up," he gasped and tried to look normal as he walked on to tend to other things that might need his attention.

When my folks would tell jokes like this about themselves, they seemed to be saying, "Yes, we are able people, but even gifted people make a lot of mistakes, have a lot of pain, and the fact is, the most serious aspects of life can wear a comic dress. Let's remember the tears—but smile at the incongruities. If you're strong enough, laughter is better medicine then pain-killers." And this was before the days when we learned about endorphins!

23

THE DAY GRANDPA BLEW UP THE TRACTOR

by Duane L. Spiess of Helotes

In 1968 my grandfather bought a used John Deere, Model H tractor for the princely sum of $75.00. Actually the tractor was manufactured in 1939, and had spent its long life sitting out in the fields. While most people referred to a John Deere as a "popping Johnny," we promptly welcomed the new addition to our family as "the Tractor." Grandpa used the tractor for pulling stumps and dragging cedar to a burn-pile, because his 1946 Chevy pickup, "Ruby," wouldn't do the job.

One particularly large cedar stump was too formidable for the tractor to pull. So, on every opportunity Grandpa would run into the stump with the blade on the front of the tractor. Incidentally, the stump remains in place to this day.

Anyway, on the day in point Grandpa slammed into the stump, thinking this might be his lucky day; but, alas, the tractor gasped under the load and stalled, killing the engine. Undaunted, Grandpa walked off to his next project. Later he returned, only to discover that he had forgotten to shut off the gasoline when the tractor stalled out. Much to Grandpa's surprise, when he went to start the tractor, he soon found the engine wouldn't turn over because the cylinders were full of gasoline.

I should mention here that the Model H is a two-cylinder, hand-crank engine. Starting is accomplished by rolling over a large flywheel, which, in turn, cranks the engine and generates a spark from the magneto.

Not to be outwitted by the situation Grandpa took out the spark plugs and slowly rolled the engine over until the last fling generated a good spark out of the magneto, which resulted in one hell of an explosion and fire.

Grandpa let out a scream. He was losing his tractor and we all stood around in horror. After the fire went out we approached the tractor and, to our surprise, found that solid, all-metal tractors don't burn. Grandpa started the tractor up and went about his business.

By the way, you can still see Grandpa and the Model H working around the place. Both are older, but they still persist in their fond partnership.

Grandpa's 1939 Model H John Deere tractor, still indestructible and still used by later generations

CUB DENMAN AND THE MOONSHINER
By Baker Denman of Nacogdoches

Charles Culberson Denman was trying a case in Federal Court in Tyler during the mid-1930s. Mr. Cub was defending a share cropper who had decided that his corn would bring a better price as moonshine than it would on the Depression market. The prosecution had him dead to rights because the revenuers had brought in the evidence of his misdeeds, a pint bottle of moonshine.

Mr. Cub, speaking for the defense, said "Your Honor, I have so much faith in my client, Mr. Ayres, that if I am convinced that what you have in that jar is whiskey, and it came from Mr. Ayres's place we will plead guilty and throw ourselves on the mercy of the court."

The federal prosecutor arose for his opening argument and asked Mr. Cub what it would take to convince him, and the defense said he would like to examine the evidence. The prosecutor handed him the jar. Cub opened it and handed it to his client and said "Did this come from your place?" The Old Man upped the jar, sampled a generous portion, and said, "Yes, it did." Cub upped the jar and killed the contents. He smacked his lips and said, "It isn't whiskey in the jar. I don't know what it is but it's not whiskey."

Mr. Cub handed the empty jar to the judge and moved that the case be dismissed for lack of evidence. Which it was.

George Oliver, infantryman, who fought the Japs from New Guinea to the Philippines, and was saved by a sergeant who didn't even like him

George Oliver, "The Rabbi," after he had given up his rambunctious ways and become a teacher and preacher, husband and father, and always a dear friend

(Pictures courtesy of Jerry and Jimmie Lee Oliver Morrow of Richardson)

24

GREATER LOVE . . .

by George N. Oliver (the Rabbi) 1923–2002 of Tyler
as told to F. E. Abernethy

We called him "Rabbi" ironically, probably because he could be so outrageously disorderly and unrabbinical. His name was George Oliver, and he was among the veterans who returned from World War II to the Stephen F. Austin State College campus on the G. I. Bill in 1946. He had been in the 169th Infantry, C Company, 43rd Division and had fought up the islands from New Guinea to the Philippines. George and I lived together in old army barracks that had been moved onto the campus to house students. We called it "The Old Folks Home," and it was a den of iniquity.

The Rabbi was one of the wildest, drinkin'est, fightin'est characters I have ever known, and we bonded early when we were thrown in jail together on one of our sprees. But the Rabbi changed. He married a good woman and he became a schoolteacher. He taught at a junior college and in one of the Texas prison units. And he got religion and became a lay preacher. And every one of us who knew him in The Old Folks Home continued to be amazed at his metamorphosis.

The Rabbi never told this war story during the early years that we knew each other. We were all too close to the war to try to impress each other with sea stories. Fifty years later, after we renewed our friendship through frequent visits, he began to tell his war stories. The following story about him and his sergeant became his main story, and I think he defined his life by that story. This episode in his war became the beginning of his redemption.

George's family knows this story better than any other of his war stories, so if the story is not legend now it probably will be if the family holds together long enough and closely enough to pass it on.

George's outfit was battling through the jungles of New Guinea when it was pulled out and sent to the rear for R&R. Before they went into town on their first pass, the chaplain called them all together and gave them the regular G. I.'s lecture on how to behave in civilization and how not to get the clap or get hauled in by the shore patrol. As usual, the soldiers were more amused than they were instructed, and the Rabbi, scorner and scoffer that he could be, was among the worst. After the lecture, he took great delight in amusing his comrades with satiric imitations of the Catholic-priest chaplain giving his lecture on sexual activities. Unfortunately, his sergeant, who was a devout Catholic and a close friend of the chaplain, heard George's performance. The result was that the sergeant took a strong dislike to George, and according to George, the sergeant for spite sent him on the most dangerous missions in the following campaigns.

A year later, in 1944, the Rabbi's outfit was in the Philippines. George's company was charged with capturing a hill and the gun emplacements contained thereon. During the advance George was pinned down and a Jap rifleman had him in his sights and was sniping at him, the bullets kicking up dust all around him. George was frantically throwing hand grenades in the Japanese direction, when he slipped and fell, turning as he fell. His hand-grenade pouch swung around and hit him square in the mouth and nose.

Blood poured down his face and front, and the Rabbi was certain that he had been hit and was mortally wounded. He screamed for the medic and then rolled up in a ball of pain waiting for something to happen.

George felt a hand on his shoulder and felt himself being rolled over on his back. He opened his eyes and saw the sergeant leaning over him. The sergeant comforted him, wiped the blood off his face, and told him, "Tex, you're hurt but you aren't shot and you aren't going to die."

Those were Sergeant Buddy Poland's last words. The Jap sniper who had been getting the Rabbi's range sighted in on the sergeant's back as he leaned over helping George. He squeezed the trigger and the sergeant dropped almost on top of George. The sergeant's body made a protective wall for George until the action moved on up the hill and George recovered and moved on with it.

George left his sergeant behind in the advance up the hill, but he never left the memory of that moment and his belief that Sergeant Buddy Poland took the bullet meant for him.

The Rabbi went to that story often as he recounted his own life's evolution from rakehell to a man of God. He got to where that incident became the turning point in his life. It wasn't. At war's end the Rabbi had not even begun to raise all the hell that life had in store from him. But between the love of his wife and some years to mature in, George did achieve a miraculous transformation. He was a naturally loving man, but he became even more so, continually concerned about his old wartime friends. And the moral of his story of a man who saved another man whom he didn't even like was "Greater love hath no man than this: that he will lay down his life for his brother."

Mt. Zion Baptist Church near Gideon Lincecum's home in Washington County, Texas (Photo by Peggy Redshaw)

25

FAMILY SAGA VS. HISTORY: HEZEKIAH LINCECUM AND THE CHURCH

by Jerry Bryan Lincecum of Sherman

Hezekiah Lincecum, my great-great-great-great grandfather, was born in 1770 in Warren County, Georgia, and died in 1839 in Lowndes County, Mississippi. Most of what we know about his life was recorded by his eldest son Gideon in an autobiography, which has been published as *Adventures of a Frontier Naturalist: The Life and Times of Dr. Gideon Lincecum* (College Station; Texas A&M University Press, 1994).

One of the most interesting Hezekian accounts which qualifies as a family saga story concerns his involvement with the Baptist church before Gideon was born. A rule about family saga stories is that they will be more interesting if you get them second- or third-hand, rather than straight from the source. In this case Gideon said, "For this portion of my narrative I am indebted to Stephen Camp, an old man whom I found dwelling in the hill country on the head waters of New River in Alabama in 1843. I spent six weeks at some mineral springs near his residence, and the old man spent many days at my camp telling me about the life of his old army friend and messmate Hezekiah before I knew him as my father." You will also notice that since Hezekiah died in 1839, this story was collected four years after his death, meaning that he could not contradict it.

However, in this age of the Internet you never know what kind of historical records will become available, and I recently discovered that the minutes of the church with which Hezekiah was involved have not only been published but also posted online. Thus I was able to compare what the church records say with the story that Gideon collected and published. Let's consider first the saga story, preceded by some background information. This version is paraphrased from *Adventures of a Frontier Naturalist* (pp. 10–15).

Hezekiah's father and two brothers had been killed in a skirmish with Indians during the American Revolution, leaving him as the only male in a household with his mother and three sisters. When he was thirteen, he fell under the influence of Thomas Roberts, an Englishman who had deserted the British service and had joined and done good service in the Rebel Army during the last three years of the Revolution. Roberts was a highly educated man but notorious for his profane and obscene language. In search of a wife, he visited the widow Lincecum's girls, but they did not fancy his bold, balderdash manner. However, Hezekiah pleased him, and he used all his powers of fascination to gain the boy's affection, in which he succeeded fully. At this time a bounty was offered to enlist two or three regiments of men to protect the border country against the Muskogee Indians. Mr. Roberts enlisted in the state service and also induced his pet, Hezekiah, to take the bounty. It grieved Hezekiah's mother, who had already lost two sons and her husband in the Army. Besides all this, Hezekiah was at that time the only male of the name Lincecum in the known world, and on this account particularly, she opposed his enlistment. But he had received the bounty, was already in camp, and all her efforts availed nothing.

At the expiration of three years, a treaty of peace was concluded with the Indians and the army disbanded. Hezekiah, now sixteen years old, had grown to be a very large and extremely active man, highly educated in all the arts, strokes, and punches of the pugilistic science. He returned to the old stamping ground fully able to (and did) whip every man in the settlement who dared to oppose him. He could also hold his hand with any of them in the use of strong drink. Roberts, who had been his teacher in these attainments, was always on hand. Soon after their return Roberts married, and he advised his pupil Hezekiah to do likewise.

At this juncture of time came Abram Brantley, a Baptist preacher, who by his earnest eloquence began to stir sinners up, and make them stop and think. It was a new thing and the first religious stirring in that vicinity since the war. Parson Brantley, viewing the irreligious condition of the people, was anxious to see what he could do towards producing a change amongst them. For this purpose he visited every family, praying with them and exercising his persuasive powers in familiar conversations. In making his rounds in the neighborhood he called at the house of widow Lincecum. Having been a conscientious religionist of the Baptist persuasion all her life, she was thankful for the preacher's attention. Her daughters were now all married and gone, leaving the household to consist only of Hezekiah and herself. Hezekiah was not only a large, portly, well-formed man but was also very handsome, with a most musical voice.

As the parson prayed and sang with them, Hezekiah took a full part in the singing, and his firm, manly, melodious voice fairly made the heavenly arches ring. The parson was surprised at the wonderful scope and power of his voice, so much so, that he could not help speaking of it. He told Hezekiah that the Lord had done a great deal for him, for which he should be very thankful. That fine form, handsome face and sweet musical voice abundantly fitted him to be a preacher of the Gospel. He should lose no time, but go right to work, studying and improving his mind and praying God to aid him in his preparation for the ministry, for that was surely what the Lord had intended for him. This flattering address waked up a new train of thought in the brain of the handsome young man.

He believed all the preacher had said and, forming a resolution to follow the advice, went to praying forthwith. He attended all the meetings, singings, and prayings, and it was but a short time till people noticed and talked of the progress he was making in his religious exercises. Soon he confessed his sins, told his conversion experience and was accepted, not only as a worthy member, but as a bright star and ornament in the fold of God. He was baptized and came out of the water shouting praises and exhorting the people to flee from the wrath to come, to renounce their sins, come to Christ and be baptized.

Hezekiah improved rapidly in singing and praying and it was but a short time till he was closing meetings and making very pretty public exhortations. No one hesitated in expressing themselves openly in reference to what was going to be the result of his unprecedented rapid growth in grace. All said the same thing: He was going to be a big preacher, sure and no mistake. The young ladies all wanted to go to heaven with the goodlooking young man. And now he, though very religious and prayerful, could not resist the flattering attentions so frankly bestowed by the young ladies. Out of the many that were being baptized, he selected one- a most beautiful, saintly creature, whose name was Sally Strange. She agreed to walk hand-in-hand with him before the Lord like Zachariah and Elizabeth. They were married, and the nuptial day was one of great religious rejoicing. It was talked about everywhere.

Under the gospel teaching of the kind, good-disposed Abram Brantley, the whole people of that vicinity seemed to be looking heavenward. The church was filling up rapidly and everything seemed to be rolling on finely. By the encouraging lectures on liberty, industry, and domestic economy, the people were enlarging their farms, improving their dwellings; thrift and better conditions of affairs were beginning to prevail everywhere. But from some cause unknown, there were some whose worldly and spiritual prospects seemed to be clouded.

It was becoming a noticeable fact that the ardor and spirit of devotion of Hezekiah had considerably cooled down. No one knew, or could say why, but it was certainly so. To his mother, who had hoped so much, the decline of his religious devotions was a source of much concern. She sent for the preacher, who endeavored to cheer him up, but he could say nothing that had any effect. He grew colder and absented himself from attending church. Then Mr. Brantley called to know his reason for absenting himself from meetings. Hezekiah did not explain. Such sad things, however, cannot long be hidden from the public. The eyes and ears of the curious will listen and peep, and they will also talk and whisper about other people's affairs.

It soon leaked out and rumor was busy circulating the precious morsel that there was a difficulty, a deadly split, betwixt Hezekiah and his beautiful and most saintly wife. No one could tell the nature and character of the difficulty, but one thing they could say was that it was awful. And sure enough, it terminated as badly as the most malicious could desire, for Hezekiah and his lovely Sally made a final separation of it. Sally went to her parental home and Hezekiah moped about, at first becoming very religious. He attended all religious gatherings, singing and praying vociferously. It had now become a settled fact among the brethren that he was to be a preacher, and a good one too.

Hezekiah began to think so himself and to prepare himself for the sacred service. He practiced the ceremonies, repeating and committing them to memory carefully. Some of the young church boys and Hezekiah being down on Powell's Creek one Sunday, amusing themselves playing in the water, they began talking of Hezekiah's prospects for becoming a preacher. It was proposed that he perform the ceremony of baptism on some of them. This he refused, but consented to baptize a cat that had followed them to the creek. And while he was performing the holy rite on the poor cat, some of the older brethren who were fishing that day happened to be passing at the time and saw him. To their notions of religious propriety, it was very offensive.

They reported the case to the leading members of the society, whereupon it was thought proper to church the presumptuous Hezekiah. While on trial he would make no penitential concessions but remained very still and intractable. His accusers said that recently he had often been seen in company with Roberts, his old army crony, whom they now looked upon as one of the emissaries of his Satanic Majesty. They finally concluded that as long as he remained friendly with the said Roberts, he would do no better. The question was read by the clerk: Shall Hezekiah Lincecum be excommunicated from the Baptist church? The vote was counted and found to be unanimous in the affirmative. So they turned him out.

Stephen Camp told Gideon that as Hezekiah walked down the aisle going out, he turned and remarked to the members, "You have turned me out of your church but you are not able to turn me out of Christ." I should have stated that Thomas Roberts was with him as he walked out of the church. And they went to a liquor shop nearby. They took some refreshments but none to excess. Hezekiah had made a resolution that he would, by a regular course of good behavior and sobriety, falsify the numerous predictions that had been made by the brethren in regard to the course he would pursue now that he was out of the protecting influence of the church.

There was a little log-cabin school started in the settlement, and Hezekiah, greatly feeling the need of an education (He was almost entirely illiterate.), enrolled. He strove with all his powers to learn the books, but he was a little too far advanced in years and had witnessed too many brain-racking vicissitudes to allow him to be a very apt scholar. And this was not all the brain-disturbing forces by which he was surrounded. The widow Hickman's daughter Sally, a most beautiful girl, fourteen-and-a-half years of age, was also entered to the same school. Her power of attraction for him was very great. He felt the want of possessing the fair young creature more than he felt the want of an education. So, from his books he turned his attention wholly to the pretty Sally and they were soon married. Roberts was at the wedding, and on this joyous occasion succeeded in leading Hezekiah so far astray as to get him intoxicated. And now, while his protégé was under the excitement of brandy, Roberts told him that he had been greatly wronged and contemptuously treated in the church. Since several of the brethren who took an active part against him during the trial were present, Roberts suggested it was a very pretty time to retaliate and get satisfaction. Hezekiah was of the same opinion and went charging into a bunch of five or six of them, knocking them down like children and kicking and cuffing them terribly.

Parson Brantley, who had performed the marriage ceremony, observed that Hezekiah turned his eyes toward him; and to avoid any difficulty with the young inebriate, the parson hurried away in a pretty tall trot. Hezekiah, seeing the hasty departure of the preacher, gave chase, pursuing him two or three hundred yards. The parson, however, made good his escape. Hezekiah returned, vociferating in a very loud voice, and asked if there were any other of the damned rascals who wished to be fed with the same spoon. But he found no one there but the bride and Roberts. The rest of the company had dispersed, so the three of them concluded to go home.

Thus ends Gideon's account of his father's dalliance with the Baptist church. This marriage turned out better than Hezekiah's first, and Gideon was the first-born of ten children, including seven sons. Hezekiah's mother's fears about the Lincecum name dying out were not well founded. As for the historical record, recently another Lincecum descendant, Bob Kelly, sent me the "URL" (uniform resource locator) for a site on the World Wide Web where the minutes of the Long Creek Baptist Church, Warren County, Georgia, have been posted. I read these minutes with considerable interest, for they include some new information about the relationship of Hezekiah Lincecum with that particular church.

First let me give you some idea about the nature of these church records, which were copied on microfilm in 1954 and have been certified by the Secretary of State of Georgia to be authentic and accurate copies. Volume I begins with this statement: "This Book is the property of the Baptist Church of Christ at Long Creek Warren County Georgia Containing a record of the Deed for the Lot of Land on which the Church was built together with the Constitution of the same, and a record of the actings and doings of the same from its Constitution, . . . which was sometime in the year 1786." Significantly, the year given for the founding of the church corresponds with the chronology in Gideon's story about the arrival of Parson Brantley and his efforts to generate some religious fervor in the community.

The record book seems to have two major purposes: one is to provide a list of the church members, with an indication of how they came in and how they went out. There is a list of the male members and a separate list for the female members. Number 114 among the male members is "Kiah Linsicomb," who came in "by Baptism" and went out by being "Excommunicated." Number 41 among the female members was Hezekiah's mother, "Milly Linsicomb," who also came in "By Baptism" and was listed as "removed & out of our fellowship," which appears to be a way of denoting former members who have moved away. This church practiced excommunication rather freely, as the three members listed right before Hezekiah Lincecum enjoyed the same status: Number 111, Zephaniah Fowler, Number 112, Samuel Jones, and Number 113, Abalom Beardon, all were excommunicated.

This brings up the second purpose of the book: to record minutes of church actions, such as excommunicating members, that were carried out in conference meetings, once a month. In this regard, 1788 was an active year in the life of Long Creek Baptist Church. Consider these excerpts from the minutes:

> **April 18th 1788.** Agreed on by the Church in Conference that any person under the censure of the Church may be admonished by the Church, but the Church is not to make application to the offender but the offender to the Church . . . Further agreed that if any member of the Church Shall neglect keeping their place in the Church in

Conference through negligence twice and still neglects to make the cause known, they shall be laid under the Sensure of the Church. . . . Proceeded to the tryal of John Berry who was charged with being concerned in stealing of an ox which being believed, it was agreed that he should be excommunicated and cut off from us.

September 3rd Sunday 1788. The Church in Conference unanimously agreed . . . that Mary Murphy should for the sin of Adultry be entirely cut off from us.

October 25th 1788. Agreed unanimously by the Church that on the first Thursday in Nov. all the male members of the Church are to meet to give an account of what they have done towards building the meeting house in order to remove difficulties from the minds of the Brethren.

2ndly–Agreed that any member exempting him or herself from the [Lord's] Supper Shall make an excuse to the Church, or have a Brother to excuse for them. . . .

4thly–Several Brethren is desired to cite the members that have neglected attending Church meetings, to remove difficulties off of the minds of some of the Brethren. [There follow the names of several members as being "cited" by other members.]

November 15th 1788. Agreed that Jeremiah Oats, George Hearn and Elisha Mason Cite Wm Washington to the Church to answer the complaint of John Castleberry.

December 17th 1788. Rhoda Fort is excommunicated for refusing to keep her seat in the Church or to hear their reproof.

Now that you have a clear idea of exactly what the church records are like and what they reveal, here is the one that directly addresses Hezekiah's case: "February 17, 1788. The Church of Christ on Long Creek of Ogechee, Being met in Conference Pursued to take into consideration the Irreligious conduct of Hezekiah Lensecom and unanimously agreed that he Should be excommunicated. First for riding a race on the Sabbath day. Secondly for refusing to hear the Church when called on. Thirdly for offering to commit a Rape on M Jonegen."

Contrary to Gideon's account, there is no mention of baptizing a cat or keeping bad company. The charge is "irreligious conduct" and there are three specific items: "riding a race on the Sabbath day," "refusing to hear the Church when called on," and "offering to commit a Rape on M Jonegen." Curiously, there is no member named "Jonegen" or any variant spelling of that name, yet the vote against Hezekiah was unanimous.

There you have it. History in the form of an official document, certified by the Secretary of State of Georgia: "The minutes of the Long Creek Church of Christ," published on the World Wide Web for all to read, contradicting the colorful Lincecum family saga account of Hezekiah's separation from the church. Nevertheless, in conclusion, I would paraphrase the famous line from the Western movie, *The Man Who Shot Liberty Valance,* to make it a rule of family sagas: "When the legend is more interesting than the facts, print the legend."

SOURCES CONSULTED

Lincecum, Gideon. "Autobiography of Gideon Lincecum," *Publications of the Mississippi Historical Society* 8 (1904): 443–519.

Lincecum, Jerry Bryan, and Edward Hake Phillips. *Adventures of a Frontier Naturalist: The Life and Times of Dr. Gideon Lincecum* College Station: Texas A&M University Press, 1994.

Long Creek Baptist Church (Warrenton, GA). "Minutes."
http://users.ticnet.com/stevem/gawalng.htm 4 November 2003.

CONTRIBUTORS' VITAS

Francis Edward Abernethy has been Secretary-Editor of the Texas Folklore Society for thirty-three years and is a retired teacher of English at Stephen F. Austin State University.

James T. Bratcher lives with his family in San Antonio. He recently rejoined the TFS after an absence of thirty years. (His Rip Van Winkle comment: "Dues have gone up!") Bratcher's main contribution to scholarship and the Texas Folklore Society is the *Analytical Index to Publications of the Texas Folklore Society* (Volumes 1–36), which he completed in 1973. He now writes short articles, mainly on literary topics.

Phyllis Bridges, a Distinguished Alumna in English of Texas Tech, is a professor of English at Texas Woman's University, where she has taught for thirty-two years. She has served as president of the Texas Joint Council of Teachers of English, the Southwest American Culture Association, and the Texas Folklore Society. She is a regular contributor to the publications of the Texas Folklore Society.

Georgia Caraway is the Executive Director of the Denton County Courthouse-on-the-Square Museum and the Bayless-Selby House Museum in Denton, Texas. Georgia has a brokerage and appraisal certification from Edinboro University of Pennsylvania and is the director of the Texas Institute of Antiques & Collectibles in Denton, an adult education certificate program for antiques brokers. She was an appraiser at *The Antiques Roadshow* when that popular PBS program was filmed in Dallas. Her book, *Tips, Tools, and Techniques,* gives more than a thousand ideas for the care and preservation of antiques and collectibles.

Tony Clark lives in Georgetown, Texas. Tony is now retired after teaching English in Texas and Arizona for twenty-seven years. He has written and published numerous short stories, poems, essays, and articles.

John L. Davis is Director of Research for the University of Texas Institute of Texas Cultures at San Antonio. He is a former teacher at The University of Texas at San Antonio, The University of Texas at Austin, and San Antonio College. Author of a number of books and articles, Davis is a freelance graphics designer, infrequent poet, and occasional metaphysician. A former resident of Center Point, Texas, and London, England, he now resides in Seguin, Texas, where his wife and cats allow him to live with them.

Kenneth W. Davis, a past president of the Texas Folklore Society, is Emeritus Professor of English, Texas Tech University, and is president of the West Texas Historical Association (2003–2004). He is interested in the oral narrative tradition in Texas folklore as well as in the lore of food—and anything else about Texas lore. Kenneth is the official spokesman for Old Bell County.

Bertha Dominguez (1940–1997) wrote her paper under Elton Miles at Sul Ross in 1972, and taught school from 1970 until her death in 1997. See the introduction to her story on "Welito."

Gloria Duarte-Valverda has taught in the English Department at Angelo State University for twenty-six years. She teaches a variety of classes, including women in literature and Mexican-American literature. Her areas of interest include Chicana writers, Mexican-American literature, and Ft. McKavett, where she grew up. She directed the exchange program with Mexico for six years.

George Ewing is a fifth-generation Texan who grew up in the Lower Rio Grande Valley and Corpus Christi, the son of a contractor who taught him the building trades. After studying and teaching electronics and radar during WWII, he finished his graduate degrees with a thesis on the temperance movement that was published as *The Well-Tempered Lyre.* Since retirement in 1992, he has done maintenance work in an apartment house for senior citizens, engaged in arts and crafts, and conducted religious services in nursing homes. He has been married to the same woman since 1946 and raised five children and one of his twelve grandchildren.

Alicia Zavala Galván is a poet, writer, translator, artist, independent scholar, and editor of Galvart Publishing. She has published six collections of illustrated poetry, three of them bilingual. As an independent scholar, she has translated a historical document written by Sor Juana Inés de la Cruz, the feminist poet-nun who lived during Mexico's early colonial period. Ms. Galván has also written, produced, and acted in *Sequestered Soliloquy,* a bilingual one-act play based on the last days of Sor Juana Inés de la Cruz, which has been presented in universities and churches in the United States, Mexico, and Argentina.

Lou Ann Herda developed a love of legend and lore while growing up on haunted land in northeastern Oklahoma. Her Cherokee roots led to her dissertation topic and to an unexpected curiosity in nineteenth-century American history. She especially loves Texas' colorful past and enjoys sharing stories with anyone who will sit still long enough. Lou Ann earned her doctorate degree in 1999 from the University of Houston and resides part-time in Galveston where she teaches speech communications courses at Galveston College. She is married to Alex Herda and has two children, Taylor Lang, who willingly attends TFS meetings, and Brittany Lang, who willingly stays home in Houston.

Mary Belle Ingram is a retired librarian who is now in charge of the archives at the Matagorda County Museum in Bay City and is Historical Marker Chairman for Matagorda County.

James Ward Lee is acquisitions editor for TCU Press in Fort Worth, where he lives in heavenly bliss after forty-two years as Professor of English at the University of North Texas. He is now Emeritus Professor of English at UNT, but he does not take that very seriously, nor is he eager to re-join the U. S. Navy, where he was once a radar pussy during the Korean War. Nor is he much interested in moving back to Leeds, Alabama, even though it bears a number of resemblances to the Underworld where Sisyphus and the Duke and Lee Marvin and Steve McQueen and Fat Fullmer are.

Jerry Bryan Lincecum, a sixth-generation Texan, holds the Shoap Professorship in English at Austin College, having taught there since 1967. Lincecum has edited three books written by his first Texas ancestor, Dr. Gideon Lincecum. In 2003 Lincecum was a coeditor of Texas Folklore Society Publication #60, *The Family Saga: A Collection of Texas Family Legends.*

Al Lowman, in business since 1935, is now retired but marches on as Stringtown's foremost sedentary lifestyle activist. He is past president of the Texas Folklore Society, the Book Club of Texas, and the Texas State Historical Association. Most recently he is founder and honorary curator of the Al Lowman Printing Arts Collection in the Cushing Library at Texas A&M University.

Charlie McCormick, after receiving his BA degree from Abilene Christian University, did graduate work in folklore and folklife at Texas A&M University and the University of Pennsylvania. He is now an assistant professor of English and Communications and the director of the Honors Program at Cabrini College in Radnor, Pennsylvania. He is currently completing a book on adolescent cruising on the commercial strip.

Jean Granberry Schnitz was born in Spur, Texas. She graduated from Raymondville High School in 1948 and from Texas A&I College in Kingsville in 1952. She and Lew Schnitz were married in 1953. They have three sons and three grandchildren. A retired legal secretary, she lives near Boerne. As of 2003 Jean has presented six papers to the Texas Folklore Society since 1990. She served as a Councilor on the Board of the Texas Folklore Society 1999–2002, and was elected a Director in 2002.

Jan Seale was born in Pilot Point, Texas. She grew up in Gainesville and Waxahachie, attended Baylor, and received degrees from the University of Louisville and North Texas State University (now UNT). Seale is the author of *Airlift,* short stories; *Homeland,* essays; *The Nuts-&-Bolts Guide to Writing Your Life Story,* and four books of poetry, the latest being *The Yin of It.* She is on the Speakers Bureau for the Texas Council on the Humanities.

Thad Sitton, a native of Lufkin, historian and writer, lives in Austin, Texas. He has explored the social history of rural Texas in a dozen books, including *Backwoodsmen, Nameless Towns,* and *The Texas Sheriff.* Sitton's latest work is *Harder Than Hardscrabble,* an oral history of the farming life (University of Texas Press, 2004). His history of Texas' freedmen's settlements, *Freedom Colonies,* is in press at UT.

Duane L. Spiess's formal education, provided at schools in Minnesota, Australia, Mexico and Texas, trained him for his professional life as a lawyer. The education that formed his avocation, that of puttering with tractors and old trucks, was nurtured by his grandfather, a farmer and self-taught mechanic in Minnesota. As a longtime resident of Helotes, Texas, he has spent, and continues to spend, many pleasurable hours "working at his trade."

Lucy Fischer West was born in Catskill, New York, but raised in El Paso. She has done freelance editing in the field of Southwestern history and is currently teaching freshman English at Cathedral High School. Her presentation, "Folklore by Osmosis: Three Decades with John O.," was included in the Writer's AudioShop *The Best of Texas Folklore Volume Two. Child of Many Rivers: Journeys to and from the Rio Grande,* a book of essays, is forthcoming from Texas Tech University Press.

INDEX